TRANSFORMING PERFORMANCE MANAGEMENT TO DRIVE PERFORMANCE

Recently a revolution has taken place in organizations around the world to transform their performance management systems from burdensome chores into valuable business practices. Many high-profile companies have announced they are getting rid of the dreaded performance review and replacing it with ongoing coaching and feedback. Although these cases are inspiring other organizations to contemplate change, many are left with more questions than answers.

While many fads and quick fixes have been proposed to answer these questions, little research exists to support them. This book provides a practical and evidence-based guide for building a performance management approach that *actually* improves performance. It cuts through the hype and gives actionable advice, useful tools, and real-world examples for organizations to build the business case for change, plan the transformation, design the new system, and implement the change effectively. Featuring research findings as well as concrete strategies from organizations that have proven successful, this book provides a roadmap for meaningful change. It will be valuable to professionals and scholars interested in evidence-based performance management and the challenges facing organizations.

Rose A. Mueller-Hanson is Associate Director/CFO of Community Interface Services. For over 20 years, she has been a champion of common sense, effective performance management practices.

Elaine D. Pulakos is President of PDRI, a CEB Company for over 25 years, she has been helping organizations drive higher performance through implementing effective performance management strategies.

Series in Applied Psychology

Series Editors
Jeanette N. Cleveland,
Colorado State University
Kevin R. Murphy,
Landy Litigation and Colorado State University

Founding Series Editor
Edwin A. Fleishman (1987–2010)

TRANSFORMING PERFORMANCE MANAGEMENT TO DRIVE PERFORMANCE

An Evidence-based Roadmap

Rose A. Mueller-Hanson and
Elaine D. Pulakos

Routledge
Taylor & Francis Group

NEW YORK AND LONDON

First published 2018
by Routledge
711 Third Avenue, New York, NY 10017

and by Routledge
2 Park Square, Milton Park, Abingdon, Oxon, OX14 4RN

Routledge is an imprint of the Taylor & Francis Group, an informa business

© 2018 Taylor & Francis

The right of Rose A. Mueller-Hanson and Elaine D. Pulakos to be identified as authors of this work has been asserted by them in accordance with sections 77 and 78 of the Copyright, Designs and Patents Act 1988.

Library of Congress Cataloging-in-Publication Data
Names: Mueller-Hanson, Rose A., author. | Pulakos, Elaine Diane, author.
Title: Transforming performance management to drive performance : an evidence-based roadmap / Rose A. Mueller-Hanson and Elaine D. Pulakos.
Description: 1 Edition. | New York : Routledge, 2018. | Series: Series in applied psychology | Includes bibliographical references and index.
Identifiers: LCCN 2017051122 | ISBN 9781138051942 (hardback: alk. paper) | ISBN 9781138051966 (pbk. : alk. paper) | ISBN 9781315168128 (ebook)
Subjects: LCSH: Performance—Management. | Performance standards.
Classification: LCC HF5549.5.P35 M84 2018 | DDC 658.3/125—dc23
LC record available at https://lccn.loc.gov/2017051122

ISBN: 978-1-138-05194-2 (hbk)
ISBN: 978-1-138-05196-6 (pbk)
ISBN: 978-1-315-16812-8 (ebk)

Typeset in Bembo
by Apex CoVantage, LLC

RMH: To Scott and Ryan—whose unwavering love, support, and unvarnished opinions on performance management were my inspirations in writing this book.
EP: To Tim—the very best coach, feedback provider, and partner in candid conversations for almost 30 years.

CONTENTS

SERIES FOREWORD

The goal of the Applied Psychology series is to create books that exemplify the use of scientific research, theory, and findings to help solve real problems in organizations and society. Mueller-Hanson and Pulakos are distinguished scientist-practitioners, and their book *Transforming Performance Management to Drive Performance: An Evidence-based Roadmap* illustrates this approach very well. Indeed, one of the themes that runs through the entire text is the way their extensive experience in developing, implementing, and evaluating performance management systems in organizations has been informed by and has informed empirical research in performance management.

Performance management represents a set of processes in organizations that are both vitally important and deeply frustrating. Supervisors, managers, and employees invest a great deal of time and effort into performance management, and often feel that they get little in return. Mueller-Hanson and Pulakos make a compelling set of arguments about why performance management is so difficult and how performance management systems can be improved.

The book is divided into three sections, the first of which makes a case for the need to change performance management systems and the barriers to the success of current performance management efforts. Mueller-Hanson and Pulakos show how a combination of attempting to pursue too many goals (some of them conflicting with others), an over-reliance on control, an under-reliance on cooperation and inflexible models for evaluating performance help to limit the success of performance management systems. They show how rigorous, data-based assessments of these systems can provide a springboard for changing the way organizations manage performance.

The second section of this book lays out concrete steps for designing and implementing successful performance management systems. It walks readers through a systematic process of defining performance, creating useful performance goals, measuring and evaluating performance, giving useful feedback, having constructive discussions about ways to improve performance, ways of linking evaluations of performance with critical organizational decisions, and finally concrete ways of defining and dealing with poor performance. This section represents a thorough roadmap to the decisions and issues that need to be faced in developing performance management systems.

The third section of this book focuses on an important topic that is too often ignored when designing human resource systems—sustaining these systems once they are implemented. It starts by considering what we know about changing behavior and wrapping this knowledge into practical programs for changing behavior in organizations. It then lays out ways of using the change management process as a framework for implementing and sustaining successful performance management programs. It closes by laying out a path forward from over-engineered, control-based performance management systems to cooperation-based systems that will direct and encourage meaningful improvements in the performance of employees.

Transforming Performance Management to Drive Performance: An Evidence-based Roadmap is an excellent exemplar of what the scientist-practitioner model has to offer in addressing important problems in organizations, and it is a wonderful addition to the Applied Psychology Series.

Kevin R. Murphy
Jeanette N. Cleveland

PREFACE

Recently a revolution has taken place in organizations around the world to transform their performance management system from a burdensome chore into a valuable business practice. Many high-profile companies have made big news by announcing they are getting rid of the dreaded performance review and replacing it with ongoing coaching and feedback. Although these stories are inspiring other organizations to contemplate change, many are left with more questions than answers. Organizations are seeking to navigate tough questions about how to get buy-in for change, how to drive better performance conversations, and how to make effective talent decisions without performance ratings.

While many fads and quick fixes have been proposed to answer these questions, little research exists to support them. Managing performance effectively is hard. If it were easy, organizations would have long ago figured out how to do it well, and there would be no need for the thousands of books and articles written about it. For many organizations, better performance management is needed now more than ever to increase performance and engagement and compete in an ever-increasingly complex world. However, practical guidance for change is in short supply. Advice to merely simplify the system or get rid of it altogether will ultimately not help organizations improve their performance.

This book provides a roadmap for meaningful change. It cuts through the hype and gives actionable advice, useful tools, and real-world examples for organizations to create a performance management approach that actually improves performance. It includes concrete techniques, examples, and wisdom from many colleagues who were generous enough to share their perspectives on this topic as well as our own experiences. Part I will help you challenge the status quo and design a more effective approach that is evidence-based and consistent with your organizational culture, goals, and values. Part II will help you create a performance management approach that actually helps drive business results: defining success, setting expectations, measuring performance, enabling meaningful performance conversations, and using data to make smart talent decisions and hold poor performers accountable. Part III will help you implement these activities and make them stick. The end goal is performance management that is not conceived of as a separate "system"—an unwelcome distraction from day-to-day work—but rather it becomes how your organization's managers and employees operate every day to achieve performance and results.

ACKNOWLEDGMENTS

We would like to thank the many generous colleagues who were gracious enough to share their insights and experiences with us. A special thanks to Renee Mack, Amy Grubb, Laura Mattimore, Ben Schneider, Matt Walter, Meredith Ferro, Lindsay Barnett, Brodie Gregory Riordan, Maya Garza, Samantha Taylor, Rob Lewis, Martha Tracy-Clowers, Herman Aguinis, Michelle Donovan, and Christelle LaPolice for sharing their thoughts. This book is better for their observations. We also very much appreciate the guidance and support of the Taylor & Francis editorial staff and series editors Kevin Murphy and Jeanette Cleveland.

PART I
Laying the Foundation for Change

1

THE CASE FOR CHANGE

Every year a familiar ritual takes place in organizations around the world—the annual performance management review. It often involves hours of filling out forms, somewhat uncomfortable conversations between employees and managers, and numerous meetings to decide how to allocate rewards. Like many rituals, its original purpose has become somewhat obscured, but we continue to do it nonetheless.

It doesn't have to be this way. Performance management has the potential to drive significant business results. Done well, it can improve individual and organizational performance, inspire employees to find meaning and purpose in their work, and promote career development. Done poorly it can hurt performance, reduce morale, and waste everyone's time. Too often performance management is done poorly.

We need good performance management now more than ever. CEB, a leading advisory company, estimates that organizations globally need an average of a 27% increase in employee performance just to meet current goals, but current practices are only likely to improve performance by 3–5%, leaving a significant gap (CEB, 2012, 2014). If performance management reached its full potential, we might be able to close this gap; however, current approaches fall short. As one human resources (HR) leader recently told us, "If we could only get performance management right, it would be a game-changer in our organization. Unfortunately, we can't seem to get it right, despite years of trying."

Why Change

Performance management is a straightforward concept. It is the collection of activities designed to improve individual and organizational performance, such as setting goals and expectations, monitoring progress, providing feedback and coaching, and measuring and evaluating results. Data produced from this process are often used to make decisions about people, including pay, job assignments, training, promotions, and terminations.

These activities appear consistent with standard business practices, so why do they fail to provide value when they are done collectively as "performance management?" It is not the activities themselves that are the problem. It is the overly bureaucratic and complicated way they have been implemented in most organizations. Performance management tends to focus heavily on documentation and process—setting goals in compliance with organizational policies, completing rating forms on time, and determining how ratings are translated into rewards. This approach largely ignores the most important drivers of performance, however, which are effective relationships and ongoing communications between managers and employees that allow for real-time performance feedback, coaching, and development (Pulakos & O'Leary, 2011).

While most HR professionals acknowledge that effective, ongoing performance conversations and feedback are critical for driving performance improvements, these ideals are hard to achieve at scale and are even harder to sustain. Many companies revert to what they can implement and track easily—documenting each performance management step. They reason that documentation at least ensures that some basic performance-related communications are occurring, even though documentation does not necessarily indicate high-quality performance conversations. Over-emphasis on process has resulted in some unintended consequences: (1) performance management activities cost organizations too much, (2) employees and even many managers have come to hate performance management requirements their organizations impose, and (3) the data generated from formal performance management documentation often cannot be trusted.

High Costs

Performance management is a time-intensive process in many organizations. Typical activities include:

- Reading communications from HR and attending required training.
- Cascading goals, in which organizational objectives are cascaded down through every level of the company before getting translated into individual objectives.
- Setting team and individual goals that meet SMART (Specific, Measurable, Achievable, Relevant, and Time-bound) criteria.
- Conducting mid-year reviews to check in on progress.
- Completing employee self-assessments, which may include rating oneself on performance criteria and writing narrative justifications to support the ratings.

- Collecting, reviewing, and providing 360-degree feedback (e.g., from peers, subordinates, customers, etc.) to use as input for performance reviews.
- Supervisory performance assessments once, and sometimes twice, a year, which may include rating each subordinate on several performance criteria and writing narrative justifications to support the ratings, along with completing self-assessments and collecting 360-degree feedback.
- Calibration sessions, in which managers meet to discuss employee ratings to ensure they are consistent and fair; these sessions may also include discussions of how to allocate raises and bonuses.
- Performance review conversations in which each manager meets with each of his or her direct reports to provide feedback and discuss performance ratings; conversations about raises and bonuses may be done as part of the review or separately.

These activities add up to a significant amount of time. According to one survey, the average manager spends about 210 hours per year and the average employee about 40 hours per year on required performance management activities (CEB, 2012). Managers in client organizations have often told us that the whole company focuses on performance management for weeks or even months, distracting everyone from getting "real work done."

All this time adds up to substantial costs. Using these time estimates at an average cost of $52 an hour for managers and $22 for individual contributors (Bureau of Labor Statistics, 2010), performance management costs $10,920 a year for each manager and $880 a year for each individual contributor. A large organization with 10,000 employees can spend up to $35 million a year on performance management (CEB, 2012). The question then becomes what return on investment (ROI) are organizations receiving for this level of effort? As one example, Deloitte found that they were spending a total of 2 million hours per year on performance management activities that most executives thought had very little value (Buckingham & Goodall, 2015), which then led to a major overhaul of their process.

This perceived lack of value is pervasive across most organizations. Satisfaction with performance management is consistently rated low on employee engagement surveys (e.g., OPM, 2016). It is important to analyze the costs of performance management against the perceived value because, in most cases, performance management has a very large cost with little return. If nothing else, it is worth considering how performance management processes can be streamlined to save time.

Criticisms From Employees and Managers

Complaints about performance management are as old as the practice itself. Just how much employees and managers dislike performance management depends on the specific activity in question. Many cite dissatisfaction with the entire process because the time invested is not seen as adding commensurate value. The most negative reactions consistently relate to the performance review, providing fodder for strong and vocal critics. For example, Samuel Culbert once described the performance review as a "pretentious, bogus practice" that should be "put out of its misery" (Culbert, 2010). A *Washington Post* headline perfectly captured the sentiment: "Study finds that basically every single person hates performance reviews" (McGregor, 2014).

Managers also loathe performance reviews. Giving and receiving feedback, especially criticism, is awkward and uncomfortable. When the stakes are raised with pay decisions riding on the outcomes, tension and conflict are further heightened. Neuroscientist David Rock has offered one explanation for why everyone hates performance reviews. He and his colleagues assert that the act of being evaluated threatens one's self-esteem and social standing in the organization. This perceived threat activates the fight-or-flight center of the brain and causes higher-level processing to shut down as the employee goes into a defensive mode. This reaction happens even if the review is positive—it is the very act of being judged that leads to defensiveness (Rock, 2008; Rock, Davis, & Jones, 2014).

Simple dislike of performance reviews is not the only problem. More concerning is that the dislike often translates into performance detriments. Research has shown that formal performance reviews are frequently demotivating to even the highest performing employees (Aguinis, Joo, & Gottfredson, 2011; Culbertson, Henning, & Payne, 2013) to the point that they can lead to apathy and less effective performance. This point is important because the demotivating effects of performance reviews, associated disengagement, and potential for decreased performance are not widely understood.

There are several reasons why formal reviews are often more demotivating than motivating, even beyond the general defensive reaction proposed by Rock. First, when an employee hears negative feedback for the first time in a formal performance review, it can cause resentment because this feedback was not shared until the review. Negative perceptions can be exacerbated when 360-degree feedback from peers and direct reports is shared for the first time in the formal review. Moreover, sometimes the performance management process is designed to constrain ratings or force a distribution. Arbitrary rules result in ratings and associated feedback that may be demotivating when there is a mismatch between actual employee performance and system-imposed rating guidelines.

Untrustworthy Data

Organizations often recognize the costs and dissatisfaction with performance management but still justify its use, citing the need for data to use in decision-making—whom to reward, promote, reassign, train, fire, etc. Is performance management data accurate enough to serve as a basis for these purposes? According to CEB, only 23% of HR leaders believe that performance data accurately reflects employee's contributions (CEB, 2012). This mistrust is well founded. In an examination of 23,339 performance ratings across 40 organizations, no relationship was found between business unit profitability and individual performance ratings in those units (CEB, 2012). Units with highly rated employees were no more likely to be profitable than units with low-rated employees.

Performance ratings may not relate to business performance for several reasons. In some companies, ratings are chronically inflated—a cultural norm that comes with strong pressure for managers to adhere to it. In these situations, very few employees are rated on the low end of the scale—most are rated in the middle or above—even when business unit performance fails to meet expectations. It is not uncommon for 98% of employees within an organization to be rated a "meets expectations" or higher on a 5-point scale, with 80% rated as "exceeds expectations" or even higher. Alternatively, the rating system in other companies comes with arbitrary distributions, such as 80% of employees need to be rated as "meets expectations," 10% (and only those who are to be promoted) can be rated as "exceeds," and 10% must be rated as "below." In either case, neither cultural norms that lead to excessively high ratings nor system "rules" that lead to arbitrary rating distributions can be trusted to lead to *accurate* ratings for each and every employee.

A second factor that impacts rating quality is that managers are not always motivated to provide accurate ratings. Telling employees their performance is "below standard" or even that it "meets expectations" can be difficult for managers to do because many employees do not take this feedback well. Managers have little incentive to upset the very people they rely on to get the work done. Alternatively, admitting to having poorly performing employees can reflect badly on the manager's leadership skills—that they selected a poor performer to begin with or failed in addressing performance issues. Murphy and Cleveland (1995) found that managers have many disparate goals when providing performance ratings, including preserving the relationship with the employee, attempting to maximize rewards, and organizational politics, among others. Therefore, many managers will try to give higher ratings when they can, which may not always accurately represent each employee's true performance level.

A third factor that can undermine rating accuracy is the sheer difficulty of the rating task. Even if managers wanted to rate employees accurately, doing so is challenging. It requires managers, with little or no formal training, to collect information over an entire year from multiple sources, carefully analyze this information to keep what is relevant and discard irrelevant data, and make an unbiased and objective judgment about the employee's performance. All of this needs to occur in environments where many managers do not observe their subordinates day-to-day and must rely on input from others in evaluating performance. However, others' observations are also not complete and may be motivated by external factors. For example, how much can you trust peer inputs when there may be inherent competition between peers for future rewards? Even objective results can be deceiving. A solid outcome can occur through others' efforts or sheer luck, while a poor outcome may likely result from factors completely outside the employee's control, so using even seemingly objective factors can result in incomplete or inaccurate views of performance. Even professional sporting judges, who have years of experience in evaluating human performance, rarely agree on athletes' scores (Adler et al., 2016). Why would we expect busy managers to do any better?

With so many factors getting in the way of accurate performance ratings, it is surprising that they would be relied on heavily to make important decisions about people. Additionally, other factors such as budget constraints and organizational performance end up being larger determinants of decisions such as pay increases, bonuses, and other rewards than performance ratings. This then raises the question of the extent to which organizations are actually using performance ratings for decision-making, even though many say this is a key reason why they need ratings. Senior leader distrust of performance data may lead them to disregard ratings and go with their own personal observations when making decisions. Although this practice varies from situation to situation, performance ratings are used less often for decision-making than one might think.

Making a Case for Change

Most organizations know their performance management approach is broken and would like to do something to fix it (CEB, 2012), but the prospect of significant change can be daunting. Just thinking about the time and effort involved, especially if changes to technology are needed, is enough to make many organizations pause—sometimes indefinitely. They justify inaction with statements such as "we have other priorities right now" or "we can't get our executives onboard." However, many organizations fail to consider or even realize the potential for decreased performance and engagement caused by poorly executed performance management.

Change need not be massive to be impactful. Sometimes even small steps can make a big difference. Organizations can start by asking some critical questions:

1. How much time are we spending on performance management activities? How much is this time costing us both directly and indirectly (i.e., through missed opportunities)? Are we getting enough value for the time we are spending?

2. How do employees and managers feel about our current performance management approach? How do these perceptions translate into performance—does our process help people do a better job or does it mostly just hurt morale?
3. How much do we trust our data? Does the data we have help us make better decisions? How do we use our data today in decision-making and do we really need it? What other factors drive decisions about people?

The answers to these questions can help organizations explore whether performance management is costing too much in terms of time spent, reduced morale, and bad data. However, until these questions are asked, the potential for performance management to help organizations close their performance gap remains unrealized.

Differing Perspectives on How to Fix Performance Management

Few experts disagree that performance management needs to be fixed, but many disagree on how. Much of the debate has been focused on whether to get rid of performance reviews and ratings. Adler et al. (2016) outlined the key perspectives in this debate. The "no ratings" advocates noted that despite decades of effort trying to improve their quality, performance ratings consistently remain inaccurate reflections of employees' true performance. Building better rating scales, providing training to raters, changing what is rated (e.g., goals, behaviors, etc.), and changing how often ratings are made, among other strategies aimed at fixing ratings, have failed. Raters frequently do not agree with each other, and ratings tend to be influenced by many factors beyond the rater's judgments of an employee's performance effectiveness (Murphy & Cleveland, 1995). Performance ratings don't motivate higher performance; they instead often hinder performance. Because performance ratings are often not accurate, feedback based on them is also not accurate and therefore not helpful. If employees perceive that feedback is not fair, they are unlikely to act upon it.

Supporting this perspective are stories from several high-profile organizations that have eliminated the annual performance reviews and replaced them with processes that center on real-time coaching and feedback. For example:

*   Adobe stopped doing formal performance appraisals and replaced them with more informal conversations. In an interview with *Business Insider*, Donna Morris, senior vice president of People and Places at Adobe, compared the typical annual performance review to a "dreaded dental appointment." She went on to explain how Adobe substituted a more informal check-in process for the annual review. Check-ins at Adobe are done throughout the year and are an opportunity for managers and employees

to discuss progress on expectations and for employees to get feedback. Adobe has noted several improvements since moving to this new approach, including better performance and engagement (Baer, 2014).

- Deloitte radically changed their performance management process after discovering that most executives did not find their traditional approach to be valuable—one that consumed over 2-million person hours per year. They eliminated activities such as cascading goals, 360-degree feedback, and calibration meetings. They also streamlined performance reviews by asking project leaders to answer four simple questions about each employee's performance at the end of every project (e.g., "I would always want this person on my team"). Data are aggregated across projects and are used to make decisions about raises and promotions. Deloitte initially reported that they were not sharing specific responses with employees for fear that managers would not give honest ratings, but they were encouraging more regular feedback (Buckingham & Goodall, 2015). While it may be too soon to know how well this process is working, Deloitte notes that the time-savings alone has yielded significant positive outcomes.

- Microsoft eliminated its longtime practice of rating and stack-ranking employees (a practice in which managers compare employees to each other and rank order them from highest to lowest performers), which the company said was killing collaboration. Instead they are moving to more real-time feedback and coaching (Warren, 2013).

- GE, the company known as the inventor of the forced-ranking system in which the bottom 10% of employees were routinely fired, has eliminated rankings and traditional ratings. They now encourage more real-time coaching and feedback and have developed an app internally that allows employees to set goals and receive continuous feedback from others (Nisen, 2015).

- Other companies such as Gap, Cargill, and Eli Lilly, among others, went through substantial reform efforts, reducing their formal performance management requirements and focusing on driving real-time goal setting, feedback, and performance adjustments. All have reported positive outcomes, especially in terms of morale improvements, cost savings, and employee engagement.

On the other side of the debate are those who believe that getting rid of performance ratings is a bad idea for the following reasons (Adler et al., 2016):

- Performance is always evaluated whether or not evaluations are explicit. Even organizations that have a "no ratings" approach still need to make decisions about individuals. Those decisions are themselves a type of rating, which equates to a judgment about the employee's future (e.g., continue to employ, promote, fire, etc.). Not sharing these "shadow ratings" is dishonest because it fails to give the employee a clear message about where he or she stands.

- The discomfort in performance reviews is necessary for growth, even if it is unpleasant. Employees are motivated to change when they see a gap between current and desired levels of performance. Employees who do not receive critical feedback as part of a formal process will carry on with ineffective behaviors.
- Organizations do not have a clear idea of what to do instead of ratings. Coaching and feedback conversations need a "forcing function" otherwise they will not occur. The fear is that managers cannot be trusted to engage in these conversations and they simply may not happen if formal reviews are not required. Organizations have difficulty identifying individuals who are ready to be promoted or given new opportunities without a systematic appraisal process and performance data.
- It is hard to justify decisions and defend against legal challenges without ratings. Although defending against a negative personnel action is possible without a formal review, most organizations lack the discipline to document employee performance without a systematic process in place.
- Specific performance management practices are required by regulation in some organizations. For example, Title 5 of the U.S. Code requires that all government employees be given periodic performance evaluations and a rating of record, making a no-ratings approach impossible for these employees. Other organizations are subject to external regulations or accreditation standards that require specific performance management practices, such as setting individual objectives for every employee. These requirements limit the flexibility that organizations might have to transform their approaches.

Some research provides support to the assertion that getting rid of ratings is a bad idea. According to a study conducted by CEB, employees who do not receive ratings are less engaged and perceive pay decisions as less fair than employees who receive ratings (CEB, 2016). However, this study did not distinguish between organizations that have replaced ratings with a robust system of coaching and feedback from those organizations that have eliminated ratings (or never had them in the first place) but did not replace them with other strategies to drive coaching, feedback, and effective and frequent performance conversations. While CEB's findings do not demonstrate a causal relationship between eliminating ratings and negative outcomes, they do suggest that organizations that are considering removing ratings proceed with caution.

One problem with the recent backlash against traditional performance management systems is that it resulted in an oversimplified focus on the ratings themselves as a root cause of performance management failure. Many organizations designed their reform efforts around eliminating ratings as the key intervention. Simply changing ratings will not improve performance. Some organizations have tried this approach only to find that managers end up avoiding feedback conversations altogether, and employees then do not see a link between their performance and rewards. On the other hand, organizations that attempt to improve performance management simply by streamlining the rating process also do not find much value from the change. Changing rating scales, goal-setting practices, and the frequency and type of review conversations in isolation are like rearranging the deck chairs on the Titanic. Cosmetic fixes are unlikely to have a real impact on behavior or performance management effectiveness (DeNisi & Smith, 2014). Thus, the important question is not "Should we eliminate performance ratings?" The better question is, "Is our performance management approach driving improved performance and high employee engagement?" If the answer is "no," then the organization is not realizing the benefits that performance management can yield.

Performance management reform needs to be tackled holistically, thinking through how the organization can best drive performance, given its strategy, other processes in place or needed, and even the work of different teams. Depending on the organization's circumstances and specific goals for performance management, it may be effective to eliminate performance ratings—or not. However, the question of whether to eliminate ratings is not the place to start. Instead, reform needs to begin with higher-level strategy and goals—system redesign then needs to follow.

Assessing the Need for Change

The ratings debate has sparked great interest in performance management reform, and many organizations have contemplated or even tried some changes as a result, with more or less success. Achieving meaningful, positive change that results in effective performance management is not a small undertaking. It takes time, effort, and commitment to achieve the kinds of culture changes around regular feedback, development, and positive performance improvement that will drive higher levels of performance and engagement. Essentially, it requires developing a culture for effective performance management. Because pursuit of this undertaking is not trivial, it is best to start by exploring the extent to which large-scale change is needed versus making piecemeal changes, such as eliminating ratings, in hopes of some improvement. Begin with a brief self-reflection, such as the example in Box 1.1, to better understand your organization's current state and the potential need for change.

BOX 1.1 ASSESS YOUR NEED FOR CHANGE

Directions: Answer each question with "yes," "no," or "somewhat" to indicate your organization's current state. Consider feedback you have gotten from employees, managers, and executives; trends in employee survey results; and your own observations about performance management practices in your organization.

In our organization . . .	Yes	Somewhat	No
1. Completing performance management tasks requires several hours of work for employees each year (e.g., setting goals, doing self-assessments, completing 360-degree feedback, etc.).	☐	☐	☐
2. Completing performance management tasks requires several hours of work for managers each year (e.g., setting goals for employees, completing performance reviews, going to calibration meetings, etc.).	☐	☐	☐
3. Employees and managers frequently complain that the performance management process is too difficult and/or time-consuming.	☐	☐	☐
4. Employees and managers frequently question the value of the performance management process.	☐	☐	☐
5. Employees frequently complain that poor performers aren't held accountable.	☐	☐	☐
6. Managers are often reluctant to give employees candid feedback about their performance.	☐	☐	☐
7. Employees frequently complain that they don't see a clear link between performance ratings and rewards.	☐	☐	☐
8. Little variation in ratings exist; it's difficult to use ratings to make distinctions in employee performance.	☐	☐	☐
9. Managers and executives don't really trust the accuracy of performance ratings when making decisions.	☐	☐	☐
10. No concrete evidence exists that the performance management approach actually leads to better performance.	☐	☐	☐

Review your answers and consider how urgent your need for change might be:

- **If you answered most questions with "yes,"** your performance management approach is ripe for transformation. It is likely time-consuming and burdensome without providing commensurate value for the investment. You can make a case for change by highlighting how much time people spend on it and the cost of that time, employee and manager dissatisfaction with the process, and the lack of useful data that results from it.
- **If you answered most questions with "somewhat,"** your performance management approach could use some improvement. It may not be your highest HR priority right now, but it is worth taking a closer look at the items you answered "yes" or "somewhat." Perhaps you can make some small improvements without changing your whole performance management approach.
- **If you answered most questions with "no,"** bravo! Your performance management process is in pretty good shape. You may have a few opportunities to make minor improvements. Focus any change efforts on those that are easy to do and will have clear benefits (e.g., streamlining time-consuming processes, improving the quality of feedback conversations, etc.).

Once you have assessed the scope of the change that may be needed, you can identify the potential benefits and costs of change. Table 1.1 lists common costs and benefits. To estimate return on investment (ROI) for the change, identify which benefits may be realistic to achieve and at what cost, given the scope of change identified previously. When benefits outweigh costs, ROI is positive.

Being upfront about the costs of change and how to mitigate them can help with obtaining buy-in and support. Although the tools in Box 1.1 and Table 1.1 provide only a rough outline for analyzing the need to change, they can help start a dialog in your organization about whether performance management change is a worthwhile goal to pursue.

★★★

Organizations are constantly seeking ways to improve performance, but performance management typically does not help. It is too time-consuming, is generally disliked, and does not produce reliable or accurate data. Why does performance management add so little value? The concept is sensible, but it

TABLE 1.1 Potential Benefits and Costs of Change

Potential Benefits	Potential Costs
• Less time spent by managers and employees on administrative performance management tasks • More time available for quality conversations between employees and managers • Easier performance management processes may lead to higher compliance and greater accuracy • Less stress and anxiety about performance reviews • Goodwill from employees and managers who feel their concerns were heard, resulting in higher engagement • More reliable and trustworthy data with which to make decisions • Improved individual and organizational performance	• Time to design and implement new approaches • Disruption to business operations resulting from both time needed to educate people about the change and distraction produced by the change • Resistance to change from managers and employees, causing delays and disruption • Money to redesign IT systems, implement new training, and other resources needed to support changes to the performance management approach • Temporary decreases in performance due to time and effort required to complete the change

is often implemented in ways that undermine its potential for effectiveness. While numerous experts have debated the relative merits of different performance management approaches (e.g., to have ratings or not), these debates often leave organizations with more questions than answers.

This book provides practical guidance for HR professionals and managers on building a better approach to performance management. Although performance management is often seen as an HR intervention, managers are key to its success. Solid relationships and good communication lie at the heart of driving effective performance—particularly between managers and employees. The next chapter presents a framework that emphasizes these relationships and provides insights for HR professionals and managers about how to transform performance management from a burden to a benefit by engaging and equipping employees to perform to their potential.

References

Adler, S., Campion, M., Colquitt, A., Grubb, A., Murphy, K., Ollander-Krane, R., & Pulakos, E. D. (2016). Getting rid of performance ratings: Genius or folly? A debate. *Industrial and Organizational Psychology, 9*, 219–252.

Aguinis, H., Joo, H., & Gottfredson, R. K. (2011). Why we hate performance management—and why we should love it. *Business Horizons, 54*, 503–507.

Baer, D. (2014, April 10). Why Adobe abolished their annual performance review and you should, too. *Business Insider.* Retrieved from www.businessinsider.com/adobe-abolished-annual-performance-review-2014-4.

Buckingham, M., & Goodall, A. (2015, April). Reinventing performance management. *Harvard Business Review*. Retrieved from https://hbr.org/2015/04/reinventing-performance-management.

Bureau of Labor Statistics. (2010). *National compensation survey*. Retrieved from www.bls.gov/ncs/data.htm.

CEB. (2012). *Driving breakthrough performance in the new work environment*. Arlington, VA: Author.

CEB. (2014). *The performance transformation: Strategies to build a workforce of enterprise contributors*. Arlington, VA: Author.

CEB. (2016). *The real impact of eliminating performance ratings: Insights from employees and managers*. Arlington, VA: Author.

Culbert, S. A. (2010, April 11). Yes, everybody really does hate performance reviews. *Wall Street Journal*. Retrieved from www.wsj.com/articles/SB127093422486175363.

Culbertson, S. S., Henning, J. B., & Payne, S. C. (2013). Performance appraisal satisfaction: The role of feedback and goal orientation. *Journal of Personnel Psychology, 12*, 189–195.

DeNisi, A., & Smith, C. E. (2014). Performance appraisal, performance management, and firm-level performance. *Academy of Management Annals, 8*, 127–179.

McGregor, J. (2014, January 27). Study finds that basically every single person hates performance reviews. *The Washington Post*. Retrieved from www.washingtonpost.com/news/on-leadership/wp/2014/01/27/study-finds-that-basically-every-single-person-hates-performance-reviews/?utm_term=.426470248841.

Murphy, K. R., & Cleveland, J. N. (1995). *Understanding performance appraisal: Social, organizational, and goal-oriented perspectives*. Newbury Park, CA: SAGE.

Nisen, M. (2015, August 13). Why GE had to kill its annual performance reviews after more than three decades. *Quartz*. Retrieved from https://qz.com/428813/ge-performance-review-strategy-shift/.

OPM. (2016). *Office of personnel management 2016 federal employee viewpoint survey results*. Retrieved from www.fedview.opm.gov/.

Pulakos, E. D., & O'Leary, R. S. (2011). Why is performance management so broken? *Industrial and Organizational Psychology: Perspectives on Science and Practice, 4*(2), 146–164.

Rock, D. (2008). SCARF: A brain-based model for collaborating with and influencing others. *NeuroLeadership Journal, 1*, 1–9.

Rock, D., Davis, J., & Jones, B. (2014, August). Kill your performance ratings. *Strategy + Business*. Retrieved from http://www.strategy-business.com/article/00275.

Warren, T. (2013, November 11). Microsoft axes its controversial employee-ranking system. *The Verge*. Retrieved from www.theverge.com/2013/11/12/5094864/microsoft-kills-stack-ranking-internal-structure.

2

WHAT TO CHANGE

What does effective performance management look like? To answer this question, we first need to understand what it typically looks like and how it evolved to its present state. We need to understand why it doesn't work, the underlying causes of this problem, and the changes we need to make to address these challenges. From this deeper understanding comes a framework that organizations can use to guide performance management transformation.

A Brief History of Performance Management

The idea of managing performance is as old as work itself. Formal approaches to evaluating performance have their roots in the industrial revolution. As work became more defined and specialized, employee performance could be assessed in a more standardized way, and information from these assessments could be used to make decisions about work assignments and rewards. This purpose fit with the scientific management theories that emerged in the early twentieth century: performance could be maximized by structuring work in the most efficient way and training employees how to follow these processes (Taylor, 1911). Performance appraisals were the means to let employees know if they were meeting expectations and help the organization make decisions about retention, promotion, and termination. By the 1950s performance appraisal was a well-established practice in organizations and was codified into law for U.S. federal government employees with the *Performance Review Act*.

By the 1960s, scientific management had given way to more humanistic theories of leadership. A professional and managerial category of work emerged that could not be reduced to a series of simple steps and instead required more judgment, creativity, and interpersonal interaction. "Management by Objectives" or MBOs became popular as a means of defining what was to be accomplished at the beginning of a year and then measuring results against those goals. Although MBOs were later criticized because they were easy to "game," they were an early step toward a more holistic approach to managing performance. In the 1970s, performance management became more formal and structured after numerous legal challenges led organizations to take greater care to align performance criteria to job requirements and to place more emphasis on defining performance standards.

In the 1980s, organizations began to fundamentally change in the face of new economic pressures, becoming flatter and leaner. Employees were urged to do more with less. Performance appraisal was expanded to "performance management" to encompass a full array of activities that were designed to drive higher performance—goal setting, 360-degree feedback, interim reviews, formal performance conversations, and calibration sessions among managers to ensure consistency in ratings (cf., London & Mone, 2014). The 1990s saw a rise in the use of technology systems to capture data and facilitate these processes.

Performance Management Today

Today work is more complex, dynamic, and interconnected than ever before (CEB, 2012), but performance management practices have not kept pace with these changes. Although most goal-setting systems encourage people to revise their goals if the situation changes, most of us don't actually do this. Yet, setting goals just once a year is not usually enough to keep pace with a dynamic and fast-paced business environment where priorities change rapidly. Success requires the efforts of diverse teams, yet performance management processes focus on rating and rewarding individuals, while ranking processes pit employees against each other and inhibit collaboration. Traditional pay-for-performance systems may undermine creativity and innovation in knowledge roles (Pink, 2009). Younger employees are demanding more career growth and feedback—stilted reviews once or twice a year is not what today's employees want or expect (Rock & Jones, 2015).

As work becomes more unpredictable and requires more agility to adapt to a changing world, performance management practices have interestingly become more rigid and complex, perhaps to exercise more control over holding employees accountable in an environment where the increased pace of work, use of sophisticated technology, interdependence, and globalization makes it difficult to track and measure performance. Instead of a holistic approach to managing talent, organizations today are faced with a dizzying array of tasks that all fall under the umbrella of "performance management," resulting in the approach shown in Figure 2.1.

The typical yearly performance cycle begins with goal setting. Goals are cascaded throughout the organization—each business unit creates its own goals and cascades these down to subordinate units until it reaches each employee

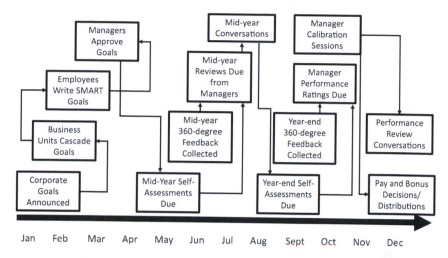

FIGURE 2.1   Typical Annual Performance Management Cycle

who creates his or her goals directly derived from higher-level goals. At the mid-year point, employees complete a self-assessment of their progress toward their goals, they (or their managers) identify others to provide input, and they are also asked to provide 360-degree feedback. The manager reviews the self-assessment and the 360-degree feedback and completes a review, which is discussed with the employee. The whole process then repeats at year end. Before communicating the final rating to employees, managers meet to calibrate their ratings (note: calibration will be discussed in more detail in Chapter 8). Final ratings then may drive pay decisions, and the ratings and outcomes are eventually communicated to the employees.

Several problems are immediately apparent. First, performance management is reduced to a series of discrete events rather than an ongoing process of improving performance day-to-day. Second, the process is complex, with many steps and dependencies. Third, the goal-setting and evaluation components take a long time, such that many employees have only a little over half the year to demonstrate performance that will "count" toward their review. Finally, the process is time-consuming, and it is not typically viewed as valuable by managers or employees.

Performance management has become the tail that wags the dog. Some managers have reported that their organization slows down the last 2–3 months of the rating cycle to devote time to collecting ratings, running calibration sessions, and having performance conversations. At the start of the next annual cycle, even more time is spent setting new goals. Managers can have up to 50 direct reports, but even with the more typical 6–10 reports, it takes a lot of time to complete the typical performance management process, with many steps, sub-steps, and handoffs that all occur within a technology system that often adds to the frustration. See Box 2.1 for one example.

BOX 2.1 TECHNOLOGY GONE AWRY

One system with which we worked required the following steps to set employee goals for the year:

- HR "unlocks" the system, making it ready for use.
- Organizational units enter their goals to be cascaded.
- Managers enter their goals and cascade to employees; the employee can't proceed until these goals are entered.
- Employees enter their goals and submit to managers for approval.
- Managers review and approve employee goals. If changes are needed, there may be additional back and forth between the manager and employee.
- Employee acknowledges final goals, which are then "submitted" as the goals of record. Once submitted, these goals can't be changed unless HR "unlocks" the system again.
- HR monitors compliance of these steps to ensure each one is completed on time.

Each of these steps was accompanied by many individual actions required in the technology system. The user interface was not intuitive, required many individual clicks, and steps had to be done exactly right or the system would not work properly. Slow system speed made data entry time-consuming and cumbersome. Many people lost data—either due to system errors or failure to save properly—and had to retype their goals multiple times. Character limits were frustrating. Employees spent more time editing their goal statements to keep them within character limits than they did making sure the goals were actually meaningful. The other system components—doing self-assessments, 360-degree feedback, and manager reviews—were equally cumbersome. Employees and managers began to associate the performance management process with the technology system. Frustration with the latter spilled over into general feelings of dislike for the entire concept of performance management.

Eventually organizational leaders got fed up and called for change. One group began by trying to change the process to make it less burdensome and more value added. They reasoned that once they redesigned the process they could buy a technology solution to meet these needs. A second group emerged that had a different view: they focused on shopping for a new technology system that was easier to use, figuring that the process that was designed into the system would be based on "best practices" and would only require minor tweaking to customize to the organization. The two groups began to compete for resources and executive sponsorship. Because frustration with the current technology system was so prevalent, the technology-focused group was given resources and authority to lead the project, and the design of effective practices took a backseat. In the end, the organization purchased a new technology system that was more user-friendly. After several years and a significant amount of money, their approach was less frustrating but did no more to actually help employees improve performance.

Despite the time and complexity of the process, most organizations have no idea if their performance management approach leads to better performance. Success is often measured by compliance—that is, how many people complete each required step on time. In our experience, compliance varies widely—approaching 100% in some organizations and less than 50% in others, depending on the strength of the HR team and the penalties for noncompliance. However, compliance is not a good indicator of effectiveness. Even in organizations where compliance is close to 100%, few managers and employees say the performance management system adds value. Even fewer (typically 20–30%) report that they see a link between their performance and important outcomes such as pay, advancement, and development opportunities.

Performance Management Failures and How to Fix Them

Gaining value from performance management starts with understanding what has worked well, what has not worked well, and why. An analysis of the root causes of performance management dissatisfaction and failure reveals the seven major challenges discussed in the rest of this chapter. Fortunately, each of these challenges can be addressed. The challenges and solutions are summarized in Table 2.1.

TABLE 2.1 Summary of Challenges and Solutions

Challenge	Solution
• Too many, conflicting goals	• Commit to a singular purpose
• Too many fads and untested assumptions	• Use an evidence-based approach
• One-size-fits-all approach	• Fit the approach to the organization's needs
• Mistrust leads to over-engineered controls	• Trade some control for flexibility
• Ignoring environmental influences on performance	• Improve performance by improving the situation
• Disconnected from day-to-day work	• Make it part of how work gets done
• Process trumps people	• Shift emphasis from process to people

Challenge: Too Many Conflicting Goals

What is the purpose of performance management? Table 2.2 shows the most common answers to this question from workshops we have led in many organizations. Answers in the left column focus on employee development while those in the right focus on administrative goals. When we ask participants what they think their performance management approach *actually* achieves, most say that it accomplishes some of the administrative goals but very few of the development goals.

Often missing from this discussion is the goal of enabling performance. Ultimately most people agree that this should be the primary purpose of performance management, but it often gets lost in myriad subordinate goals, many of which work against each other. For example, development goals can be at odds with administrative goals. Development requires employees to engage in self-reflection about how their performance needs to be improved and seek help from others. In turn, managers need to be able to offer feedback and coaching focused to help employees grow their skills. When performance ratings are used as the basis for rewards, employees are reluctant to openly discuss their development needs with their managers and instead feel compelled to argue for higher ratings and rewards. It is also difficult for managers to switch gears—at one moment serving as a coach and in the next moment judging performance, applying a rating, and rewarding the employee. Performance reviews that are used both to develop and reward employees create a situation in which neither purpose is done well. Discussing ratings and rewards always trumps development and coaching—which takes a backseat.

Even if an organization tries to prioritize development or administrative goals, the performance management process can still suffer from trying to do too much. For example, one HR leader told us that his organization uses a

TABLE 2.2 Typical Answers to the Question: What Purpose Should Performance Management Serve?

Development Goals	Administrative Goals
• Inspire and motivate employees • Set clear expectations for employees • Align employees' work with organizational goals • Help employees develop their skills • Ensure employees get coaching and feedback • Foster communication and good working relationships between employees and managers • Provide career development and growth for employees	• Differentiate employee performance to use as the basis for decisions about pay, promotion, training, or termination • Protect the organization in case of legal challenges • Hold poor performers accountable—gather documentation needed to support performance improvement plans • Analyze performance ratings across the organization to identify low- and high-performing business units

single performance rating to inform all people decisions: distribute raises and bonuses, determine promotions, nominate employees for special development programs or awards, and identify and provide consequences to poor perform- ers. Each of these are different decisions that have different business goals, but this organization uses a single rating for all of them, which places an enormous amount of pressure on a single, arguably flawed, number. Managers agonized over the ratings and consistently tried to increase them so employees would not miss out on all possible rewards. In the end, ratings were not viewed as a real reflection of performance but rather how managers needed to game the system to best distribute rewards to their employees.

Solution: Commit to a Singular Purpose

A system that tries to do too many things will ultimately do none of them well. Therefore, organizations should commit to a singular purpose for performance management: to improve performance. A clear, written statement of purpose serves as a litmus test to evaluate any proposed performance management prac- tices. If the proposed practice does not have a clear link to improving performance, it should not be implemented. Once this criterion has been met, the organization can determine how to meet secondary goals, such as making pay decisions.

In our experience, this clarity of purpose has been enormously helpful for organizations as they design their new performance management approaches. We have seen many productive debates about whether to include a particular practice (e.g., self-assessments), and they were almost always resolved by an hon- est discussion of how much the practice would actually contribute to improv- ing performance and at what cost. This type of discussion helps overcome the temptation to add complexity that does not provide incremental value.

Clarity of purpose does not eliminate other needs such as the desire to defend against legal challenges or provide substantiation for pay decisions. However, an important question to explore is the extent to which the cur- rent performance management approach meets these needs today. For example, organizations are often fearful of streamlining or eliminating documentation requirements because they feel these are needed to defend against legal chal- lenges. However, performance documentation by itself is rarely sufficient to fully defend against a challenge. Further, when we have evaluated performance documentation as part of legal challenges, written comments often do not align with ratings or rewards, which can exacerbate legal problems. Frequently an employee will have prior reviews that say he or she was doing a great job before being fired or reassigned. The reality is that additional documentation is almost always needed to substantiate any negative performance actions. Therefore, we are not suggesting that secondary goals for the performance management sys- tem are unimportant, but rather that some secondary goals organizations may think they are achieving today are not being achieved well.

Challenge: Too Many Fads and Untested Assumptions

Performance management is probably the HR practice most vulnerable to fads and untested assumptions about what drives and motivates human behavior. Many HR leaders tell us that they implemented a particular practice because the CEO read it in a popular business book, but they had no research or evidence to back up the practice. For example, one HR leader told us that her CEO insists on using forced-ranking to identify the bottom 10% of employees each year for termination or remediation. Employees hate the system, but the CEO insists on keeping it, believing that the organization needs it to improve sagging performance. Research shows that these forced-ranking systems can provide a short-term boost to performance if low performers are terminated and good performers remain. However, within a few years this approach provides diminishing returns and can cause unintended negative consequences. Cutting out the "bottom" every year leads to terminating satisfactory employees over time, and good employees may be more likely to leave on their own, leading to decreased performance (Scullen, Bergey, & Aiman-Smith, 2005).

Solution: Use Evidence-Based Approaches

Instead of relying on fads and untested assumptions, organizations should use evidence-based approaches to performance management. Evidence-based means that proposed practices should have research that supports their use. Unfortunately, performance management research is sparse. Much of the research that does exist is focused more on perceptions rather than outcomes. One exception was a comprehensive study by CEB that found that some practices do in fact greatly improve performance, some have little impact, and some have a negative impact (CEB, 2002). Table 2.3 summarizes research on these specific practices and their impact.

A few themes emerge from the data. The practices with the most positive impact are those that focus on improving communications and relationships, especially among employees and managers—clarifying expectations, providing effective feedback, and ensuring good development opportunities are available. Those with more marginal impact are associated with administrative processes such as measuring and rewarding performance effectively. The few with negative impact are those that employees tend to dislike the most: stack-ranking, focusing on weaknesses in reviews, and requiring multiple, formal reviews.

The size of the impact will determine ROI of any intervention. That is, for the time and money invested in carrying out the practice, what is the return that can be expected? A positive ROI occurs when every monetary unit (dollar, pound, Euro, etc.) invested yields more than a unit of return. A negative ROI occurs when more is invested than returned. For example, if we invest

TABLE 2.3 Summary of CEB Research on Effectiveness of Common Performance Management Practices

High Effectiveness (More than 25% impact on performance)	Moderate Effectiveness (Between 25% and 10% impact on performance)	Minor Effectiveness (Less than 10% impact on performance)	Ineffective (Zero or negative impact on performance)
• Employees get informal feedback from a knowledgeable source that is fair and accurate, and that helps them do their jobs better • Employees understand the performance standards for which they are held accountable • Managers emphasize performance strengths in performance reviews • Internal communications are effective • Employees assigned work that plays to their strengths	• Managers clearly communicate expectations • Managers translate long-term goals into step-by-step plans • Managers help employees solve problems and access resources • Employees can develop and grow through stretch experiences • Employees can work on challenging projects and assignments	• Managers recognizes and rewards achievements • 360-degree feedback is used • Employees have development plans • Managers measure performance and results • Employees receive effective training • Employees perceive a connection between performance and rewards (pay, promotion)	• Rank order employees from best to worst performers • Do more than one formal performance review per year • Emphasize weaknesses in formal performance reviews and informal feedback

Source: Performance Management Survey (CEB, 2002)

$10,000 in a new system but only get $8,000 of value from it, our ROI is negative. It is difficult to quantify many of the benefits of performance management with specific monetary amounts, but we can still use the concept of ROI to determine if performance management activities are worth the time they take to conduct.

While many common practices do provide a small positive impact, they are extremely time-consuming to implement, yielding a small or even negative ROI. Therefore, interventions should have a demonstrable and evidence-based positive impact and be practical and cost effective. The value that they add must outweigh the costs of implementing them.

Challenge: One-Size-Fits-All Approach

Many organizations are risk-averse and unwilling to try something unless other organizations have done it first. However, using only "tried and true" approaches stifles innovation and prevents experimenting with new ideas. Whole industries exist just to collect and disseminate case studies and best practices. The problem is that most organizations have ineffective performance management processes so emulating the practices of others will likely lead to more bad practices. Even if the practice has worked well in one organization, trying to replicate it in another may not lead to the same positive results. Performance management is both a reflection of and a contributor to an organization's culture (London & Mone, 2014) and must fit the organization's strategy, culture, and goals to be effective.

Solution: Fit the Approach to the Organization's Needs

Every HR leader with whom we have worked to implement change has emphasized the importance of fitting the performance management approach to the organization's strategy and culture. While it may be tempting to imitate what large, prestigious organizations have done, blindly transplanting best practices from one organization to another rarely works. Instead, practices must often be tailored to fit each unique organization.

A prime example is the use of performance ratings. Some cultures are very data-driven, take performance ratings very seriously, and use these ratings to make significant decisions about people. The bestselling book, *Work Rules*, about talent practices at Google, has a chapter entitled "Pay Unfairly," which advocates rating and paying high and low performers very differently (Bock, 2015). Bock notes this is an effective strategy at Google, which has a strong engineering culture that values data and the resources to make big distinctions in pay. However, pay-for-performance systems have failed spectacularly in other cultures where performance has not historically been differentiated, such as in government agencies. Similarly, some organizations have managed to successfully eliminate performance ratings while others have tried and failed. Choices about ratings as well as every other aspect of the performance management approach must fit the organization's strategy, resources, and culture to be successful.

Challenge: Mistrust Leads to Over-Engineered Controls

As illustrated in Figure 2.1, performance management processes are often overly complex. This complexity arises out of mistrust: a fundamental belief that managers and employees will fail to do the right thing without numerous checks and balances. The process is over-engineered to take away possibility of error. A prime example is the requirement to have a formal, mid-year review (complete with ratings and written narratives) because it is believed that managers won't have feedback conversations more than once a year otherwise.

This mistrust is not without basis. A chief complaint of organizations that have removed formal processes such as ratings is that sometimes employees then do not get any feedback at all. Without ratings as a forcing function, managers will avoid the uncomfortable task of having performance conversations—especially if the organization has not done anything else to develop manager skills or hold them accountable. The same concern is true for other components such as goal setting. Without HR to enforce standards for SMART goals, managers may not set expectations at all. When mistakes are made, the solution is often to add another step, process, form, requirement, or approval. For example, if managers cannot be trusted to make unbiased ratings, then a second-level review is needed, adding to the time and effort required. The result is the heavy processes we see today with new steps, processes, and rules bolted onto the old.

An over-emphasis on control results in complexity and rigidity—the opposite of the dynamic nature of today's work environment. Goals must be set at the beginning of the year, even though that timing may not fit with how work is actually done. Employees must be rated on how well they achieved their year-old goals even though conditions changed during the year, goals are no longer relevant, and no updates to goals have been made. Managers must complete extensive written documentation to justify performance ratings and defend against legal challenges even though these challenges are rare and usually require additional documentation or other processes to take defensible negative action against employees, such as termination. HR's role ends up being one of policing the performance management process rather than serving as a strategic partner in driving organizational performance.

Solution: Trade Some Control for Flexibility

A truly valuable approach to performance management must be flexible enough to accommodate change and fit the unique requirements of different departments, functions, and regions in an organization. Allowing more flexibility necessitates giving up some control. It also requires HR to operate as more of a strategic partner than rule enforcer.

We are not suggesting a free-for-all with no requirements or accountability. On the contrary, managers and employees function best when they understand what they are supposed to do. However, building a flexible approach requires letting go of some control. In later chapters, we provide specific ideas for developing more flexible approaches for each major performance management activity. The important underlying principle to our approach is parsimony. Each requirement in a performance management process should be carefully evaluated to ensure it is important in driving high performance. Activities should be included only if their value outweighs their costs (e.g., Effron & Ort, 2010).

Challenge: Ignoring Environmental Influences on Performance

W. Edwards Deming once observed that "A bad system will beat a good person every time" (Deming, 1993), meaning that even the most talented employees will struggle in a dysfunctional environment. Behavior is a function of the person and environment (Lewin, 1936): performance is a result of not only an individual's talents and motivation but also the extent to which the environment supports or inhibits performance. Individuals who are star performers in one role may be only average in another. For example, one study showed that 46% of stock analysts who were star performers at one firm did poorly after moving to another firm. The researchers concluded that a myriad of environmental factors led to the decreased performance (Groysberg, Nanda, & Nohria, 2004).

The importance of the environment is largely ignored in the typical approach to performance management. Individual goals are set and performance is evaluated as if each employee had full control over the results. This is rarely the case, of course. Numerous factors can impact performance, such as:

- Market and economic conditions.
- Siloed organizational structures that make it difficult to collaborate across boundaries.
- Knowledge, skills, abilities, and motives of team members whom individuals rely on to get things done.
- Organizational or external rules, policies, or procedures that slow down work and delay approvals.
- Lack of resources or technology needed to perform efficiently.
- Poorly defined expectations and criteria for success.

Solution: Improve Performance by Improving the Situation

If performance falls short of expectations, the first place we should look to fix it is the environment. In what ways has the individual employee been set up for success or failure? What can we do to change the environment to increase our chances of success? If we want to maximize performance, we must set the environment up to support it. This includes:

- A greater awareness when setting expectations of the real constraints and barriers that might hurt performance and an honest discussion about if and how these can be overcome.
- More shared responsibility for results—rather than evaluating individuals only, balancing individual and team evaluations.
- More real-time analysis of results so that problems can be spotted and course corrected early.
- A willingness to scrutinize and if necessary revise business processes and workflows to remove barriers that block performance.

Not all performance challenges can be overcome by altering the environment. Good selection decisions are essential. No amount of changing the environment will improve performance if the employee lacks the essential knowledge, skills, and abilities to succeed. Either the job must be changed to better fit the employee's skillset, the employee needs to be placed in a different role that is a better fit, or the employee needs to be let go. In Chapter 9, we discuss how to diagnose the root causes of poor performance and how to address it.

Challenge: Disconnected From Day-to-Day Work

Managers and employees alike view performance management tasks as taking them away from real work. This criticism has a lot of merit. Many activities do take place outside of day-to-day work and seem misaligned with how real work gets done. For example, goal-setting practices don't fit with real work cycles. Goals are often set at the beginning of the year, but this is not necessarily in sync with when new projects begin. Projects may start and stop throughout the year, and different parts of the organization may have different work cycles. Some projects may span multiple years with few milestones along with way. Other projects may span just months or weeks. Some employees don't work on "projects" but rather on daily tasks they are assigned, with little control over their workloads. The classic example is a call center where employees answer calls as they come in and help customers by placing orders or resolving problems. Daily or weekly metrics (e.g., number of issues successfully resolved, customer satisfaction) are likely more relevant for these roles than year-long goals.

Several organizations with whom we have worked took goal-setting requirements to extremes. One decreed that every employee needed individualized goals, regardless of whether their work was largely identical to their peers. This resulted in managers spending an inordinate amount of time trying to make artificial distinctions in goals among employees. The organization also insisted that goals include only things that were "above and beyond" day-to-day activities. This requirement worked well for employees who did primarily project-based work. However, employees whose main role was to do the same tasks every day had difficulty setting these types of goals. Employees ended up creating "make-work" goals, such as serving on a special committee or task force outside of their normal responsibilities. Because goal attainment factored heavily into rewards, many employees would focus more on these extra duties than their core work assignments.

Solution: Make It Part of How Work Gets Done

Instead of treating performance management as something separate from work, it should be a natural part of how work gets done. Goals should be set in accordance with the natural rhythm of work—at the start of a project, or the beginning of a financial quarter, or whenever it makes sense for a particular role. The format of the goal should be allowed to fit the work—some will be in the form of daily or weekly metrics, some will be in the form of quarterly sales targets, and others may be in the form of long-term projects whose success can only be measured by qualitative means. Performance measurement and feedback should also fit the work and be embedded in it.

For example, imagine an employee is tasked with developing a marketing campaign for a new product. Ideally the employee and her manager would start by discussing what the campaign should include, when it should be complete, and what success would look like. As the campaign materials are developed, the employee gets feedback from various stakeholders. The employee then uses this feedback to refine and improve the materials—seeking out the manager's assistance if needed. Once complete, the success of the campaign could be measured in a variety of ways such as customer feedback, the "click-through rate" in an email campaign, website traffic, and increased product sales. All these activities are part of performance management—setting expectations upfront, monitoring progress, getting feedback, and evaluating end results. Requiring additional steps outside this process—setting a formal goal before the need for a campaign is even defined, getting feedback at prescribed times during the year instead of in real time, and evaluating success way after the work is done and in an indirect manner (e.g., an overall rating on a 5-point scale)—is of questionable value if the goal is to maximize performance and drive a successful marketing campaign.

Instead of requiring separate processes that occur totally outside of work, organizations should consider how to better embed performance management into the work itself. Performance management is most effective when it occurs naturally as part of day-to-day activities. Employees and managers may not even recognize these activities as performance management. What's more important than the label is that performance-enabling behaviors (ongoing expectations, feedback, coaching, and measuring progress) are embedded in the organization's culture and viewed as a natural part of how work gets done.

Challenge: Process Trumps People

Pulakos and O'Leary (2011) noted that the primary problem with performance management is that it has been reduced to a sequence of administrative activities that tends to alienate rather than empower people. Technology systems tend to exacerbate this problem because they are usually focused exclusively on process. An automated performance management system can help HR leaders determine whether all steps were completed on time, but it doesn't indicate the quality of relationships and communications among coworkers and between managers and employees.

In the quest for more rigor, organizations often implement processes that undermine engagement and morale. For example, stack-ranking and forced distributions are often used to promote more differentiation in performance ratings and rewards. However, employees despise these processes because they feel like no matter how hard they work, it's impossible to get one of very few high ratings. Their commitment and performance then suffer as a result.

Solution: Shift Emphasis From Process to People

Effective communication and ways of working together should be the primary focus of performance management. Building better communications and relationships should not be limited to managers and their direct reports. Managers may not work closely with their direct reports or even be in the same geographic region. Matrix organizational structures, in which employees are aligned to a business unit, region, and functional area are common. Employees may work with colleagues and project leaders from multiple groups. These individuals may be in a better position to set expectations and provide feedback than an employee's direct manager.

In the new work environment, performance management activities are not just the manager's responsibility, they are everyone's. Managers and employees alike need to understand the value of clear expectations for everyone on a team, coworker to coworker, not just manager to team member. Everyone needs to understand how measuring progress on important factors enables higher performance through early detection and course correction, and how discussing and diagnosing performance misses unlocks blockers. Improving the quality of performance conversations at multiple levels and among all employees will yield much more impact on outcomes than focusing on refinements to administrative processes.

What Good Performance Management Looks Like

The foregoing solutions are incorporated into a framework for effective performance management shown in Figure 2.2. This framework has a singular purpose: it is first and foremost focused on the actions that organizations can take to improve employee performance. It is evidenced-based and includes practices most likely to have a positive impact on performance. It is general enough that it can be tailored to fit individual organizational cultures. It balances control with flexibility and parsimony; while there are many things that could be done to improve performance, it focuses on the most powerful levers that organizations can pull. It recognizes the importance of the broader organizational environment in influencing performance. It is tied closely to work—instead of specifying a sequence of events, it represents a more dynamic and ongoing way to embed performance management in work. Finally, it is centered on relationships rather than administrative processes.

The core of the framework represents the most significant driver of performance: the concept of *partnership*. Partnership reflects the nature of the

FIGURE 2.2 Effective Performance Management Framework

relationships between managers and employees and among peers, and this concept permeates all other performance management activities. A partnership is based on mutual respect, trust, and open communication. It differs from the traditional top-down dynamic in which the manager gives direction, the employee carries out orders, and the manager judges the results. The assumptions inherent in the traditional dynamic are 1) a permanent imbalance of power in the relationship—managers are the superiors and employees are the subordinates, 2) one-way communication from the manager to the employee, and 3) employee solely responsible for performance and results. In contrast, a partnership assumes a balance of power, two-way communication, and shared responsibility for results.

Figure 2.3 summarizes the different behaviors that contrast the typical top-down relationship with partnership. The type of relationship between employees and their manager and peers has a direct impact on individual employee

Top-down Management	**Partnership**
Imbalance of Power	*Balance of Power*
• Managers hold the power to make assignments, set goals, and judge results	• Managers and employees work together to decide how work will be accomplished and success will be measured
• Employees can attempt to influence, but managers have the final say	
One-way Communication	*Two-way Communication*
• Most feedback is communicated from the manager to the employee	• Managers and employees communicate openly with each other about what each needs from the other to be successful
• Managers may get feedback anonymously through 360 reviews	• Feedback for both employees and managers comes from multiple sources
Employee Ownership of Results	*Shared Ownership of Results*
• Employees are accountable for their results and receive rewards or consequences based on them; employees are expected to solve problems and overcome barriers to meet their goals	• Managers and employees each acknowledge how they impact results and work collaboratively to improve performance; managers see their role as helping employees to solve problems and overcome barriers

FIGURE 2.3   Top-down Management Versus Partnership

performance (Peterson & Hicks, 1996). Employees who see their relationship with their manager as one of partnership will perform better than those who don't, regardless of the other performance management processes in the organization. If organizations do nothing else to drive high performance, fostering partnerships can still yield significant improvements. Chapter 10 tackles the issue of how to change behavior to be more partnership-oriented.

The inner circle surrounding the partnership concept illustrates the performance management activities that most directly support partnership and improved performance: setting expectations and performance goals, measuring performance, and providing feedback and coaching to help employees improve their performance. Most organizations do some version of these activities today. However, there are some key differences between the way they are typically done and the way they should be done to maximize performance:

• Set goals and expectations. The most common approach to goal and expectation setting is to sit down at the beginning of a rating cycle and establish objectives that must be accomplished by the end of the year. A significant amount of effort is often expended to get the objectives worded just right and to meet corporate standards for SMART goals. Too often these objectives are then put in a drawer and forgotten until the end of the year, when they form the basis of the performance evaluation. By this time, circumstances may have changed and employees have been working on different priorities. This static and rigid way of setting goals undermines the attributes that make them powerful. In Chapter 5, we discuss how to make the process of setting goals and expectations more dynamic and meaningful.

- Measure performance. Performance measurement is often synonymous with end-of-year performance reviews. Employees may receive a rating on overall performance as well as individual facets of performance. However, this information comes too late for employees to use it to impact the quality of their work. Additionally, performance ratings are often so disconnected from the work that employees have a difficult time understanding why they got the ratings that they did. Moreover, ratings are often driven more by political, social, and economic factors than one's performance. Performance measurement that occurs in real time is more useful in driving high performance so that employees can use this information to monitor and improve throughout the year. Performance measurement should also be tied closely to the work that people perform so that employees can clearly see a link between their actions and the results. In Chapter 6, we distinguish performance measurement from performance evaluation and discuss how to use performance measures to enable performance on an ongoing basis.

- Coach and provide feedback. Like performance reviews, feedback and coaching often come only once or twice a year, which is too little and too late to be useful. Feedback must be delivered in real time and in the right way. Feedback done poorly does not usually improve performance and sometimes it can undermine performance by crushing potential and enthusiasm. In Chapter 7, we discuss how to conduct high-quality performance conversations so that feedback and coaching are productive, happen in real time, and lead to improved performance.

These activities are core responsibilities of managers, and it is thus managers who have the greatest potential to positively impact performance. In each of these chapters, we provide guidance and implications for managers as well as HR professionals, who can serve important strategic partnership roles in supporting these activities.

The outer circle of the framework represents activities in the broader organizational environment that are essential for supporting effective performance management. These set an upper boundary on what levels of performance can be achieved. For example, even when employees have solid partnerships with others and performance management practices are executed well, performance will suffer if they face insurmountable barriers to getting things done. While there are many factors in the organizational environment that can affect performance, we focus here on four that have a significant impact on the extent to which well-executed performance management activities between managers and employees and among coworkers can drive performance:

- Communicating purpose. Employees perform better when they believe their work contributes to the organization's mission and that the organization's values align with their own. Employees need to feel they are working toward a higher purpose. A clear vision and strategy communicated widely will help employees identify where they fit and why their work matters.
- Defining success. Organizations must both define the work to be done and the standards for success. Without thoroughly understanding the work and what success looks like, performance management activities are likely to be inconsistent and misaligned.
- Removing barriers. Barriers come in many forms: organizational structures that make it hard to work across boundaries, resource limitations, government regulations, uncooperative colleagues, outdated technology, etc. Some of these barriers can be removed or worked around, while some are more intractable. "Overcoming" barriers first entails defining what the barrier is and its scope, thinking creatively about what can be done to eliminate or mitigate it, and helping employees take the right actions. Some of these solutions might require larger organizational interventions (e.g., changing organizational structures, purchasing new technology) and some might be more limited (e.g., establishing better communications with other business units). Good leaders help employees overcome barriers. Employees perform better when they have leaders who roll up their sleeves and help them solve problems. This is a key behavior in the partnership mindset that is at the core of our framework—when performance is not ideal, it's important to dig in and identify barriers and participate in working to overcome them rather than simply passing judgment on others for performance failures.
- Use data for decisions. Decisions about people (including selection, promotion, training, and development) are better and fairer when they are based on good data. Organizations typically use some type of performance rating to inform these decisions. However, as discussed in Chapter 1, these data are notoriously inaccurate and often ignored in favor of "gut instincts." Better data aligned to the decisions that need to be made yields better results.

This outer layer of the framework contributes to the climate and ultimately the culture in the organization. While a full discussion of these elements is beyond the scope of this book, we address communicating purpose in Chapter 5, defining work and success in Chapter 4, overcoming barriers to performance in Chapter 9, and using performance data to make people decisions in Chapter 8.

★★★

Understanding the root causes of performance management system failure is important to overcoming them. Many of these failures stem from the view of performance management as an HR-driven process rather than a people-driven process, which has the relationship between managers and employees at the center. An effective approach to performance management begins with recognizing that this partnership is at the heart of good performance management. All subsequent activities should support accomplishing work with a partnership mindset—setting flexible goals, measuring performance, and providing real-time feedback. Organizations and HR can support these activities by communicating a strong sense of purpose, clearly defining success, helping to remove barriers, and using performance data in the right way to make effective talent decisions.

References

Bock, L. (2015). *Work rules! Insights from Google that will transform how you live and lead.* New York: Twelve.

CEB. (2002). *Building the high-performance workforce: A quantitative analysis of the effectiveness of performance management strategies.* Arlington, VA: Author.

CEB. (2012). *Driving breakthrough performance in the new work environment.* Arlington, VA: Author.

Deming, W. E. (1993, February). *Deming four day seminar in Phoenix, Arizona* (via the notes of Mike Stoecklein). Retrieved from http://quotes.deming.org/authors/W._Edwards_Deming/quote/10091

Effron, M., & Ort, M. (2010). *One page talent management: Eliminating complexity, adding value.* Boston, MA: Harvard Business Press.

Groysberg, B., Nanda, A., & Nohria, N. (2004, May). The risky business of hiring stars. *Harvard Business Review.* Retrieved from https://hbr.org/2004/05/the-risky-business-of-hiring-stars.

Lewin, K. (1936). *Principles of topological psychology.* New York: McGraw-Hill.

London, M., & Mone, E. M. (2014). Performance management processes that reflect and shape organizational culture and climate. In B. Schneider & K. M. Barbera (Eds.), *The Oxford handbook of organizational climate and culture.* Oxford: Oxford University Press.

Peterson, D. B., & Hicks, M. D. (1996). *Leader as coach: Strategies for coaching and developing others.* Minneapolis, MN: Personnel Decisions International.

Pink, D. H. (2009). *Drive: The surprising truth about what motivates us.* New York: Riverhead Books.

Pulakos, E. D., & O'Leary, R. S. (2011). Why is performance management broken? *Industrial and Organizational Psychology: Perspectives on Science and Practice, 4,* 194–197.

Rock, D., & Jones, B. (2015, September 8). Why more and more companies are ditching performance ratings. *Harvard Business Review.* Retrieved from https://hbr.org/2015/09/why-more-and-more-companies-are-ditching-performance-ratings.

Scullen, S. E., Bergey, P. K., & Aiman-Smith, L. (2005). Forced distribution rating systems and the improvement of workforce potential: A baseline simulation. *Personnel Psychology, 58,* 1–32.

Taylor, F. W. (1911). *The principles of scientific management.* New York: Harper & Brothers.

3

A ROADMAP FOR TRANSFORMATION

Armed with a desire for change and a vision of the future, the next step is to design your new performance management approach. The design should include the guiding principles, key components of the performance management process, and preliminary ideas for how these components will be implemented. Figure 3.1 overviews the design process that we have used successfully with many clients; each of these major phases is described in detail.

Planning the Project

Time invested upfront to plan will keep the project well organized and on track. Begin with a kick-off meeting with a few key stakeholders to brainstorm your approach, decide who to involve, and create a written project plan. Initial kick-off meetings are most efficient when they are limited to the vital few individuals who will be responsible for the effort. A broader kick-off meeting can be held with a full range of stakeholders later to present the project plan.

Discussion topics for this initial meeting may include:

- Why are we pursuing this effort—what problems are we trying to solve?
- What do we want to achieve with the redesign effort?

  - If this effort is wildly successful, what will we have achieved by the end?
  - Beyond a new performance management approach, what do we want to get out of this process?

- What's in and out of scope? Will it be limited to performance management or will it include related talent processes such as compensation, development, succession planning, etc.?

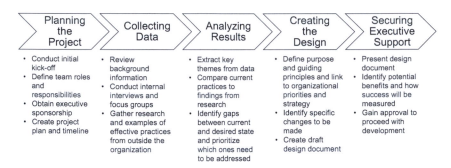

FIGURE 3.1 Roadmap for Performance Management Design

- Which employee groups will be impacted? What employment laws, regulations, or agreements will apply? (For example, labor laws vary by country, which may impact your ability to implement a single approach that applies to everyone.)
- What stakeholders do we need to engage in this process and what is the best way to engage them (both HR and business leaders)?
- Who will be involved in this project, and what will be their roles and responsibilities, such as:

  - Executive sponsor
  - Project leader
  - Logistical coordinator
  - Other key contributors to the design
  - Stakeholders we should consult along the way

- What other major initiatives are happening in our organization and how might these help or hinder our efforts?
- When do we want to implement the new approach? What other organizational events should we plan around?

The results of this session should provide the basis for a written project plan with key activities, milestones, timelines, responsibilities, and resource needs. Regular team meetings should be part of the project schedule to check progress and make course corrections as necessary. Indicators of success are also helpful to keep everyone aligned on the same goals.

The project plan can help to secure executive support and resources, such as external consulting help, additional staff support from inside the organization, and time from stakeholders to participate in interviews and focus groups. Depending on the organizational culture and norms, the project concept may first need to go through multiple rounds of review and approval before creating a final project plan. Support from the highest possible levels in the organization is needed to give the plan the best chance of success.

Getting senior level support is essential. Failure to obtain the right level of sponsorship will doom the effort from the start. We have seen numerous examples of HR teams that worked tirelessly on a redesign concept only to have it shot down by the CEO in the first meeting. Before investing a lot of time, ensure your executive team believes that changing the organization's performance management approach is a priority. They don't have to agree on what the new approach should look like at this point—just that it is a problem worthy of solving. Research from the first two chapters can hopefully help you build the business case that your performance management approach can and should be fixed.

Collecting Data

Data collection entails gathering information from internal and external sources. Internal information is used to assess the organization's current state: the policies and procedures in the current performance management process, what employees and managers think about it, and how effective it is. External information puts the internal information into perspective. It helps you to envision your desired state and assess how your current state fits with this vision.

Data From Internal Sources

Data from internal sources typically includes organizational documents, interviews with key leaders, and focus groups with employees and supervisors from a diverse cross-section of the organization. Useful organizational documents may include:

- Organizational chart.
- Strategic plan/mission/vision/values.
- Organizational demographics: number of employees and managers in various business units, functions, and regions.
- Current performance management policies, process, and procedures, including any forms or templates used throughout the process.
- Information about the organization's broader talent philosophy or strategy.
- Compensation philosophy, policies, and procedures.
- Competency models and rating standards currently used for performance management.
- Performance appraisal forms, including self-appraisals, 360-degree feedback, and manager reviews.
- Ratings data if available (i.e., ratings distributions for each major business unit).
- Employee satisfaction or engagement survey data.

Spend some time mapping out your current approach and reviewing how performance management activities are carried out in any technology systems. This includes how activities are presented, sequencing, time required to complete each step, etc. Examine the process from both the manager and employee's perspective. If available, system metrics can provide a baseline of current participation (e.g., what percentage of the population completes each step).

Interviews and focus groups are useful not only to collect information but also to engage a wide array of stakeholders in the design process. The more that members of diverse groups are represented, the more that key constituents will feel that they have input into the process, which is essential for adoption of the new approach. Interviews and focus groups can be conducted by internal staff or external consultants. Each approach has pros and cons. Internal staff have more first-hand knowledge of participants and their work. However, they may have preconceived ideas that will bias their conclusions. External consultants will have more of a learning curve on the organization and key players, but they can bring a fresh perspective, new insights about the organization, and sometimes additional credibility to the process.

We suggest scheduling 30–60-minute one-on-one interviews with key stakeholders, such as:

- Process owners in HR, such as leaders in Centers of Excellence focused on talent management, performance management, compensation, and development.
- Senior HR Business Partners (HRBPs) who support critical business units.
- Senior business leaders who have expressed frustration with performance management or a desire to change the current approach.
- Leaders of groups that may want to pilot a new performance management approach.
- Senior executives who are especially influential in the organization and whose support is essential to the success of the project.
- Legal counsel if needed (e.g., high risk exposure, prior lawsuits involving performance ratings, current consent decrees in place).

Face-to-face interviews are ideal, but phone or web-based interviews can work equally well, depending on cultural norms. Invitations to participate should include language that clearly explains the purpose of the interview, why the interviewee has been selected, and the questions or types of questions to expect. Interview topics may include:

- Key business priorities: skills and behaviors from staff members needed to meet these priorities and how the performance management approach helps or hinders achieving business goals.

- Perceptions of the current performance management approach: what works well and what could be improved.
- Feedback culture: how often do employees get high-quality feedback and what gets in the way of effective feedback.
- Implementation considerations: key groups to include, communication strategies, etc.

Focus groups can be a useful supplement to interviews, especially if getting employee input is an important part of the organization's culture. Usually 4–6 focus groups of 8–12 participants each is sufficient to get a broad array of input; however, more may be needed to give enough people an opportunity to contribute. Tips for selecting the right participants include:

- Conduct separate meetings with individual contributors and managers so that everyone feels more comfortable being candid.
- Ensure participants in each meeting are diverse in terms of demographics (age, sex, race, etc.) as well as business units and functions. Having people from different units and functions in the same group is especially useful, as it gives participants valuable perspectives on other parts of the organization.
- Ask for volunteers (reluctant participants are ineffective participants) but feel free to invite participants who would be especially valuable contributors (e.g., high performers who have good ideas and can clearly articulate them).
- Include people who are known to have different opinions on the topic of performance management. However, be careful of individuals who have a reputation of arguing for argument's sake. The conversation can quickly get derailed if a vocal minority uses the focus group as the opportunity to air personal grievances.
- Include newer hires as well as tenured employees; however, employees should have been with the organization long enough (usually at least a year) to have an informed opinion of how performance management works.
- Keep group size to 12 maximum if possible. Larger groups make it difficult to ensure everyone has a chance to speak.

Additional coordination is required for organizations with bargaining unit employees. If bargaining unit employees will be affected by the redesign, union representatives should be consulted during every step of the process. Depending on the specific contract terms, they may have varying rights with respect to providing input into the performance management process. However, it's usually in the organization's best interest to try and work with the union as a partner rather than an adversary. Even if their role is consultative, they will likely appreciate the opportunity to share their views. Union representatives are more apt to embrace performance management changes when they believe it will increase transparency and fairness and provide better support and opportunities for employees.

Two hours is usually enough time to conduct each focus group. As with interviews, focus group invitations should clearly describe the purpose of the meeting, why participants have been invited, and a preview of the discussion topics. Focus groups are most effective when conducted face-to-face, though we have had success with virtual focus groups as well. Video (e.g., through Skype or WebEx) is the next best thing to in-person. As a last resort, a simple phone conference can work as well. In general, if the group is virtual rather than meeting in person we suggest making the group smaller and inviting participants from the same general geographic region to make it easier to coordinate across time zones. Groups where some participants are face-to-face with the facilitator and others are virtual are less than ideal. It's hard for virtual participants to stay as engaged, especially if employees who are physically present dominate the conversation. A better approach is to go with a group that is either all in-person or all virtual.

If possible at least two project team members should attend each meeting—one to lead the group and facilitate the discussion and one to take notes. Taking notes on a computer and projecting them for participants to see can be especially useful, as it shows participants that their ideas are being recorded. Any off-topic comments can be placed in a "parking lot"—a separate space to capture any questions and concerns that are not directly relevant to the questions at hand (e.g., bringing up concerns with compensation if that's outside the project scope). If participants get off-track, placing their comment in the parking lot can assure them that their concern was heard and allow the group to move on with the conversation.

Data From External Sources

External data can bring a much-needed outside perspective to the design effort. In addition to the research cited in this book, sources of external data may include academic research, applied research, benchmarking studies, case studies from business publications, business books, websites and blogs, external consultants, and guidance from professional practice organizations. The amount of external data collected will depend on the time and resources of the project team and the extent to which the organization's culture values external research. As noted in Chapter 2, performance management is often subject to fads and an over-reliance on best practices. Therefore, findings from research should be prioritized over singular examples from case studies. We suggest identifying key principles from research and then finding examples of how these principles have been applied in practice.

Analyzing Results

Analysis entails reviewing collected internal and external data to answer questions that will inform the strategy development. Sample questions include:

1. What are our most pressing business priorities as an organization? How is our performance management approach helping or hindering these priorities?
2. What purpose(s) does our current performance management approach serve? What purpose(s) should it serve? How are performance data used today and how does that differ from how they should be used?
3. Can we apply consistent practices to all employees in the organization or will we need different approaches for different groups? What principles or practices will be common across the organization and what will be defined at local levels?
4. How much time do employees and managers spend on the current performance management process? Which components take the longest? Is the time spent in proportion to the perceived value?
5. What is our current approach to each major performance management activity: goal setting, measuring performance, providing feedback, and linking performance to rewards?

    a. Do managers and employees find this approach to be valuable?
    b. What do we know from research and real-world examples about effective approaches to doing this?
    c. How does our current approach compare with evidence-based practices?
    d. Where are our biggest gaps and how much of a problem are these gaps (e.g., in terms of time spent, employee dissatisfaction, etc.)?

6. What do we say we value as an organization? How well does employee and manager behavior fit with these values?
7. How did our current performance management approach evolve to its present state? How does our current approach reflect our organizational culture? What changes are we trying to drive in our culture and how can performance management support those changes (e.g., organizations that are trying to drive innovation will want to avoid rigid goal-setting practices and rewarding based on narrowly defined outcomes)?
8. How much risk exposure do we have? Do we use performance ratings as the basis of significant pay, promotion, or other decisions? Have we been sued for performance management practices in the past?
9. What do we need to do to successfully implement change (e.g., timing, communication methods, fit with other organizational initiatives, new materials, new technology, training, etc.)?

Answering these questions usually entails an iterative process among project team members. Once the analysis is completed, you will have a clear vision of your current state, how well it is working, and some indications of what needs to change to improve the efficiency and effectiveness of your performance management approach. It can be especially helpful to review the results of this analysis with key stakeholders to get a reality check on your findings. In our experience, the findings from the analysis are rarely surprising, but organizations find it very valuable to summarize the current state and identify the most pressing priorities for improvement.

Creating the Design

In this step, you will use the results of the data analysis to develop your new performance management design. The design is conceptual and high level rather than an in-the-weeds description of how everything will work. It may include the following:

- A statement of purpose and guiding principles for the new performance management approach.
- Whether a single performance management approach will be used throughout the organization or if different processes will be used for different units or geographies.
- General guidelines for how goals and expectations will be set, such as establishing consistent standards and expectations (e.g., tasks, behaviors, values, standards, etc.) and parameters for individual goals (e.g., frequency, content, etc.).
- Current sources of information for measuring performance and any additional needs (e.g., 360-degree feedback, objective data).
- Whether performance ratings will be used and if so for what purpose.
- General ideas for improving the quality of coaching and feedback, such as how to improve training and how technology might be used.
- General ideas for evaluating employee performance and using data to inform decisions, such as whether and how to use performance information to inform compensation and other talent decisions.
- Ideas about how performance management will relate to other key talent processes, such as selection, development, succession planning, compensation, etc.
- A description of how to hold managers and employees accountable and how to measure success.
- An overview of planned implementation: key milestones and timelines, resources needed, technology implications, training and communication approaches, etc.

Depending on the size and complexity of the organization, and the need to engage multiple stakeholders, developing the design document may require multiple working sessions or meetings. Participants should include core project team members along with HR and business leaders. The final product can be used to start developing a new performance management approach. The design document should include the statement of purpose and guiding principles, a description of the current state of performance management, high-level recommended changes, and the rationale for the changes.

Defining the purpose and guiding principles for the new performance management approach is an important component of the design document. If participants can agree upfront on what these principles are, it will make the rest of the design work go much smoother. These principles serve as the ultimate litmus test for any design decisions (i.e., does this proposed design feature fit our intended purpose and key principles?). They are essentially statements about what the organization believes to be true about driving high performance (e.g., a focus on transparency, clear expectations, good feedback, etc.).

Table 3.1 provides a concrete example of how one organization, Cargill, went about identifying areas to target for performance management reform. Table 3.2 then outlines how Cargill translated their findings into a new performance management design and guiding principles that evolved directly from the organization's business strategy to address key gaps uncovered in Cargill's

TABLE 3.1 How Cargill Targeted Performance Management Areas for Change

---

Step 1: Started with Cargill's Strategic Business Priorities
Cargill's strategic business priorities were to:

- Become more agile in response to rapid, external market changes
- Reduce complexity
- Simplify processes to focus on creating value for customers
- Generate sustainable profits
- Reinforce its strong culture of valuing employees

Step 2: Aligned Performance Management Reform to Strategic Business Priorities

Goal: Increase employees' alignment with organizational strategy and goals; focus on work that affects business results and agility to quickly make changes in priorities

Step 3: Evaluated the Current State of Performance Management

- Reviewed engagement and performance management survey results and interviewed employees, managers, and leaders globally
- Identified performance management process waste and estimated potential savings from streamlining
- Identified three key pain points that the performance management strategy was designed to address:
  - Disconnect between performance management process and daily work
  - Managers reluctant to give candid feedback to employees
  - Managers view performance management as an administrative drill

TABLE 3.2 Cargill's New Performance Management Mindset and Process: Everyday Performance Management

Everyday performance management is a new mindset, built on a few foundational principles:

- Effective performance management is an ongoing process, not an annual meeting and a form to complete
- Day-to-day activities and practices predict the performance management quality rather than forms and scales
- Employee-manager relationships are at the heart of effective performance management
- Performance management systems need to be flexible to address different business needs

To reinforce this new mindset, Cargill determined that performance management had to be intertwined with the daily work performed by employees. It could not be a separate process marked by semiannual or annual events and requirements. Accordingly, the new approach and process focused managers and employees on engaging in ongoing, effective conversations and de-emphasized and simplified administrative requirements substantially. Ongoing employee-manager discussions were the mechanism to set and align on expectations, build trust, seek and provide feedback and coaching, and develop and engage employees. Results of Cargill's efforts showed increased satisfaction and perceptions of performance management value among both managers and employees.

performance management evaluation research. More information about Cargill's design process can be found in Pulakos, Mueller-Hanson, Arad, and Moye (2015).

One question that frequently comes up is whether to rebrand the performance management process. The term "performance management" may have a negative connotation in the organization or may be unfamiliar if the current process is called something else. Box 3.1 describes some considerations for rebranding.

BOX 3.1 SHOULD "PERFORMANCE MANAGEMENT" BE REBRANDED?

Given the mental baggage associated with the term *Performance Management*, many clients ask whether it should be rebranded. They reason that if the process undergoes a major change so should the name—otherwise employees will fail to be energized by the transformation. In our experience, there is some merit to this idea. If employees and managers have negative reactions to the current process, it will be hard for them to think positively about a new process that constantly reminds them of the old one.

We've seen many approaches in naming a new performance management process. Some organizations have tried to align it more with a career or developmental focus (e.g., "Career and Performance"). Others have tried names that emphasize the performance aspect, such as "Plan to Perform." We've seen this idea taken to extremes with some organizations spending many hours debating names that will make clever acronyms and searching for the perfect logo, tagline, graphic, etc. that will grab attention and engage employees.

After going down the renaming road many times, our advice is this: don't overthink it and keep it simple. It's fine to call your performance management process something other than "Performance Management." It may even be a good idea if your employees hate the current approach. Make sure the new name is intuitive and that it accurately reflects what the new process is all about. A catchy name and slogan are fine, but don't expect employees to get excited by the marketing campaign alone. They will be engaged when they see that the new process is easier and more helpful than the old—regardless of what it is called.

Securing Executive Support

In most organizations, the proposed design will require some form of executive support and perhaps approval before it is implemented. Gaining support early before the project plan is even developed and involving key executives during data collection can smooth the way for final approval. The specific steps to get executive support will of course vary by the organization and should fit the values and culture. For example, some executive teams will want to see the background research and data collected while others will want to just focus on recommended changes. Some executive teams may want to weigh in on various aspects of the design and make major changes while others may simply give HR the green light to proceed. In some organizations, a formal presentation to the executive team is expected. In others, support is best gathered by meeting with key executives individually before meeting with the larger group.

The path to gaining executive support will be swifter if proposed changes can be linked to better business results. For example, demonstrating that changes will save employees and managers time, which translates into money saved, is important. A simple way to do this is to show that new rating forms will be streamlined and take less time complete. Other benefits may include anticipated increases in employee engagement, better alignment of individual goals to organizational priorities, more accountability for effective feedback and coaching behaviors, etc.

Showing how success will be measured via multiple methods is also important. Most organizations measure process compliance; however, that is only the first step. A successful approach will increase compliance, positive perceptions, and actual business outcomes. Figure 3.2 illustrates examples of how to measure success of the process, perceptions, and outcomes.

Regardless of the approach taken to obtain support, it is important to ensure that all the key players are fully engaged and willing to actively help the new process get implemented. Actions may include speaking to employee groups about the changes, modeling new behaviors, personally holding managers who work for them accountable to implement the new process, appearing in videos or other training materials to speak about the changes, etc. Ask the executives what they are willing to personally commit to doing and especially ask the most senior leaders if they are willing to hold the others accountable for their commitments.

Process	Perceptions	Outcomes
• Increased percentage of employees and managers who complete each major activity on time, as measured by data in HRIS • Reduced time required to complete each major activity, as measured by time to complete in HRIS and survey of employees and managers • Faster resolution to performance issues, as measured by speed and ease of implementing performance improvement plans	• Percentage of employees and managers who say they have had quality performance conversations at regular intervals, as measured by periodic pulse surveys • Percentage of employees and managers who say the new process is easy to use and valuable, as measured by periodic pulse surveys • Positive comments from employees and managers on internal discussion forums (e.g., Yammer)	• Increases in employee engagement scores, as measured by annual engagement survey • Improved individual performance, as measured from subjective (e.g., customer feedback) or objective (e.g., productivity) sources • Improved business performance, as indicated by key metrics (e.g., revenue, profit, KPIs, etc.) • Decreased regrettable turnover (i.e., fewer high performers leave voluntarily)

FIGURE 3.2   Example Measures of Success

★★★

The design is a living document that provides a roadmap for subsequent development and implementation. In the process of implementing the design, new information will be discovered and changes may be needed to the design concept. Having a strong statement of purpose and guiding principles to refer to and test ideas against helps ensure that the final performance management system stays true to the intent. Specific suggestions for developing each component of the performance management approach, using evidence-based methods, are presented in the chapters that follow.

Reference

Pulakos, E. D., Mueller-Hanson, R. A., Arad, S., & Moye, N. (2015). Performance management can be fixed: An on-the-job experiential learning approach for complex behavior change. *Industrial and Organizational Psychology: Perspectives on Science and Practice, 8,* 51–76.

PART II

Creating a Performance Management Approach That Drives Performance

4

DEFINE THE PERFORMANCE YOUR ORGANIZATION NEEDS TO SUCCEED

Before performance can be declared successful, success must be defined. Without a clear definition, it is impossible to communicate expectations to employees, measure their progress, and provide meaningful feedback and coaching to help them improve. Defining success is the foundation of all other performance management and indeed all talent management processes. It informs talent acquisition, talent development, performance management, and career and succession management. For example, if successful performance is defined in part by how well employees collaborate, then selection processes should include an assessment of interpersonal skills, development programs should expose employees to others from across the business to help them build professional relationships, performance expectations should be set around collaborative behaviors, and promotion decisions should be based in part on how well employees make and use connections for getting things done. Figure 4.1 illustrates these relationships.

Defining success in a performance management context requires identifying: 1) the organization's priorities and strategic objectives, 2) the work activities or tasks that need to be done to accomplish these objectives, 3) the behaviors employees should demonstrate to carry out work tasks effectively, and 4) the standard to which activities and behaviors need to be performed and the resulting outcomes that should be achieved. For example, a cashier's work activities might include scanning customer purchases and processing payments. Important behaviors for this role might include effective communication and customer service. Standards may include the number of customers that should be served per hour, accuracy of calculating payment and making change, ability to quickly answer customer questions, and attaining a particular customer satisfaction score on a follow-up survey.

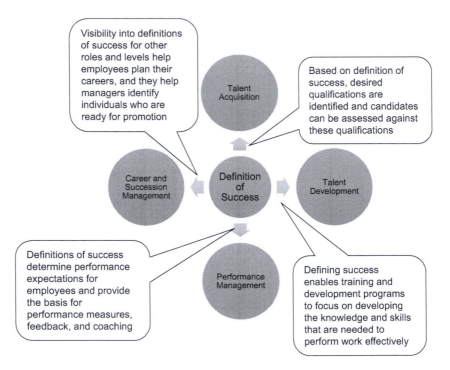

FIGURE 4.1   Talent Management Relationships

Identify Organizational Priorities and Objectives

A strategic approach to performance management begins with a thorough understanding of the organization's priorities and objectives. Without this understanding, employee efforts may be focused on the wrong activities. While a complete description of organizational strategic planning is beyond the scope of this book, this section provides a few thoughts on how to best align performance management efforts to meet organizational goals.

First and foremost, managers should clarify their own understanding of the organization's purpose and critical current objectives. Many organizations have lofty vision and mission statements with aspirational language, such as "deliver unparalleled value for customers and stakeholders." These statements do little to help focus employees' efforts and inspire them to action. A useful exercise is to translate these statements into plain language for employees and describe what makes the organization unique. For example, a plain-language statement of purpose is, "We produce cars that appeal to a broad range of people because they are well-designed and affordable."

In addition to putting the organization's purpose into plain language, it is often useful to do the same for business unit priorities. For example, if the overall goal of a car company is to make high-quality, affordable cars, each major function will have a unique contribution to that goal. For example, research and development creates and tests new designs that use high-quality and cost-effective materials, manufacturing assembles parts and produces a finished product in an efficient manner, supply chain management focuses on strategies to minimize costs from suppliers, and so on. When business unit goals are misaligned with organizational goals, managers struggle to communicate how goals fit together. It may be outside the scope of the performance management transformation to engage senior leaders in a strategic planning exercise. However, if business goals and priorities are unclear, it is worth convening the executive team to try and define these goals more clearly. At the very least, HR leaders can help the teams they support find their purpose by linking up to higher-level goals.

Beyond understanding the organization and individual business unit's purpose, it is helpful for employees to know how the organization's specific strategic goals relate to their work. For example, the organization may have goals to grow revenue in China by 20%, develop a new product that receives at least 10% of market share in the first year, and cut operating costs by 15%. Managers can help employees understand where they fit by identifying the goal(s) most relevant to the work of each employee and describing how their work contributes. In this example, a marketing manager may point to an employee's role in designing materials to promote the new product, while an administrative manager may help employees see how their work contributes to increasing operations efficiency as a way to reduce costs.

Define Important Work Activities

Defining the work that needs to be accomplished to meet organizational goals begins with an understanding of the job or occupational structure in the organization. Many organizations have well-defined job structures already. Organizations that don't need not spend an extensive amount of time doing a large-scale job or occupational analysis. It may be sufficient to define a basic job structure that includes the following elements:

1. Job categories. These categories are usually functional in nature, grouping jobs together into similar skillsets and professions, such as finance, engineering, manufacturing, sales, etc. Often these categories are distinguished as "line" or "staff" roles. Line roles are those that are directly involved in producing and delivering the products and/or services that are at the core of the organization's business. Staff roles are those that support line functions. For example, in a consumer products manufacturing organization, line roles might include research and development, manufacturing, marketing, sales, and distribution. Staff roles might include finance, HR, information technology (IT), and administrative support.

2. Job levels. Job levels show progression of scope and responsibility through-out a typical career lifecycle for individual contributor roles as well as leadership roles. In some job categories, there may be parallel tracks of individual contributor and leadership positions available. For example, in many government agencies, employees may move into executive roles through either a leadership track or a senior expert track. Leaders have formal management responsibilities, and senior experts do not but are expected to be leaders in their area of expertise and share this knowledge with others.

Figure 4.2 illustrates a high-level example of a role structure in a professional services organization. The first column shows different job categories and the subsequent columns show the different job levels. The intersection of each job category and level shows example job titles. Not all categories need have job titles available at every level. For example, administrative support positions do not have any roles defined at the senior leader level.

The value of mapping out a basic job structure is to identify the major types of work that have different requirements for success. Once job categories and levels are identified, more specific performance requirements can be defined. For example, Figure 4.3 illustrates example requirements for consultant roles at different career levels within a professional services organization. This information now provides a basis for what is expected within each major role. The language is simple and straightforward. It

	Job Levels				
Job Categories	**Entry Level**	**Mid-level**	**Senior Contributor**	**Leader**	**Senior Leader**
Consulting	Associate Consultant	Consultant	Senior Consultant	Team Leader Managing Consultant	Director Vice President
Finance	Payroll Clerk Receivables Clerk	Accounting Specialist	Senior Accountant	Finance Manager	CFO
IT	Help Desk Support	Application Developer IT Specialist	Senior Developer Senior Engineer	Project Manager	CIO
Administrative Support	Administrative Assistant	Administrative Coordinator	Executive Assistant	Administrative Support Manager	

FIGURE 4.2 Example Job Structure in a Professional Services Organization

	Job Levels				
Work Activities	**Associate Consultant**	**Consultant**	**Senior Consultant**	**Team Leader**	**Managing Consultant**
Client Interactions	Participates in client meetings	Leads client meetings and serves as day-to-day point of contact on specific projects	Responsible for managing overall client relationship for existing clients	Develops new client relationships	Develops new client relationships and strategic partnerships
Project Work	Completes basic project tasks as assigned with minimal guidance	Leads moderately complex project tasks with minimal guidance	Leads complex tasks and projects independently	Leads multiple, complex projects, involving the creation of new content or service approaches	Oversees a portfolio of projects and develops new products and service offerings
Leadership		Provides on-the-job training to new associates	Mentors and develops colleagues	Leads a team of 2–4 consultants	Leads a group of 5–10 consultants
Business Development	Does research to support proposals	Writes proposal sections and helps in sales pitches	Leads proposal efforts and sales pitches	Develops $500K–$1M in new business each year	Develops $2–$3M in new business each year

FIGURE 4.3 Example Consulting Job Level Requirements in a Professional Services Organization

highlights the most important distinctions among levels rather than listing every responsibility for each role. Level guides of this nature are useful summarizing expectations and providing career guidance—they show in clear terms how expectations differ and the skills and capabilities that will be needed to get to the next level.

Methods for defining work activities include observing employees performing work tasks, interviewing employees and managers about their work, and gathering information from published sources, such as existing job descriptions, procedural manuals, and databases such as O★NET (e.g., Aguinis, 2013). Once identified, work activities should be reviewed with job experts to ensure their clarity and completeness. For jobs with many incumbents, it is useful to gather data on the importance of each activity and the frequency with which it is performed. These data serve an important purpose in establishing the job relevancy of the performance management approach. When decisions are based on performance data, they are more defensible if there is a clear line of sight between performance criteria and job-relevant activities.

Define Effective Behaviors

If work activities define *what* is to be done, behaviors define *how* work should be done. Behaviors are often expressed as values, such as integrity and appreciation for diversity, or as competencies, such as teamwork, communication, and critical thinking. Values typically apply organization wide, and competencies may apply to specific roles or organization wide, though they may be defined differently for different job levels. Figure 4.4 shows an example of an organization-wide competency defined at multiple job levels.

Teamwork: Works effectively with others and contributes to creating and maintaining an open, team-oriented environment.

Entry-level Contributor	Mid-level Contributor	Senior Contributor	Leader
Treats all others with courtesy and respect.	Treats all others with courtesy and respect and encourages others to do so as well.	Serves as a role model for treating all others with courtesy and respect and encourages others to do so as well.	Creates a team climate that fosters courtesy and respect by acting as a role model and holding others accountable.
Provides regular updates on progress upon request.	Proactively keeps others informed of progress and issues that affect them.	Ensures others are kept informed of progress and proactively raises concerns before they become issues.	Facilitates communication on progress among team members, ensuring everyone is kept abreast of emerging issues.
Provides assistance to others when requested.	Proactively provides assistance to others.	Actively seeks opportunities to assist and mentor others.	Ensures team members are receiving and providing assistance.
Listens to and demonstrates respect for differing points of view.	Seeks out diverse perspectives and demonstrates appreciation for differing points of view.	Seeks out diverse perspectives and incorporates them into decisions to ensure a broad array of ideas are represented.	Facilitates open communication and actively solicits differing views to make sure a broad array of ideas is heard and incorporated into team discussions.

FIGURE 4.4   Example Competency Defined at Multiple Job Levels

Competencies define the collection of knowledge, skills, abilities, behaviors, and other attributes needed for success (Green, 1999). They can be defined at multiple job levels with behavioral benchmarks to more precisely articulate how the competency manifests at different career stages. These benchmarks can be useful in giving managers the right language for defining behavioral expectations. However, some organizations have recently begun to question whether competencies are valuable. Competency models are often overly complex and are too unwieldy to be useful. Moreover, behavioral statements that define competencies are often written in such a generic way that they become meaningless. When organizations attempt to create more specific libraries of competencies for several occupations, they become even more unwieldy, are difficult to maintain, and almost always collapse of their own weight.

Competency models have advantages and disadvantages. The following guidelines can help ensure competencies are helpful rather than burdensome (note: for more detail on competency best practices, see Campion, Fink, Ruggegerg, Carr, Phillips, & Odman, 2011):

- Distinguish values (universal characteristics expected of all employees) from competencies (behaviors that can be developed over time and that may have varying requirements for different roles). For example, integrity and appreciation for diversity are core values that everyone in the organization is expected to demonstrate. Typically, these attributes are expected from all employees on day one and are often part of the selection process. While employees can be educated on them somewhat, they are based more on enduring characteristics than knowledge or skills. When they are not present, it is usually obvious and immediate actions must be taken (e.g., a demonstrated lack of integrity would result in disciplinary action). It is difficult to measure values on a traditional 5-point performance rating scale (e.g., what is the difference between "meets expectations" and "exceed expectations" on integrity?), and as such they should not be lumped in with other competencies that can be more easily defined at different levels. For example, competencies such as communication, teamwork, leadership, technical expertise, etc. can be developed to some extent. Employees may vary in their ability to demonstrate effectiveness in these competencies and can, with coaching and guidance, often increase their proficiency.
- Limit competencies to the vital few. Having too many competencies leads to overlapping definitions among them, and employees have difficulty understanding the distinctions. When competencies are used as part of performance management, four to seven are usually the maximum needed to define the most important success factors for the work.
- Keep the structure simple. Competency models can be constructed in several ways. At a basic level, competencies have a label (e.g., "Communication") and a definition (e.g., "presents information verbally and in writing in a clear, concise, and compelling manner that is tailored to the needs of

the audience"). Competencies may be defined at different levels of proficiency with behavioral benchmarks for different job levels, such as the example shown in Figure 4.4. More complexity does not result in better performance management. Make the structure only as elaborate as needed to clearly define expected performance.

- Use vivid and powerful language. One challenge with competencies is that they tend to look the same from organization to organization. They are often so generic that employees have trouble remembering them and understanding why they are important. Often a string of adjectives is used to distinguish among roles and job levels. Competencies are more powerful when the language is clear and vivid and tailored to the organization's culture. For example, Amazon's *Leadership Principles* include phrases such as "Customer Obsession" and "Have Backbone; Disagree and Commit."[1] Descriptions that evoke emotion and passion are more memorable and easier to connect to the organization's unique value.

Define Performance Standards

Performance standards define how well work must be performed for it to be considered successful. Performance standards can be based on objective or subjective measures. Objective standards are those that ostensibly do not rely on human judgment. They can be verified by multiple observers (e.g., sales or production numbers). In contrast, subjective standards are based on judgments—by managers, direct reports, peers, customers, etc. They are subjective because reasonable people might observe the same behavior and come to different conclusions about it. Table 4.1 lists examples of objective and subjective standards.

While employees and managers bemoan standards that are "too subjective," the reality is that even objective standards may be partially subjective. For example, a quarterly sales quota may seem like an objective performance standard for a salesperson working in a retail store. However, the quota itself is based on a subjective judgment about how much each salesperson ought to sell. Also, a variety of other factors may impact the number of sales, such as store location (busy shopping area or isolated building), the days and times the salesperson is working, and environmental factors such as the local economy and sales taxes. It is difficult to completely define success with objective standards. For example, a salesperson might sell a lot of merchandise by pressuring customers to buy things they do not need or by exaggerating their benefits, leading to a high number of returns and low customer satisfaction. Therefore, a successful salesperson will not just sell a lot of merchandise, he or she needs to sell it in the right way that makes customers happy.

Many organizations struggle with finding the right balance between objective and subjective measures of success. Numerous media stories illustrate the pitfalls of performance standards that over-emphasize some results and neglect others. Box 4.1 illustrates one of the more egregious examples.

TABLE 4.1 Examples of Objective and Subjective Performance Standards

Objective Performance Standards	Subjective Performance Standards
• Timeliness—whether tasks are completed within a specified time frame • Attendance—number of absences or late arrivals to work • Speed—how quickly tasks are accomplished • Productivity—how many items are produced or processed within a specified time • Utilization—percentage of employees' time that is billable to customers • Accuracy—how few errors are made in completing a finished product • Efficiency—how much can be accomplished with the fewest amount of resources (e.g., reducing scrap or waste) • Sales—how much of a product or service is sold in a given time frame • Turnover—proportion of staff who leave the organization within a given time frame • Adherence to procedures—correctly completing observable tasks (e.g., performing the necessary steps to change the oil in a car)	• Quality—judgments about whether work produced is of high quality; may apply to physical products (e.g., user-friendly, durable, reliable, etc.) as well as informational products (e.g., thorough, well researched, insightful, etc.) • Creativity— judgments about whether work produced is new and innovative • Proactivity— judgments about whether employees take initiative to seek out new responsibilities • Teamwork/collaboration— judgments about whether employees work effectively with others • Communication— judgments about whether employees can communicate verbally and in writing in a clear, compelling, and concise manner • Customer service—customer feedback about their satisfaction with services received • Capability— judgments about whether employees can handle difficult and complex situations and problems

BOX 4.1   WHEN PERFORMANCE STANDARDS GO AWRY—THE WELLS FARGO FAKE ACCOUNT SCANDAL

In 2016, news broke that Wells Fargo was setting up fake bank and credit card accounts for customers without their permission. As many as 3.5 million fake accounts were set up (Mehrotra & Keller, 2017), thousands of employees were fired, CEO John Stumpf was forced to resign, and Wells Fargo paid millions of dollars in fines. As of the writing of this book, lawsuits are ongoing, and it may be years before the full implications of the scandal are known.

How did such a well-respected banking institution have such a tremendous misstep? According to several reports, at the root of the problem was a performance culture that valued new sales above all else. CEO John Stumpf's mantra to employees was "eight is great," meaning that each customer would ideally buy eight separate Wells Fargo products. This mantra translated into enormous pressure on managers and employees to engage in cross-selling customers on new products. Despite this pressure, cross-selling was difficult to achieve, and employees resorted to fraud to meet their aggressive performance goals. Employees set up fake accounts for customers without their knowledge to make it appear as if they success-fully cross-sold products. Customers were charged for the fake accounts, and employees received credit for meeting sales targets, earning them higher commissions and bonuses.

This example highlights the importance of balanced performance standards. When organizations prioritize revenue and profit above all else, employees may resort to unethical practices to meet these goals. A more balanced approach includes not just financial goals but also demonstrat-ing behavior that aligns with organizational values such as integrity and customer service. It is not enough, however, simply to have strong mission and values statements. In fact, Wells Fargo's vision and value statements emphasized customer service and declared trust was a core value. However, the actual behavior that was rewarded with raises, bonuses, and promo-tions was achieving financial targets. Employees who failed to meet overly ambitious sales goals or who complained about unethical practices were fired. These practices led to predictable unintended consequences (Lawler, 2016). Wells Fargo has since ended sales targets in retail banking and is redefining its standards for success to include a more balanced approach.

Where to Set the Bar with Performance Standards

Organizations are seemingly obsessed with "raising the bar" on performance. Increasing competition and shrinking resources often means that employees are urged to "do more with less" and "strive for continuous improvement." These mantras translate into the superman/woman syndrome in performance manage-ment, which is the unrealistic expectation that everyone be good at everything.

A more strategic approach to setting performance standards is to link the level of necessary performance to the organization's strategic objectives (Boudreau, 2015). For example, consider the different business objectives of Southwest Airlines and Emirates Airlines. Southwest's competitive advantages are low costs, reputation for on-time arrivals, and friendly service. In contrast, Emirates is known for its high-end service and a luxurious flying experience in first class. These different business goals drive differences in what makes for successful employees. Southwest employees need to work efficiently and provide good, but not necessarily overly attentive, service. In contrast, Emir-ates employees, especially flight attendants, need to provide passengers with an extraordinary experience. Consequently, performance standards should target the factors that most matter to the business rather than expecting employees to excel in every area.

Similarly, organizations need to think about how good is "good enough" to meet business needs. For example, fast food franchises provide food and service that is inexpensive and "good enough" to meet the needs of the masses. Predictability is a key competitive advantage. A Big Mac should taste basically the same in Los Angeles or London. To be successful, employees need to follow established procedures and work efficiently. Serving customers with a smile and leaving them satisfied is important. However, would there be a business advantage to greatly raising the bar on customer service in a fast food restaurant? Perhaps, if customer service was deficient, but if the service is already satisfactory little is likely to be gained from encouraging employees to attempt to "delight the customer." In fact, this strategy may backfire if it takes away from the core business goals of fast service and low prices.

These examples highlight the importance of setting realistic expectations that are in line with business needs. Analyzing the work to be done will provide insight into the behaviors that employees need to demonstrate and the level of performance needed to meet business goals.

Communicating What Success Looks Like

Clearly defining success gives everyone a common language with which to communicate what is valued in the organization and what effective performance looks like for each major job category and level. Descriptions of success are typically codified into role or job descriptions. These are useful tools for guiding all the talent management processes discussed earlier in this chapter. Role descriptions should:

- Describe the minimum and desired qualifications of the role along with the knowledge, skills, and abilities needed to be successful. From these, hiring criteria can be established to select new employees who are most likely to succeed.
- Establish the work activities that need to be performed and serve as the basis of defining training and development requirements.
- Include the standards to which employees will be held accountable and are therefore the foundation of performance management; these standards will be the basis for setting performance expectations, measuring progress, and providing feedback and coaching.
- Show how role expectations progress from one level to the next, providing useful information to employees about how to progress in their careers and to managers to inform promotion decisions and succession management activities.

Once the role descriptions have been created, they can be a catalyst for a meaningful conversation between employees and managers about how each person's work contributes to organizational goals. These conversations are best accomplished using plain language. The manager's role is to discuss in clear terms how employees' work contributes to organizational success, for example:

- Sales professional: "you connect our customers with our products and services, which enrich their lives in the following ways. . . . You bring in new business and money, which gives us the resources we need to keep producing great products and services."
- Marketing professional: "you help get the word out about our products and services so that our customers can make an informed choice about what to buy. You let people know about products and services they may not have known about before that could improve their lives, work, etc."
- Administrative professional: "you help others do their jobs quickly and efficiently. You are like the oil in an engine—you make sure everything runs smoothly; without this support, we can't effectively deliver our products, serve our customers, etc."

For some jobs, it may be very clear how the role connects to the larger success of the organization; for other roles, managers may need to help employees connect the dots. In either case, employees appreciate knowing how they fit in the larger organizational scheme and why their work matters. These conversations provide a good foundation for communicating performance expectations. Once employees have a clear understanding of the importance of their work, the next step is to discuss the work activities and behaviors that need to be demonstrated to perform the role and to what standard that work should be performed to contribute to the organization. From there, more specific performance goals can be identified. Figure 4.5 illustrates how these elements are can be connected in a robust conversation, with both the manager and employee working in partnership to define success.

★★★

A clear definition of success is the foundation for all performance management efforts and indeed all other talent management processes. Defining success begins with a clear understanding of the work to be performed and how it contributes to broader organizational goals. Understanding the work entails creating a job structure that defines the key functions and significant job levels and the important work activities accomplished by each function at each level. From there, more specific performance standards are defined that describe how well each activity must be performed for it to be considered successful. Setting the right bar in performance standards requires careful thinking about what

Key Discussion Topics

Role Purpose
- Describe in plain language the core purpose of the organization and how the employee's work contributes directly or indirectly
- E.g., "This role is important because it helps our clients become more effective and therefore more likely to be repeat customers because they find value in our services."

Work Activities & Behaviors
- Discuss the most important activities and behaviors required to carry out this purpose and how they are distinct from other roles
- E.g., "The primary responsibilities of a senior consultant are to lead complex projects, build lasting relationships with clients, and help mentor more junior staff to develop their skills."

Performance Standards
- Discuss the standards to which these activities and behaviors must be performed.
- E.g., "Success in this role means that projects are completed on time and within budget, clients are happy and purchase more services, and junior staff develop greater skills and independence."

Performance Goals
- Develop specific goals that will be a near-term focus for meeting or exceeding standards. Link these back to the organization's purpose
- E.g., "Your goal is to lead the XYZ project with Client ABC and complete it by ____. Ensure the client's criteria for success are met and that junior staff on the project are well-utilized...This project is important to our business because..."

FIGURE 4.5   Example Conversation Guide for Defining Success

level of performance and in what areas is essential for the organization to meet its business objectives. A good definition of success is typically captured in a role description, which can be used to inform many talent management processes. In addition, it provides a catalyst for robust performance conversations. These conversations give employees a clear sense of how their work fits into the organization and why it matters, which gives them a sense of purpose and empowerment.

Note

1 As shown on the Leadership Principles page at www.amazon.jobs/principles

References

Aguinis, H. (2013). *Performance management* (3rd ed.). Boston, MA: Pearson.

Boudreau, J. W. (2015, October). *Trouble with the curve: Redefining performance using strategy differentiation*. Presented at the SIOP Leading Edge Consortium, Boston, MA.

Campion, M. A., Fink, A. A., Ruggegerg, B. J., Carr, L., Phillips, G. M., & Odman, R. B. (2011). Doing competencies well: Best practices in competency modeling. *Personnel Psychology, 64*, 255–262.

Green, P. C. (1999). *Building robust competencies: Linking human resource systems to organizational strategies*. San Francisco, CA: Jossey-Bass.

Lawler, E. E. (2016, November 1). The Wells Fargo debacle: How proper reward practices can remedy a toxic culture. *Forbes.com*. Retrieved from www.forbes.com/sites/edwardlawler/2016/11/01/the-wells-fargo-debacle-how-proper-reward-practices-can-remedy-a-toxic-culture/2/#d9bebe22ff53

Mehrotra, K., & Keller, L. J. (2017, May 12). Wells Fargo's fake accounts grow to 3.5 million in suit. *Bloomberg online*. Retrieved from www.bloomberg.com/news/articles/2017-05-12/wells-fargo-bogus-account-estimate-in-suit-grows-to-3–5-million.

5

INSPIRE ACTION AND DIRECT ENERGY

Setting effective performance expectations is one of the most significant drivers of performance. When employees are clear about what they are supposed to do and the standards against which their performance will be measured, their performance is better (CEB, 2002). One of the most common ways organizations apply expectation setting to performance management is by requiring individual performance goals or objectives for each employee (note: while much has been written about the difference between a goal and an objective, as a practical matter the two terms are often used interchangeably, as we use them in this chapter). A performance goal specifies what the employee is expected to achieve within a given time frame.

Goal setting leads to higher performance, as shown in numerous studies (e.g., CIPD, 2016; Smith & Pulakos, 2010; Latham & Locke, 2006). Unfortunately, the way organizations implement goal setting as part of performance management often undermines the effectiveness of goals. Guidance to managers and employees is often based on an idealized view of how goal setting should work:

1. After the organization sets its strategic goals for the year, they are cascaded down through business units to managers and finally to employees. The rationale for the cascade is ensuring a clear line of sight between individual and organizational goals.
2. Employees set their annual performance objectives in consultation with their managers. To ensure quality, goals often must be SMART (Specific, Measurable, Aligned, Realistic, and Time-bound) and meet other organizational requirements, such as:

    a. Emphasis is placed on quantitative measures, which are perceived to be more objective and easier to measure than qualitative measures.

    b.   Goals must not focus on day-to-day work; instead, they should stretch employees to go above and beyond normal duties.

    c.   Goals must be individualized and unique to each employee, irrespective of how similar one employee's work may be to another's.

    d.   Goals can be adjusted throughout the year, as priorities change.

3.   At the end of the year, employees are evaluated on the extent to which they met the goal, usually using a rating scale (e.g., "1" = not met, "2" = partially met, "3" = met, "4" = exceeded, and "5" = far exceeded).

4.   Managers calibrate their ratings to ensure fair distribution of rewards across employees (e.g., a "5" is eligible for 130% of target bonus and a 4–5% merit increase, a "3" is eligible for 100% of target bonus and a 2–3% merit increase, and so on).

This ideal state is based on several assumptions: that organizational performance is better when employee goals are aligned to organizational goals, that SMART goals ensure consistency and accountability, that goals motivate high performance, and that rewards can be distributed fairly based on individual contributions. While these assumptions seem logical on their face, goal-setting practices rarely work as intended for several reasons:

1.   It often takes so long to cascade goals down through the organization that several months can pass before individual goals are set. In the meantime, employees carry on with their work, which leads to questions about how essential goals are to driving performance.

2.   Individual work unit and manager goals often don't have a clear link to higher-level goals. With the many translations that happen as part of a cascade, the connection between individual goals and organizational objectives can be obscured. It is like the game of "telephone," in which multiple retellings of a story evolve and alter it in ways not originally intended (Mueller-Hanson & Pulakos, 2015).

3.   Employees and managers struggle mightily to make their goals "SMART." Measures are sometimes included just for the sake of having an objective measure of performance, but these may not be realistic (e.g., statements such as, "reports will be 98% accurate" when there is no easy way of measuring accuracy) or meaningful (e.g., "produce three reports on X topic" when the number of reports is not important but can be easily measured). Additional requirements levied on managers (e.g., goals must be individualized and cannot focus on day-to-day tasks) make goals even more difficult to write. The reality is that many employees have jobs in which 100% of their time is devoted to getting day-to-day tasks done and going "above and beyond" requires them to divert from core work requirements. Moreover, when all employees in a given work unit do the same job, it is

difficult to write individualized goals that are consistent and fair across employees. Some organizations attempt to ensure consistency by "calibrating" goals (i.e., meetings among managers to ensure equivalent challenge for similarly situated employees). However, in practice these calibration sessions end up taking up a lot more time than the value they provide.

4. Once written, performance goals are frequently set aside and employees get on with doing their jobs; goals are not reviewed during the year and do not have much of an impact on performance. When priorities change, employees rarely go back and update their goals because the whole process of rewriting goals and getting them reviewed and approved simply takes too much effort.

5. At the end of the year, it is often difficult to ascertain if a goal has been met or exceeded. Employees may have taken on new assignments that don't neatly fit into the goals that were set earlier in the year, but they still want credit for these accomplishments. Some goals may not have been met because of factors outside of the employee's control. Much effort can be spent writing justifications for why an unexpected goal was met or exceeded while one of the planned goals was not, rather than reflecting on what went well and what could be improved.

6. Because rating inflation is a pervasive problem in organizations, most employees may be given an above-average rating on goal attainment. However, not everyone can get an above-average bonus and merit increase, and managers must then negotiate like horse-traders to get the biggest rewards for their people. Managers also need to consider organizational realities, such as budget constraints and the extent to which the overall unit, division, or entire organization met its financial goals. These factors typically have a lot more to do with how much bonus an employee receives than an individual employee's goal attainment, which adds to perceptions that there is not a clear link between individual goal attainment and rewards. See Box 5.1 for an example of difficulties one organization encountered using goal attainment as the basis for rewards.

BOX 5.1 POTENTIAL PITFALLS OF REWARDS BASED ON GOAL ATTAINMENT

In one organization, bonuses were tied directly to goal attainment. Bonuses could theoretically range from 0 to 200%, with a target of 100% for employees who met their goals. The intention was to make significant distinctions in performance and consequently rewards, which would motivate employees to higher performance.

The reality was that no one ever got less than 100%. Even 100% was rare—most people got somewhere between 110–120%, with a few people getting up to 130%. Employees might start out with a rating of 200%, but after calibration the number was usually changed significantly because it was hard to "sell a bigger bonus to corporate" and because budget constraints did not allow for too many big bonuses. The few employees with less than 100% were often changed as well, unless the organization was "trying to send a message to them."

Taken together, these factors greatly reduced the link between performance and rewards. Ratings for low performers were artificially inflated while ratings for high performers were artificially reduced to conform with political realities and budget constraints. Not surprisingly, less than a third of employees in this organization said that they could see a clear link between their performance and rewards, even though bonuses tended to be very generous overall.

Despite these challenges, goals can be powerful drivers of performance and a valuable part of performance management. The key to harnessing their power is to implement them in a way that is consistent with how they improve performance.

How Goals Work

Goals increase performance when they provide direction, energize action, and increase persistence to overcome obstacles. Goals provide direction when they guide employees to focus on the most important contributions they can make to the organization. Goals motivate action when they bring attention to the gap between a current and desired state. Under the right conditions, this gap creates discomfort, which leads to increased effort and a willingness to persist in the face of obstacles to close the gap (Latham & Locke, 2006). For example, if Jasmine has a goal to finish a complex project on time and within budget, there is a gap between the current state of the project (not finished) and the desired state (completed on time and within budget). This discrepancy creates discomfort for Jasmine and a desire to close the gap. She is therefore more likely to put in the effort needed to achieve a successful result if the conditions described in the following sections are met. Attributes of effective goals are discussed in the sections that follow.

Importance

The goal must be meaningful to the individual in order to motivate effort (Klein, Wesson, Hollenbeck, & Alge, 1999; Locke & Latham, 2002). This does not mean that the individual must set the goal himself or herself. In fact, some evidence suggests that goals are more impactful when managers set them and evaluate progress because it creates external accountability (Harkins & Lowe, 2000). While someone else can set the goal, the individual must understand the rationale for the goal and believe that it is an important and worthwhile endeavor. For example, if Jasmine does not care very much about the success of the project, she likely will not put much effort into it. However, if she was inherently interested in the work and believed the project was important to the organization's priorities or to her own career prospects, she would be more motivated to do well. She may be even more motivated to perform well if someone else, such as her manager, was involved in setting the goal and holding Jasmine accountable for making progress.

The implication in an organizational setting is that goals can be perceived as important regardless of whether the manager or employee sets them. To increase the goals' perceived importance, they should:

- Be few in number: the more goals that one has, the less time and attention that can be paid to each one. A maximum of three to five high impact goals is recommended. If the individual has more than five goals, each of them will receive less than 20% of the individual's effort, unless the goals are weighted differently. In that case, some goals could be "worth" far more than 20% and others far less. Weighting is usually not that useful because it overly complicates the goal-setting process and results in some goals being worth too little for the employee to attend to.
- Be linked to higher-level goals: goals that clearly contribute to the broader purpose of the organization will be more meaningful to employees. This does not mean a lengthy cascade is needed. Individual goals can be "linked up" to organizational goals from any level (Mueller-Hanson & Pulakos, 2015), often more efficiently and effectively than cascading down.
- Have a clear rationale: when employees understand the purpose of the goal and why it is important to the organization, they will be more committed to it.
- Be aligned to the employee's personal values: employees who believe the goal is consistent with their own beliefs and values will be more committed to it.

Challenge

Goals motivate behavior and increase performance when they are moderately challenging (Locke & Latham, 1990). The discrepancy between the current and desired state must be large enough to create some discomfort but not so large that if feels impossible to achieve (e.g., Atkinson, 1958). For example, if Jasmine's project was very simple, the gap between the current and desired state would be small, unless she was new to leading projects. Completing the project on time must feel like it will be a bit difficult to attain, otherwise it won't be much of a motivator. If the goal is too difficult, for example to finish the project in half the scheduled time at half the cost, Jasmine might feel it is unattainable and give up in frustration.

The implication for performance goals is that they should be aspirational. They should push employees to perform beyond their current abilities. However, if employees know they will be rewarded on goal attainment, they will likely try to sandbag—make the goals easily attainable so that they are guaranteed a reward. Goals in a performance evaluation context are often too easy—more so than goals set in a learning context, which are usually more challenging (Winters & Latham, 2006) and may be more apt to drive high performance, especially for complex work. Rewarding attainment can undermine the ability of goals to motivate performance.

Because aspirational is not a component of the "SMART" acronym, it often gets missed when setting goals. One well-known example for setting effective aspirational goals is the OKR (objectives and key results) system popularized by Google (Yarrow, 2014). OKRs consist of an objective and several key results. The objective is a broad statement about what is to be accomplished (e.g., "Implement a new marketing website that contributes to increased sales.") and the key results are the measurable milestones that help achieve the objective (e.g., "Launch website on X date," and "Achieve XX number of unique visits to the site within the first week."). Google's use of OKRs differ from traditional SMART objectives in that they:

- Are set quarterly rather than annually.
- Are transparent—everyone's OKRs are visible from the top of the organization down.
- Are ambitious to the point of being somewhat uncomfortable.
- Have several measurable results for each objective, each of which is "graded" on a 0–1 scale to indicate the extent to which the result was achieved.
- Are not intended to be fully achieved. The "sweet spot" for the average grade is .6–.7 per objective. The rationale is that if every result is fully met (earning a score of 1) then the OKR was too easy in the first place.

OKRs can be the basis of rewards, but their primary purpose is to drive performance by focusing attention on the most important priorities for each employee. They are aspirational and intended to push employees outside of their comfort zones. While they are graded, the focus is on driving higher performance.

Control

Individuals must expect that working toward the goal will produce a positive result, and they must be able to measure their progress along the way to see if they are on track (Harkin et al., 2016). For example, Jasmine must believe that she can meet project deadlines through her efforts. If deadlines slip because of forces outside of her control or even if she believes it is outside of her control (e.g., she is unable to attain leader support to move forward), her motivation and performance may suffer. The implication for performance goals is that employees must believe they have the knowledge, skills, and abilities to achieve the desired outcome and that achievement is within their personal control.

Specificity

Specificity is a double-edged sword in goal setting—it can both help and hinder performance, depending on the situation. Goals for straightforward tasks work best when they are specific with respect to what outcome is expected and how success will be measured. For example, Jasmine's goal is quite specific—she has a due date and a budget to meet. If the timing and budget were vague (e.g., "finish as soon as possible"), she would be more likely to take longer and potentially spend more. On the other hand, given that her project is complex, specifying what the project's result should be in advance may quell innovation and the potential for achieving exceptional performance.

In today's dynamic work environment, it is difficult to set specific goals over long time horizons for many jobs. Shorter time spans are better for driving performance because employees can get more immediate knowledge of how they are doing (Latham & Locke, 2007). For example, if Jasmine's project were broken up into smaller milestones, it might be easier to predict what specific outcomes should be achieved at each stage. Employees must feel they are making good progress to remain engaged and motivated (note: the importance of assessing progress toward goal attainment is discussed in more detail in Chapters 6 and 7). Near-term goals can be more quickly achieved, and therefore provide more sense of accomplishment than longer-term goals. If longer-term goals are needed, they can be broken up into interim steps and milestones.

The more specific and measurable the goal, the more likely it is that employees will achieve it. Goals that provide specific details about what success looks like and how success will be measured remove ambiguity. Ironically, the more specific the goal, the more similar performance will be among people who have that same goal, which may make it difficult to use goal attainment as a basis for distinguishing performance (e.g., Locke, Chah, Harrison, & Lustgarten, 1989). This paradox is an example of where the different aims of performance management can conflict with each other. Goal specificity increases performance but decreases the ability to use goal attainment as the basis for making distinctions in rewards. Therefore, organizations need to choose whether their aim is to improve everyone's performance or highlight distinctions in performance. It will be problematic to use the same process to achieve both outcomes.

The downside to specificity is the potential for goals to stifle innovation and to interfere with performance on complex tasks. If desired results are specified in advance and employees know they are rewarded on achieving these results, they will be focused on doing that and may miss unanticipated opportunities to achieve even better results. Additionally, highly specific goals can result in an overly narrow focus when the task is complex and requires abstract and divergent thinking. For example, a pharmaceutical researcher may have a goal of conducting a certain amount of experiments within a given time frame. However, research often leads to new and unexpected discoveries that may take the experiments in an entirely new direction. Trying to specify how the research will go in advance can lead to missed opportunities for new learning and discovery.

Given today's dynamic work environment, it may be better to trade some specificity for flexibility to allow for capitalizing on new opportunities without having to go through the effort of revising an employee's performance goals. The extent to which this is feasible will depend on the nature of the work and level of the employee's role. Establishing broad priorities and expected behaviors rather than setting specific SMART goals can be more effective in some cases, especially for complex work (CIPD, 2016). For example, broad priorities might include creating innovative products that capture additional market share, making discoveries that advance a field or enable revenue growth, gaining operational efficiencies through automation, etc. Measuring success on broad priorities is more subjective because the criteria is less about whether a specific metric or outcome was achieved and more about the impact an employee's accomplishments and activities had on the overall success of the business.

How to Drive Effective Expectation Setting in Organizations

Link Up Rather Than Cascade Down

Cascading goals are intended to align individual actions to organizational priorities. Traditional cascades work like a waterfall; goals flow from above and touch every level before reaching individual employees. As described earlier in this chapter, cascading goals may not work as intended because they take too long and are too distorted by the time they reach individual employees.

Rather than cascading down, managers and employees should work together to link individual goals up to larger organizational strategies. As discussed in Chapter 4, a key role for managers is to help employees understand where their work fits and why it matters to the organization. Armed with this information, employees and managers need not wait for a cascade to set their own goals. They can simply identify how the employee can best contribute to supporting organizational priorities and set individual goals and expectations around those contributions. To link up goals, managers and employees can:

- Discuss their understanding of the organization's purpose and priorities in the short and long term.
- Discuss the employee's role and how his or her work contributes to the organization.
- Together, develop one or more performance goals that will focus the employee's effort on the activities most likely to positively contribute to the organization.

In this manner, connecting individual goals to organizational priorities is more like a fountain than a waterfall—direction comes from a single source but fans out across all levels at once rather than running through each level successively.

Allow Flexibility

Organizations usually try to mandate when and how performance goals will be set. Often these requirements apply to the entire organization—even employees in different business units, regions, and functions who are doing vastly different work. Behind these requirements is a desire to ensure consistency and fairness; controlling the process feels like the only way to achieve these aims. Unfortunately, the result is goals that meet requirements but don't always fit the realities of the employee's work (Pulakos & O'Leary, 2009).

Letting go of standardization in the goal-setting process can be important to ensuring that everyone's goals are relevant and meaningful to the work they are performing. A more flexible goal-setting process allows for goals to be:

- Set at any time during a performance cycle and for any duration that makes sense for the work at hand. For example, employees involved in project work may need quite irregular goals that align with this work while those in customer service may need weekly or monthly goals, while at the other extreme, those involved in R&D may need multi-year goals (Pulakos & O'Leary, 2009).
- Focused on the employee's most important responsibilities. For some, this may be performing specific day-to-day tasks. For others, this may be milestones achieved for specific projects.
- Realistic and meaningful measures of success. Some work lends itself to quantitative measures of success (e.g., sales quotas), while other work is more appropriately measured by quality indicators (e.g., customer perceptions). The extent to which quantifiable outcome measures can be defined and rigorously measured should be allowed to vary across employees and types of work.
- Set at the level that is most relevant for important outcomes—this can be at the individual, team, or business unit level. When work is team-oriented and highly interdependent, setting goals at the team level may be more

appropriate than setting individual goals (Lawler, 1994; Ployhart & Weekley, 2009). Specific expectations can still be set for how individuals will contribute to the team's success, but the team as a whole and not the individual should be evaluated when the outcome is produced and measured at the team level. This strategy also helps drive improved collaboration that is needed to perform in many roles today.

- More informally documented. One argument for making goal setting standardized is so that goals can easily be documented in the performance management system. However, organizations should consider whether this documentation is necessary. The value in documenting goals is that it can help those involved, namely the employee and manager, to be clear on what the expectation is. However, entering goals into a formal performance management system does not ensure clarity or aligned understanding, especially if the requirement is handled as a check-the-box activity. By requiring documentation in a system, HR leaders may feel assured that everyone has at least has some expectations set, but this does not ensure high quality and may result in goals that are less relevant and meaningful than they could be. See Box 5.2 for an example.

BOX 5.2 UNANTICIPATED CONSEQUENCES OF GOAL-SETTING REQUIREMENTS

One of our long-term projects involved evaluating the extent to which performance objectives met organizational standards for quality across multiple organizations. These standards included ensuring the goals met SMART criteria and adhered to other policy requirements (e.g., that goals be individualized). These requirements were implemented at great expense; managers and employees spent a significant amount of time in training and learning how to write SMART goals, HR spent time monitoring goals to ensure they met these standards, and the performance management technology systems needed custom adaptations to ensure goals could be entered and tracked.

In our work across multiple organizations and review of over ten thousand individual objectives we discovered that:

- Managers and employees found goal setting difficult, and most objectives didn't fully meet SMART criteria. Organizations that had more experience with SMART objectives tended to do a better job, but there was a limit to how effective the objectives were—even in the most experienced organizations.

- The most difficult SMART criteria to meet were specificity and measurability, which often go together.
- Almost all goals were achievable, relevant, and time-bound, as these attributes are relatively easy to include in goal statements.
- Goals were not individualized, and many people had the same goal as their peers. Although this was against organizational policy, it made sense for the work, as most employees in each major job category performed similar tasks and should be held to the same standards.
- Ratings on goals were correlated highly with ratings on competencies— often with the exact same language used to justify both the goal rating and competency rating.
- Goals had to be set each year and were therefore rather broad and vague because conditions and priorities changed frequently. They often read more like job descriptions than specific outcomes to be achieved for the year.
- Many goals were "recurring"; that is, rather than specifying a longer-term desired outcome they specified the ongoing recurring tasks that employees performed (e.g., respond to service requests within 24 hours).
- The implementation of required SMART goals did not yield better employee performance when compared to prior methods of expectation setting.

Our conclusion from many years of study is that the time and focus on creating SMART goals often does not pay off. Goals are not as "SMART" as the organization would like, and there is no evidence they improve performance. A more effective use of resources would have been to provide training and resources to help managers set effective expectations in whatever format made sense for the work and to place less emphasis on "SMART" and more on setting meaningful and challenging expectations.

HR leaders may be understandably hesitant about allowing these flexibilities. A valid concern is that without some accountability and oversight, managers may fail to set any expectations or goals at all. Several strategies can be leveraged to mitigate this concern, for example, employee pulse surveys can be used to determine if employees are clear on their expectations and if they are driving toward work outcomes that they feel are meaningful and motivating. Feedback from these surveys can be used to identify and provide additional guidance to groups that have unclear expectations. Second, HR can sometimes help identify goals and performance standards that apply to broad groups of employees. These standards are especially useful when many employees do similar work because they help hold them to similar goals and standards of performance that endure over time. Finally, HR can serve in a consulting capacity by coaching managers to identify appropriate expectations for different employee groups. This type of support is an essential part of being a strategic partner—helping business leaders identify the results they need to achieve to drive important business goals.

The main point, however, is that over-engineered goal-setting processes can yield a false sense of security that employees will be clear on what they need to do and equipped to perform well. In all but the most rudimentary cases, having expectations and performing against them is a fluid process that requires setting clear goals, working toward them, receiving feedback that clarifies expectations, adjusting, and so forth until the goal is fully understood and successfully achieved. High performance is facilitated and eventually engrained in an ecosystem in which managers are intentional about their important role of checking in, clearing away obstacles, coaching, and altering expectations, as needed. This goes beyond our current narrow focus on goal setting at the beginning of the annual rating process and embeds it more fluidly in the ongoing processes of monitoring, driving, and adjusting performance in real time to ensure important business outcomes are achieved. To drive high performance, we need to reimagine how goal setting can best be evolved into a more holistic goal accomplishment processes.

Choose the Right Type of Expectation for the Role

Different types of expectations are relevant for different roles or even types of work within a role. Table 5.1 lists some examples.

TABLE 5.1 Expectation Examples for Different Roles

Type of Expectation	Examples	Best For
Performance standards describe qualitative expectations for results and behaviors such as communication, collaboration, customer service, etc. Standards should be described in enough detail that reasonable people can agree on whether they were met. Typically, standards endure over time and apply to a large group of employees.	Treat all coworkers with courtesy and respect. Embrace diversity by seeking and incorporating a variety of ideas from different groups when making decisions. Communicate clearly, concisely, and in a manner appropriate to the audience. Provide effective service to customers by meeting their expectations.	Performance standards can be used for nearly any job and are especially useful in jobs for which few quantitative measures of success exist. Standards may include different benchmarks for different groups or career levels (e.g., individual contributors are expected to embrace change and managers are expected to lead it).

Type of Expectation	Examples	Best For
Metrics provide quantitative measures of success; similar metrics are typically established for all individuals doing similar work at similar levels, though metrics can be individualized for some roles. Metrics are usually enduring standards that change at an organizational rather than individual level (e.g., new sales targets introduced each year for everyone).	Sales quotas. Number of items produced, processed, distributed, etc. Number of calls or customers served and effectiveness (i.e., no call-back for same problem). Customer satisfaction ratings. Error rates or accuracy Timeliness or speed (e.g., respond to customer requests within 4 hours).	Jobs in which tangible outcomes can be measured objectively and are within the individual's control. Particularly relevant for jobs that include repetitive and recurring tasks (e.g., clerical, sales, manufacturing, customer service, etc.). Note that these are best when the measure itself has meaning. Just because something can be counted does not mean it should be. For example, the number of reports written may be irrelevant when it is the quality that matters. Metrics should only be used when there is an effective and efficient way of measuring the outcome.
Performance goals describe specific results to be achieved within a given time frame. They can be written in a variety of ways such as SMART goals, OKRs, etc. They can be set for individuals or teams.	By X date, analyze the widget manufacturing process and provide recommendations to improve its effectiveness and efficiency. Present findings to the executive oversight committee. Complete the ABC project on time and within budget to meet project specifications: • Conduct weekly progress meetings. • Provide monthly status reports to the customer. • Finish system testing by X date. • Complete user training by Y date.	Jobs in which work responsibilities may vary by individual or team and for which goals can reasonably be tailored. If everyone in a given job is doing the same work, performance standards or metrics may be more efficient than individual goals. Individuals may still have unique goals to help them better meet standards if there is a performance gap (e.g., complete work tasks on time).
Ongoing, informal expectations are usually not tracked in a formal way. They may be discussed verbally or in emails. They are set as needed, are highly individualized, and driven by work demands.	Complete the XYZ report by Tuesday at 5:00 p.m. Convince client X to sign the new contract at the meeting next week. Get marketing to agree to support our product launch next month by creating a new flyer and adding it to the website.	Are used across many jobs and are often easy to make SMART because they are specific and have a clear indicator of success.

As shown in the table, expectations can vary widely, depending on the nature of the work, and flexibility in format is essential for ensuring that expectations are appropriate to the work. Providing examples of different types of expectations and advising on which type of expectations are most relevant for different types of work is an important part of helping managers set expectations that will drive high performance.

Organizations often require that expectations include both "what" is to be achieved and "how" it is to be achieved. For example, the "what" might include concrete business results such as items produced, sold, etc., while the "how" might include collaboration, communication, and appreciation for diversity. In organizations where there has been a history of focusing on business results at the expense of collaborative behaviors, the "how" may be particularly important to articulate.

Every organization has its urban legends about the manager who always "delivers the numbers but leaves a path of dead bodies in his or her wake." The idea that one can deliver high results but exhibit poor behavior on the job, or vice versa, has led many organizations to mandate that employees be evaluated on distinct "how" and "what" expectations, for example:

- Evaluating employees separately on performance goals or objectives (business results) and competencies (behaviors).
- Writing different goals for what is to be achieved and how it should be achieved (known as "what" and "how" goals).
- Evaluating employees on separate standards for results and behaviors (e.g., have a set of standards for "achieving results" as well as standards for other dimensions such as "collaboration" and "communication").

Organizations often end up over-complicating these "how" and "what" distinctions. Clearly distinguishing between "how" and "what," especially in separate goal statements, can be difficult and confusing for employees. Further, when employees are rated separately on business outcomes or goals versus competencies, these ratings are usually highly correlated, leaving questions about the value gained for the extra work and potential complexity added.

Although stories of employees who get results but treat others badly are ubiquitous, these individuals tend to be rare in reality, and their behavior is unlikely to change simply because they are rated separately on goals and behavioral competencies. The reality is that many will still get high ratings and rewards because they get results—regardless of how expectations are structured. What really changes behavior is not having parsed outcome goals and behavioral expectations but rather holding employees accountable for their actions, which requires managers to give feedback, withhold rewards, administer discipline, or take other appropriate action when they observe bad behavior. It is this willingness to take action to address poor behavior, and not how expectations are structured, that makes a difference in driving high performance. Real consequences also send a clear message to others about what is valued. Therefore, holding employees accountable who behave poorly or violate organizational values and even terminating them if necessary sends a much stronger message about the importance of both behaviors and outcomes than any expectation-setting process will.

Although behaviors and outcomes are separate conceptually, they come together and are both important in achieving high performance. For example, to achieve revenue targets often requires collaborating across groups and communicating effectively with customers. Combining what and how together in setting expectations helps employees understand the big picture of what they need to achieve and provides guidance (i.e., the how) for doing so. Therefore, when behaviors and outcomes are integral parts of a goal, we recommend incorporating both into expectations rather than parsing these into separate goals that can obscure the relationships between them. This blending can occur when setting informal expectations, performance goals, and performance standards. A 50/50 balance of results to behaviors is not always necessary—and rules of thumb like this actually detract from what is most important, which is communicating in clear terms what the employee should achieve and any behavioral expectations associated with the achievement. For example, instead of setting separate goals for developing a new product and collaborating with colleagues, set a single goal for developing a new product by working collaboratively with colleagues.

Some organizations struggle with blending behaviors and results because they worry employees won't understand that both are important. Some HR leaders have told us that creating separate performance elements for the "how" and "what" is necessary to drive culture change and to send a message that both elements are equally valued. While there is merit to this perspective and different organizations will have different views about the value of behavioral expectations, more holistic expectation statements that incorporate both tend to be easier to grasp. In the end, employees will attend to what they see valued and rewarded by the organization. If effective behaviors as well as results are rewarded (not just financially but with praise and recognition), employees will be more likely to demonstrate them. Providing managers with guidance on how to incorporate both behaviors and results in expectations as appropriate should result in more straightforward expectations for employees and avoid over-complication that does not add clear value.

Provide Practical Guidance and Tools

Allowing flexibility in the timing and content of expectations and goals does not negate the need to provide guidance on how to set these effectively. This should minimally include:

- The number of goals that each employee should have (e.g., three to five).
- A few examples of effective goals and expectations for different types of work, such as those presented in Table 5.1.

- A checklist for effective goal setting that includes attributes of effective goals from research (importance, challenge, control, and specificity).
- Tips for connecting individual goals to larger organizational priorities.
- A how-to guide that gives instructions for how to set effective expectations and explicitly states the flexibilities available to managers when setting goals. It can also be useful to include discussion topics for employees and managers to engage in effective goal-setting conversations.

Some organizations present this guidance in the form of training courses, including e-learning, webinars, and in-person classes. In our experience, the most effective training for goal setting is a hands-on workshop in which managers spend time writing actual goals they will use themselves or with their employees. Writing goals in a workshop enables immediate feedback from facilitators and peers, which leads to higher-quality goals. Beyond initial training, managers may benefit from ongoing consulting by HR partners who can coach them on setting goals for specific employees.

Separate Development and Performance Goals

The focus of this chapter is performance expectations; however, development goals frequently appear as part of the performance management process. Some organizations require employees to set both performance goals and development goals (e.g., to acquire a new skill or complete a training program) at the same time. While development goals can help improve performance over time, the impact is usually more indirect, as the focus is on gaining new knowledge and skill rather than achieving a work outcome.

In keeping with the principles for effective performance management outlined in Chapter 2 (parsimony, a primary focus on driving high performance), development goals should be part of employee development and not part of the performance management process. Adding development goals to performance management complicates the process and is only indirectly related to the goal of driving high performance. Development goals should follow performance expectations where appropriate. For example, if an employee has a performance goal of implementing a new software system, he may first need training on how to administer the new system. Completing the training is not the end goal, but it is useful for helping him achieve the desired performance result.

Be Cautious in Using Goal Attainment as a Basis for Performance Ratings

When goals are used as the basis for performance ratings, they are rarely challenging enough. An exception is Google's OKR process described earlier in this chapter in which the expectation is that most goals won't be fully achieved.

However, in the typical organization, goals are graded on a 1–5 or similar scale with the midpoint being equivalent to the goal being fully met. Lower ratings indicate that the goal was not met, and this is usually looked upon so negatively in the organization that these scores are rarely given. Higher ratings indicate the goal was exceeded, and employees strive to achieve these higher ratings because they are often associated with higher rewards. This type of grading scale encourages sandbagging, however, which is making the goals too easy so that employees are assured of meeting if not exceeding them. This practice undermines a key factor that makes goals effective—challenge. If every goal is met or exceeded, then the goals were probably not challenging enough.

If goal attainment is tied to rewards, ensure the linkages make sense. Rewards for goal attainment work best when results are easily quantifiable and under the employee's direct control (e.g., sales targets). However, it may be difficult to reward attainment of individual goals in jobs that require a high degree of teamwork to achieve results. In those cases, it may be more meaningful to set a goal at the team level and distribute rewards based on team rather than individual performance.

A variant on rating goal attainment is for employees to describe their most meritorious accomplishments and the impact of these on the organization's overall success. Self-reported accomplishments can be very rich sources of performance information, especially when managers do not have extensive opportunity to directly observe performance. If employees are motivated to achieve impactful accomplishments and can be trusted to invest and deliver results in those areas that most benefit the organization, setting broad priorities and evaluating the impact of accomplishments post-hoc can work well to drive effective performance. The strategy is also effective when work is more nebulous and timelines for goal accomplishment are more difficult to predict, such as research or discovery-based work.

★★★

Setting clear expectations, like providing effective feedback in real time, is essential for driving performance. Although expectations and feedback are often thought of as separate steps of a performance management system, they in fact go hand in hand as fluid features of a larger end-to-end process of how employees need to engage with managers and others to continuously achieve goals that positively impact the team's and organization's overall performance. While goal setting is a potentially powerful tool for communicating expectations, the way it is implemented in most organizations undermines its potential value. A more successful approach is to focus on the attributes of effective goals (importance, challenge, control, and specificity) and allow managers and employees flexibility in using goals in ways that best align with their work to advance important outcomes and contributions. Many HR leaders will be hesitant to give up control of rigid goal-setting processes because these provide comfort that at least some performance expectations are communicated. However, a bolder shift to the goal accomplishment processes discussed here will enable leveraging goals much more effectively to drive performance, rather than merely checking a box that goals have been documented in an automated system.

References

Atkinson, J. (1958). Towards experimental analysis of human motivation in terms of motives, expectancies and incentives. In J. Atkinson (Ed.), *Motives in fantasy, action and society* (pp. 288–305). Princeton, NJ: Van Nostrand.

CEB. (2002). *Building the high-performance workforce: A quantitative analysis of the effectiveness of performance management strategies.* Arlington, VA: Author.

CIPD. (2016, December). *Could do better? Assessing what works in performance management.* Research Report.

Harkin, B., Webb, T. L., Chang, B. P., Prestwich, A., Conner, M., Keller, I., Benn, Y., & Sheeran, P. (2016). Does monitoring goal progress promote goal attainment? A meta-analysis of the experimental evidence. *Psychological Bulletin, 142,* 198–229.

Harkins, S. G., & Lowe, M. D. (2000). The effects of self-set goals on task performance. *Journal of Applied Social Psychology, 30,* 1–40.

Klein, H., Wesson, M., Hollenbeck, J., & Alge, B. (1999). Goal commitment and the goal-setting process: Conceptual clarification and empirical synthesis. *Journal of Applied Psychology, 84,* 885–896.

Latham, G. P., & Locke, E. A. (2006). Enhancing the benefits and overcoming the pitfalls of goal setting. *Organizational Dynamics, 35,* 332–340.

Latham, G. P., & Locke, E. A. (2007). New developments and directions for goal-setting research. *European Psychologist, 123,* 290–300.

Lawler, E. E. (1994). *Motivation in work organizations.* San Francisco, CA: Jossey-Bass.

Locke, E. A., Chah, D., Harrison, S., & Lustgarten, N. (1989). Separating the effects of goal specificity from goal level. *Organizational Behavior and Human Performance, 43,* 270–287.

Locke, E. A., & Latham, G. P. (1990). *A theory of goal setting and task performance.* Englewood Cliffs, NJ: Prentice-Hall.

Locke, E. A., & Latham, G. P. (2002). Building a practically useful theory of goal setting and task motivation: A 35-year odyssey. *American Psychologist, 57,* 705–717.

Mueller-Hanson, R. A., & Pulakos, E. D. (2015). Putting the "performance" back into performance management. *SIOP-SHRM Science of HR White Paper Series.* Retrieved from www.siop.org/SIOP-SHRM/SHRM_SIOP_Performance_Management.pdf

Ployhart, R., & Weekley, J. (2009). Strategy, selection, and sustained competitive advantage. In J. L. Farr & N. Tippins (Eds.), *The handbook of employee selection* (pp. 195–212). New York: Psychology Press.

Pulakos, E. D., & O'Leary, R. S. (2009). Defining and measuring results of workplace behavior. In J. L. Farr & N. T. Tippins (Eds.), *Handbook of employee selection.* Mahwah, NJ: Erlbaum.

Smith, K. G., & Pulakos, E. D. (2010). *An examination of the use of goal setting as a basis for performance management: What we know from research and practice.* Arlington, VA: PDRI.

Winters, D., & Latham, G. P. (2006). The effect of learning versus outcome goals on a simple versus a complex task. *Group and Organization Management, 21,* 236–250.

Yarrow, J. (2014, January 6). This is the internal grading system Google uses for its employees—and you should use it too. *Business Insider.* Retrieved from www.businessinsider.com/googles-ranking-system-okr-2014-1.

6

MEASURE AND EVALUATE PERFORMANCE

A fierce debate has raged in HR circles about the relative merits of perfor-mance ratings. As discussed in Chapter 1, critics say ratings are dehumanizing, burdensome, and ultimately unhelpful for improving performance. Supporters counter that performance evaluation occurs no matter what you call it, and that ratings are the best and fairest way to make important talent decisions. Lost in this debate is the importance of performance measurement, which is distinct from performance evaluation or ratings and is essential to performance improvement.

Performance measurement is the bridge between performance expectations and feedback. Performance expectations specify what needs to be done, perfor-mance measurement is the observation of progress toward these expectations, and performance feedback is how these observations are communicated to the employee, which can be used to change behavior and improve future perfor-mance. Performance evaluation is often used synonymously with performance measurement; however, the distinction between them is important:

- **Performance measurement** is the ongoing collection and analysis of information about employee actions relative to expectations. Its purpose is to assess progress and provide information needed to adjust and improve future performance.
- **Performance evaluation** is a judgment about the adequacy of perfor-mance over time. Its purpose is to inform decisions about people, but it often comes too late to impact performance.

Imagine employees in a call center who are responsible for taking customer calls, answering questions, and solving problems. Performance measures may include the number of calls they handle in a given time frame, the quality of calls, customer satisfaction after the calls, etc. Knowing the results of these measures on an ongoing basis can help employees change their behavior and get a better result. In contrast, performance evaluation is a judgment about whether the employee's performance over time on those metrics meets or exceeds standards, and it is commonly done once or twice a year and communicated in the form of a performance rating. These ratings may then inform decisions about raises, bonuses, promotions, etc.

Good measurement provides the knowledge of results that is necessary to give effective feedback. It can also be diagnostic—helping employees to understand specifically what is working well and what needs to be improved. If measurement is done on an ongoing basis as work is performed, it can provide feedback that is timely enough to help employees make corrections to get better results before the work is completed. If it comes from multiple sources, especially if some of those sources are objective rather than subjective, it can reduce defensiveness and resistance to feedback. Well-conceived performance measures can even be a substitute for manager feedback, addressing a major problem in organizations—manager's reluctance to give candid feedback—and taking pressure off managers to be the sole providers of feedback (as discussed in more detail in Chapter 7).

Organizations frequently forego ongoing performance measurement and instead substitute a once- or twice-a-year performance evaluation, missing the opportunity to impact performance. Performance evaluation has less impact on performance than ongoing measurement because:

- It is usually too broad and general to provide the diagnostic information needed to improve performance. For example, if an employee is rated a "3" on a 5-point scale on "communication," little additional information may be available as to what specifically the employee said or did that merited this rating and what could be done to earn a higher rating. Performance is complex and requires a more nuanced conversation to help employees improve.
- It lacks detail and nuance represented by the full range of an individual's performance. One of the major challenges with performance management feedback or ratings that occur annually is that they summarize many instances of performance into a single rating or set of ratings, only a fraction of which the rater may see. Incidents of performance that are especially ineffective or effective tend to stand out and be weighted higher. Thus, performance evaluation will be an average or more likely an overall impression. Performance evaluations that merely summarize performance do not provide enough detail to help employees improve or deliver praise for their noteworthy accomplishments.
- It involves passing judgment on the employee's performance, which often is interpreted as passing judgment on the employee as a person. How often

have you heard people referred to as "she's a 5" or "he's only a 3," as if the people were merely the sum of their ratings? Because of this labeling and judgment and the stakes that often accompany ratings, evaluation tends to be more emotionally laden than measurement. Emotional reactions to the psychological threat of being judged can interfere with subsequent performance (c.f., Culbertson, Henning, & Payne, 2013; Rock, 2008).

• It is often only done once or twice a year, long after the events in question have occurred and therefore comes too late to impact performance.

In summary, performance measurement and evaluation serve different purposes, each of which has a place in a performance management process.

• Performance measurement is primarily for improving performance.

   • It is an ongoing process of gathering information in real time that can be fed back to employees to help them improve for the future.
   • It is more detailed and uses multiple sources of data.
   • Employees are less likely to have an emotional reaction to it—if its focus is informational and delivered in the spirit of continuous improvement, leading to greater acceptance.
   • It is often welcome, especially when things go wrong. Employees expect and appreciate after action reviews or post-mortems to discuss what happened and identify lessons learned for the future.

• Performance evaluation is primarily for decision-making.

   • It is inherently backward-looking.
   • It is usually communicated with ratings that capture an overall impression once or twice a year.
   • It tends to be emotionally charged process because it applies numbers and/or labels to people.

Measuring Performance Effectively

We define performance measurement broadly: it is any means of gathering information on an ongoing basis about employees' actions and results. Ideally, performance measurement involves obtaining real-time indicators of success from multiple sources that help employees gauge their progress and improve. Sources of data might include customer satisfaction surveys, website analytics, informal feedback from colleagues while working together, supervisor observations, objective measures, etc. Table 6.1 shows examples of performance measures.

Performance measures provide information about how much was produced, how fast, with how many errors, at what cost, etc. This feedback is neither

TABLE 6.1 Examples of Performance Measures

Example Measurement Methods

- Productivity/efficiency metrics (e.g., how much is produced/accomplished in a given time frame and at what cost)
- Error rates/amount of scrap generated
- Timeliness of deliverables
- Adherence to budget
- Adherence to schedule
- Utilization metrics as measured by percentage of time that an employee is engaged in "billable" activities
- Attendance and punctuality as measured by timekeeping systems (e.g., timeclock, timekeeping software)
- Website analytics (e.g., number of unique visits, length of time on site, etc.)
- Amount of sales, returns, etc.
- Cost savings
- Call volume, time to resolve issues, number of callbacks for same problem, as measured by call records and monitoring software
- Number of safety incidents, injuries, etc. caused by the employee's actions or inactions
- Observations of task performance or behavior (e.g., supervisor monitoring of phone calls or other customer interactions, supervisor monitoring of task completion)
- Comments and ratings from peers or direct reports done on an ongoing basis (e.g., pulse surveys, online comments/feedback)
- Customer satisfaction survey results

negative nor positive—it simply is information. It is only when we assign meaning to it that it becomes an evaluation (e.g., did the amount produced meet the quota, are the number of errors acceptable, etc.). This distinction is useful because employees respond better to measuring performance when the purpose is to help them improve for the future rather than an evaluation of their worth as an employee.

Many jobs already use performance measures extensively, such as:

- Technician performance may be measured on the number of repair jobs completed in a day and the number of callbacks received (customers who call back after the repair, complaining of the same problem).
- Call center employee performance may be measured on the number of calls handled and customer ratings in follow-up surveys.
- Professionals who provide billable services (lawyers, accountants, consultants) may be measured on the number of billable hours delivered, new clients acquired, and percentage of clients retained.
- Healthcare professionals' performance may be measured on the number of patients treated, number of medication errors, and a variety of patient outcomes.

When jobs lack standard metrics, performance evaluations often become the sole means of measuring performance. This practice is unfortunate as it fails to provide employees with real-time feedback and the chance to improve their performance. Jobs less likely to use real-time performance measures include knowledge work or team-based work where it is challenging to isolate the performance of one individual. Despite these challenges, performance measurement is worth doing for all the performance benefits discussed. To be meaningful, performance measurement must be tailored to the target job; however, the following sections describe some general principles for developing effective measures.

Measure Performance as Directly as Possible

The cardinal rule of performance measurement is to measure performance as directly as possible. Start with the employee's core responsibilities and focus on the behaviors or results the employee can control. Make the measure as objective and tangible as possible—even if the quality of the employee's results is usually only assessed in a subjective manner. For example, many knowledge workers regularly produce reports and other documents. Instead of waiting until the end of the year to give an overall performance rating, measure the timeliness, quality, etc. of output as documents are produced. Break more subjective evaluations down into more tangible criteria. For example, instead of simply declaring the quality to be poor, fair, good, exceptional, etc., identify the criteria that matter and indicate their presence or absence. For example, does each document:

- Use clear and concise language that is free from grammar and spelling errors?
- Contain all required elements?
- Support assertions with data and research?
- Present a recommended course of action that is well-supported?

It may be tempting to change this type of data into a rating scale, such as rating document quality on a 5-point scale. However, we suggest resisting this temptation. As soon as raw data gets converted to some type of rating, it starts to take on evaluative meaning for the employee. Moreover, important information may be lost in converting the data to a rating, reducing its accuracy. At the performance measurement stage, it is better to present the data in its original form when communicating it to employees. The process of interpreting this data and comparing it to a standard (e.g., quota, behavioral benchmark, etc.) is a useful exercise for employees and managers to do in partnership. It allows for employees to have a voice in how their work is measured, increases understanding and acceptance of the results, and reduces defensiveness.

Figure 6.1 shows a partial example of a monthly performance measure developed for a social services position. Performance in social services is challenging to measure. Employees often work one-on-one with clients, and supervisors may have little insight into their client interactions. The nature of the work is to help people with chronic problems: poverty, abuse, disability, homelessness, addiction, etc., and true progress on these issues is rare. Clients may not have good outcomes due to factors outside the social worker's control. However, as shown in Figure 6.1, there are still important measurable behaviors that effective social workers demonstrate. Achieving these outcomes does not guarantee success for clients, but they make it more likely for success to occur. Measuring these outcomes gives the organization a better handle on overall service quality, and this process is the foundation for giving employees feedback that helps them improve and identifies training needs.

Staff Member Name	*Pat Sample*			
Month	*May*			
Number of Client Hours Delivered	*120 (95% of hours assigned)*			
Mileage	*362*			

Behavioral Criteria

Client Services	*Yes*	*Somewhat*	*No*	*Not Observed*
1. Used client-centered language when speaking about and to clients	X			
2. Created specific plans for helping clients reach their program goals	X			
3. Involved clients in planning their own services		X		
4. Clients showed evidence of actively working toward program goals			X	
5. Clients provided positive feedback on services received	X			

Documentation

	Yes	*Somewhat*	*No*	*Not Observed*
1. Client case notes were detailed and thorough		X		
2. Client documentation was turned in on time	X			
3. Documentation was provided for all service hours delivered	X			
4. Client records were up to date		X		
5. Timesheet and mileage reports were accurate and on time	X			

FIGURE 6.1 Example Monthly Performance Measures for Social Work Position

Health, Safety, and Ethics	Yes	Somewhat	No	Not Observed
1. Reported client incidents in a timely manner				X
2. Followed safety protocols during client service delivery	X			
3. Conducted emergency safety drills with each client	X			
4. Verified each client's medication to ensure correct dosage				X
5. Communicated questions and concerns to supervisor in a clear and direct manner	X			

Comments/Follow-up Needs

Clients need to be more involved in planning their services so that they feel ownership of their service plans and actively work toward their goals. Next month, suggest Pat set up a meeting with each client specifically to get their input on their plans and adjust accordingly.

FIGURE 6.1 (Continued)

As shown in the figure, important behaviors are simply indicated by their presence or absence. This aids in communication and feedback because it allows the manager and employee to focus on specific areas that may need improvement as well as highlighting areas in which the employee is doing well. Objective data like service hours delivered and mileage is reported along with behavioral data for a more balanced perspective on performance. Note that the data are not evaluated at this stage. Over time, data can be aggregated and then compared to standards to give an indication if performance is acceptable or needs improvement (e.g., 80% is considered acceptable)—see Figure 6.2 for an example. Relative percentages may be compared across employees for use in decision-making if needed.

Use Multiple Sources of Data

As illustrated in Chapter 4, performance requirements that focus on a single metric, such as revenue or profit, at the expense of other criteria often result in unintended consequences, such as ethics violations. Similarly, if a single source of data is used to measure performance (e.g., sales figures), employees are more likely to focus on it to the exclusion of other important aspects of performance. A more balanced approach to performance measurement includes observing important aspects of the employee's performance without making the measurement too burdensome.

One emerging trend in gathering data from multiple sources is the use of crowdsourced feedback. This type of feedback uses social media platforms to gather information in real time from a wide variety of individuals (Ledford, Benson, & Lawler, 2016). Crowdsourced feedback works by providing a

Staff Member Name	*Pat Sample*		
Year	*2018*		
Average Monthly Client Hours Delivered	*110 (90% of hours assigned)*		
Average Monthly Mileage	*340 (Mileage within acceptable limits)*		

Behavioral Criteria

Client Services	*Yes*	*Somewhat*	*No*
1. Used client-centered language when speaking about and to clients	92%	8%	0
2. Created specific plans for helping clients reach their program goals	92%	8%	0
3. Involved clients in planning their own services	75%	8%	17%
4. Clients showed evidence of actively working toward program goals	68%	16%	16%
5. Clients provided positive feedback on services received	84%	16%	0

Documentation

1. Client case notes were detailed and thorough	84%	16%	0
2. Client documentation was turned in on time	75%	17%	8%
3. Documentation was provided for all service hours delivered	92%	8%	0
4. Client records were up to date	75%	25%	0
5. Timesheet and mileage reports were accurate and on time	100%	0	0

Health, Safety, and Ethics

1. Reported client incidents in a timely manner	100%	0	0
2. Followed safety protocols during client service delivery	100%	0	0
3. Conducted emergency safety drills with each client	100%	0	0
4. Verified each client's medication to ensure correct dosage	92%	8%	0
5. Communicated questions and concerns to supervisor in a clear and direct manner	84%	16%	0

FIGURE 6.2   Example Aggregate Performance Measures for Social Work Position

platform for peers to rate or comment on any individual's performance at any time. This feedback is typically more free-form than a structured 360-degree process and is therefore easier and faster to do. Ledford et al.'s research suggests that crowdsourced feedback, when paired with ongoing feedback, has a positive impact on increasing organizational performance, providing useful feedback to employees, and supporting company values.

Ensure Measurement Is Feasible and Sustainable

Performance measurement can be time-consuming, and if it is too burdensome, managers and employees will quickly abandon it. Therefore, the most effective measures are those that can be somewhat automated so that they take little to no extra effort. For example, if an employee is responsible for creating online content, website analytics can provide ongoing measurement of how often that content is accessed, how long people spend on the site, how they consume the content, etc. These metrics will be easier to maintain if analytics reports can be generated automatically on a regular basis.

If performance measures can be gathered from processes that already exist in the organization, they will be easier to sustain. For example, any metrics that are already generated for business purposes are potentially performance measures, such as sales numbers, call center logs, customer satisfaction results, turnover, attendance, production metrics, etc. Likewise, if measurement can be embedded in standard workflows and processes it will become just a normal part of how the work gets done and will not feel like an extra step. If the performance of interest is behavioral and requires a more subjective judgment, make the judgments as easy as possible. Checklists that simply indicate whether desired behaviors were observed can be especially useful, particularly if completing these checklists are embedded in routine work processes. For example, supervisors can easily complete checklists like the one shown in Figure 6.1 monthly as part of their normal supervision duty. One organization with whom we worked uses this approach with great success. Completed checklists are one way the organization's leadership ensures service quality and are therefore considered a core business requirement and not simply a "nice to have." Employees get feedback on their performance every month, and scores are aggregated annually to identify broad training needs and to make promotion decisions.

Another particularly effective method for embedding behavioral performance measurement into work was developed by the U.S. Army: The after action review (AAR—U.S. Army, 1993). The AAR is a routine part of every operation and training event. After the event is complete, participants meet briefly to review what happened and lessons learned. The typical process is to:

1. Review what should have happened—recap the original plan and commander's intent.
2. Review what actually happened.
3. Discuss why actual events might have deviated from the plan.
4. Discuss what went well and what did not.
5. Discuss lessons learned for future operations.

The purpose of the AAR is learning. Each soldier is expected to participate, and lower-ranking individuals can speak as freely as higher-ranking individuals. Effective AARs use open-ended questions and a non-judgmental tone to elicit candid feedback from participants. The FBI has adopted a similar strategy with its special agents that they refer to as the "Hot Wash" (Grubb, 2015). Like the AAR, the Hot Wash is an opportunity to reflect on recent performance and learn from it. Results from informal AARs and Hot Washes are not documented nor are they part of formal performance evaluation processes, which is likely why these techniques have proven to be successful strategies for reflection and learning.

Acknowledge and Mitigate the Potential for Error

No measurement method is comprehensive and free from error, and many measurement methods can be "gamed." For example, field repair technicians who are measured on the number of jobs they complete can achieve better numbers by contriving to be assigned "easier" jobs and jobs that are closer together to reduce drive time. Technicians who take on more complex and time-consuming jobs will thus be penalized for completing fewer of them.

It is impossible to account for all sources of error and to design a measurement system that cannot be gamed, but these issues can be mitigated:

- Use multiple measures that cover different aspects of performance (e.g., not just production metrics but satisfaction, quality indicators, etc.).
- Acknowledge external impacts on performance measures and address them if performance is less than desired (e.g., if work is late, address external causes such as lack of manpower, inadequate resources, missing information, inefficient work processes, etc.).
- Keep the primary goal performance improvement rather than judgment or decision-making. Be cautious about tying financial incentives directly to performance measures, as this will increase motivation to game the system.
- Measure processes as well as outcomes. Sometimes overall outcomes are outside of an employee's control. In that case, focus on the process used to achieve that outcome.

Because measurement error can be mitigated but not eliminated, managers and employees need to recognize the limitations of performance measurement. No one measure or set of measures tells the whole story about an individual's performance—there will always be factors outside an employee's control that impact results. If the focus of the measurement is simply to gather information that can be used to help employees improve, employees will be less likely to try and "game the numbers" to look more successful than they are. It is impossible to take all emotion out of performance measurement—most employees want to put their best foot forward and will become defensive if they believe the measures make them look bad. However, to the extent measurement processes are transparent, use data from multiple sources, and are used to improve performance and not pass judgment, defensiveness can be reduced.

Evaluating Performance

Performance evaluation is the process of making a judgment about an employee's effectiveness in his or her role and overall value to the organization. Most organizations evaluate performance at least annually, and some do semiannual or quarterly evaluations. Performance evaluations usually include one or more performance ratings accompanied by narrative descriptions. Evaluation criteria typically include:

- The extent to which employees have met, not met, or exceeded their performance goals.
- The extent to which employees have successfully demonstrated key performance dimensions (e.g., communication, teamwork, etc.).
- Overall effectiveness.
- Some combination of the above.

Performance on these criteria is then rated with a scale consisting of 3, 4, 5, 6, or 7 rating levels, with five levels being the most common.[1] Rating scales may consist of numbers and labels or just labels, along with a description of what each rating level means. Two example rating scales are shown in Table 6.2. Both are known as behaviorally anchored rating scales because each rating level is anchored with examples of behavior that define that level. The first example is a broad rating of effective job performance, and the second example illustrates how rating scales can be developed for specific performance dimensions.

Organizations use a variety of methods to combine ratings from different dimensions. Some simply ask managers to provide one overall rating. Others allow weighting of each performance factor and then calculate an overall score based on the weighted average or sum of the individual performance ratings. While weighting may emphasize the importance of certain performance dimensions, it does not tend to impact the overall rank order of employees' scores. In other words, employees who are rated highly with weighted criteria also tend to be rated highly with unweighted criteria because performance criteria are rarely independent of each other. Employees who perform well in one area are likely to perform well in other areas.

Although there is often lively debate about the merits of different numbers of scale points and scale formats, research has shown that neither has much impact on rating accuracy (DeNisi & Murphy, 2017; Landy & Farr, 1980). Despite this finding, employees often attach great importance to rating scales and labels. Some organizations use a three-level scale to simplify ratings because, as a

TABLE 6.2 Sample Performance Rating Scales

Overall Performance Rating

Label	Description
1. Unacceptable	Completes assigned tasks only with extraordinary guidance and oversight. Work is frequently late or fails to meet standards and may include major errors that require correction or rework.
2. Needs Improvement	Completes assigned tasks with extra guidance and supervision. Work may occasionally be late or fail to meet standards and include errors that require correction or rework.
3. Fully Successful	Completes all assigned tasks on time and within standards with minimal guidance. Work is generally error-free, requiring little correction or rework.
4. Excellent	Completes all assigned tasks on time and within or above standards independently and without errors. Takes initiative to seek out new tasks and responsibilities.
5. Outstanding	Completes all assigned tasks on time and within or above standards independently and without errors. Takes initiative to seek out new tasks and responsibilities. Develops new ways of improving effectiveness and efficiency. Trains and mentors others to help them improve their performance.

Specific Performance Rating Scale—Teamwork Dimension

Label	Description
1. Unacceptable	Frequently treats others disrespectfully and unprofessionally and ignores differing points of view. Contributes in meetings and discussions only reluctantly. Assists others rarely, grudgingly, and only after repeated requests.
2. Needs Improvement	Needs reminders and prompting to treat others professionally and respectfully, and to listen to differing points of view. Contributes occasionally in meetings and discussions. Helps others only when requested.
3. Fully Successful	Treats others professionally and respectfully. Listens to differing points of view. Contributes actively in meetings and discussions. Helps others when needed.
4. Excellent	Treats others professionally and respectfully. Seeks out and listens to differing points of view. Contributes actively in meetings and discussions. Proactively offers assistance without being asked.
5. Outstanding	Role model for professionalism and respectful behavior. Ensures diverse perspectives are sought, heard, and incorporated into discussions and decisions. Leads meetings and discussions effectively and facilitates contributions of others. Proactively offers help and gets others to help when needed.

practical matter, managers rarely use the end points of the scale anyway (e.g., with a 5-point scale, most employees receive a rating of "3" or "4"). However, changing from a 5-point scale to a 3-point scale can yield resistance—employees who used to be rated a "3" on the 5-point scale are now unhappy with a rating of "2" on a 3-point scale).

Employees also have strong reactions to rating labels. If the midpoint of a rating scale sounds like average performance (e.g., "satisfactory," "successful"), employees may resent that rating because most people believe they are above-average performers (e.g., Headey & Wearing, 1988). Some organizations attempt to address this by using an even number of rating levels that allow most employees to receive above-average ratings. For example, a four-level scale might have the labels "unacceptable, successful, excellent, and outstanding." If most employees are rated "excellent" or "outstanding," they feel better, and the organization can make some distinctions among employees to distribute rewards.

Rating scale design is more art than science. Organizations that use performance ratings (more about this debate follows), can develop a good scale by following a few key principles:

- Use clear and descriptive language for each rating level.
- Ensure each level can be clearly distinguished from the others.
- Fit rating labels to the organization's culture, the messages it wants to convey, and its intended use.
- Consider how rating scales have been used historically and the psychological impact of rating labels and levels. If employees are used to receiving high ratings, they will resist a new rating scale that makes them feel their performance is less valued—even if rewards remain unchanged.

Performance ratings happen in the context of the larger performance evaluation process, which can involve the following activities:

- Employees complete a self-assessment, which may consist of both ratings and narrative descriptions of performance.
- Ratings from peers, direct reports, and others may be sought in the form of 360-degree or multi-source feedback. Typically, this feedback includes both ratings on performance dimensions as well as open-ended comments about strengths and development needs.
- Managers review employee self-assessments and 360-degree feedback (if available) and complete their own evaluation, consisting of both ratings and narrative justifications of performance.
- Managers may need to submit their evaluations to a higher-level reviewer and/or attend a calibration session in which ratings are debated with other managers (discussed in more detail in Chapter 8).
- Managers and employees meet to review and discuss the performance evaluation.

Employees and managers frequently complain about this process because review forms are long, complex, and require too much time and effort to complete. The review process is often reduced to a process-heavy "check-the-box activity," and little attention is paid to having high-quality conversations. Documentation requirements vary widely by organization and range from one overall summary rating and narrative statement that fits on a single page to multiple ratings and narratives that can require up to 20 pages. However, there is no evidence that longer and more complex performance evaluation requirements provide more accurate evaluations or ultimately lead to better performance.

Use of Self-Assessments

As noted earlier in the chapter, self-assessments, in which employees provide ratings and narrative descriptions of their own performance, are frequently included as part of the evaluation process. The rationale for their inclusion is that they provide employees with more of a voice in the process and provide managers with useful information they may not otherwise have known. However, self-assessments can be time-consuming to complete and can create unnecessary conflict between managers and employees.

The primary question to consider when deciding whether to include self-assessments is if they contribute to improving performance. The answer appears to be that they do not improve performance and may in fact be harmful. While employee perceptions of fairness are important, research suggests that external appraisals of performance are more powerful for motivating future performance than self-appraisals (Harkins & Lowe, 2000). Moreover, if employee self-assessments do not match supervisory assessments, employees are more likely to have a negative view of the evaluation process. Employees who have negative reactions to performance feedback are likely to receive lower subsequent performance ratings (Smither, London, & Reilly, 2005).

This research does not suggest that employees should not be involved in the performance evaluation process, but it does suggest the nature of the involvement should be different than self-appraisals. Employee involvement is best achieved by engaging in meaningful two-way dialog during performance conversations in which the employee's perspective is sought and genuinely attended to (CIPD, 2016). A formal, written self-assessment is not conducive to improving performance, but asking employees to reflect on their accomplishments informally and come prepared to performance conversations to share their reflections is a sound approach for giving employees a voice in the process.

Use of Multi-Source Ratings

Use of multi-source or 360-degree ratings for performance evaluation is somewhat controversial. On one hand, gathering feedback from multiple sources can provide performance information that managers may not be able to observe. On the other hand, research suggests that raters are less candid when they know the ratings will be used for evaluation purposes rather than development (Greguras, Robie, Schleicher, & Goff, 2003). Additionally, gathering ratings from multiple sources can be time-consuming and logistically challenging.

If multi-source feedback will be used as part of the evaluation process, it works best if:

- the feedback providers have credible, first-hand knowledge about the employee's work.
- the process is perceived as fair.
- feedback delivery is provided in a non-threatening manner.
- emotions are effectively managed.
- the recipient uses the feedback to take action that leads to changed behavior.
- feedback providers are anonymous and can provide feedback without fear of reprisal.
- internal consultants and champions are available to support the process.

Understanding Rating Accuracy

Accuracy is a primary concern when ratings are the basis of important decisions about people (e.g., compensation, promotion, termination, etc.). However, the concept of "accuracy" in ratings is problematic for a variety of reasons. First and foremost, there is no single objective measure of performance to which ratings can be compared to assess their accuracy. Objective measures, such as production or sales, may not entirely align with supervisory assessments of performance that cover broader performance areas such as teamwork, communication, and so forth. Additionally, there is little to no relationship between performance ratings and business metrics such as revenue and profit. For example, in one-large scale study of rating accuracy, performance ratings were entirely uncorrelated with business unit performance. Business units with high performance ratings were no more likely to be profitable than units with low performance ratings (CEB, 2012). In the following sections, we discuss a number of different factors that impact rating accuracy and strategies that have been tried to address these.

The Impact of Human Information Processing Limitations on Accuracy

Even if managers had no other goal than to rate employees accurately, the task of evaluating job performance is extraordinarily challenging. Managers see thousands of performance examples in many different contexts across a year-long rating period. To objectively summarize these into an accurate overall rating, managers would need to remember, appropriately weight, and correctly combine their observations. This is impossible, so they revert to their overall impressions or noteworthy examples of performance that stand out from the rest, consistent with how we naturally process large volumes of information (Landy & Farr, 1980). Because ratings draw on overall judgments, attempts to increase accuracy with more complex rating scales or more rating levels with finer distinctions have not been successful—managers simply cannot recall the details about different employees' performance that are required to make fine-grained distinctions in ratings (Pulakos & O'Leary, 2009).

Complicating matters further is that different raters bring their own "frames-of-reference" or viewpoints and standards to any rating situation. These develop over time based on raters' past experience, personal rating tendencies, and individual views about what good performance looks like (Pulakos, 2009), which makes performance ratings inherently subjective. The result is that different individuals rarely agree, even when they are observing the same behavior. Intensive rater training can provide some improvements in agreement (DeNisi & Murphy, 2017), although much of the research that has shown training to improve accuracy comes from artificial laboratory settings (e.g., Pulakos, 1984, 1986). These results are difficult to replicate in real work situations that are much more complex and in which rating accuracy is not always an important goal.

The Impact of Role Relationships on Accuracy

Research on 360-degree ratings provides additional insights into the challenges associated with rating accuracy. Ratings from different rating sources (managers, peers, customers, etc.) rarely agree. In some cases, disagreement stems from raters seeing different aspects of performance; for example, direct reports see how their managers set expectations, provide feedback, and so forth, while other rating sources (e.g., peers, customers, managers) have little knowledge of this area. Employees sometimes behave differently with different groups or individuals. For example, an employee may collaborate very effectively with managers but poorly with peers, resulting in a high rating from the manager, a low rating from peers, and an average rating overall. Another employee may collaborate at an average level with everyone and also receive an average rating overall. Are both employees performing the same? How should we think about rating accuracy in this case?

The Impact of Political and Social Factors on Accuracy

In light of these issues, the idea that we can define and achieve rating accuracy becomes highly questionable. But what may make this idea entirely out of reach is that raters have strong motives for giving ratings that have nothing to do with accuracy. Murphy and Cleveland (1995) summarized these in terms of four competing political and social goals that managers need to balance as part of the performance management process.

- Task performance goals: using performance evaluation to influence the subsequent performance of ratees.
- Interpersonal goals: using appraisal to maintain or improve interpersonal relations between the supervisor and subordinates.
- Strategic goals: using the performance management process to increase the supervisor's and/or the workgroup's standing in the organization.
- Internalized goals: goals that are the results of raters' beliefs about how he or she should evaluate performance.

These goals often carry so much weight in managers' rating behavior that accuracy and differentiation are simply not relevant drivers of performance evaluation. As a practical matter, what ends up being more important is managers being able to avoid conflict and protect their relationships with the people they count on to get work done, so they can succeed themselves.

Strategies to Mitigate Rating Inaccuracy

Many different strategies have been tried to increase rating accuracy, including use of different types of rating scales, different types of rating criteria, and different types of training, among others—all with little success. One approach that has gotten quite a bit of traction in organizations, however, is to implement a forced-ranking process. The theory behind forced-rankings is that ratings are normally distributed, meaning there is an approximately equal—but small—number of very high and very low performers and most employees fall in the middle. Forced-rankings require raters to categorize employees into groups that match what would be expected in a normal distribution, which forces more differentiation in ratings and rewards than is typically observed with traditional rating scales. This process has been shown to decrease rating inflation, a pervasive problem in performance ratings in which most ratings are clustered at the high end of the rating scale and do not differentiate well between employees. An example of a forced-ranking approach is:

- The top 10% of employees are rated highest.
- The next 20% of employees receive the next highest rating.
- The middle 50% of employees receive the middle rating.
- The bottom 20% receive the lowest ratings and potential termination.

A much more complex variant on the above ranking approach is stack-ranking, in which all employees in a group are individually ranked from highest to lowest performers (e.g., 100 employees would be ranked 1, 2, 3 through to 100). In either approach, the highest performers earn the biggest rewards and the lowest performers may earn no rewards or are at risk of losing their jobs.

The genesis of forced-ranking is attributed to GE's "rank and yank" performance management approach in which each employee was categorized based on her effectiveness relative to other employees, and those deemed the lowest performers were separated. Proselytized by Jack Welch, this practice quickly gained popularity. In a particularly contentious version of forced-ranking, Microsoft rank-ordered all of its employees from 1 to N, although executives eventually came to believe this resulted in unhealthy competition and poor performance, which caused them to abandon this approach in 2013 (Warren, 2013). While forced-ranking has diminished in popularity since its GE heyday, it is still used by about 20% of organizations (CEB, 2014). A recent example was its use at Yahoo during Marissa Mayer's tenure as CEO as a mechanism to separate lackluster talent.

At least initially, forced-ranking can have a positive impact, provided that high-performing employees do not leave voluntarily as their lower-performing colleagues are let go (Scullen, Bergey, & Aiman-Smith, 2010). In organizations in which there are significant numbers of poor performers, forced-ranking can accelerate moving out the lowest performers. In the longer-term, forced-ranking provides diminishing returns and can become counterproductive if a high percentage of the lowest performers in a relative sense are actually solid contributors. Employees tend to despise forced-ranking because they can't earn better performance ratings through their efforts alone; their ratings and subsequent outcomes are dependent on how they stack up against their peers.

Forced-ranking systems were implemented and used broadly over many years, based on the belief that that reduced rating inflation implied corresponding increases in rating accuracy. However, recent research has raised questions about the foundational assumption that performance is normally distributed—and has shown that in many cases, it is not (Aguinis, Gottfredson, & Joo, 2013; O'Boyle & Aguinis, 2012). Further, if organizations are managing their talent well, coaching low performers out, and retaining high performers, their rating distributions should have more high performers than low performers, rather than follow a normal distribution. In this case, ratings would actually cluster into a narrower range, with an average rating above the midpoint. Force fitting ratings to a normal distribution when they are not in fact distributed normally increases rating error and decreases rating accuracy; hence, these approaches are not recommended. The past five years have shown a significant decline in the use of forced-rankings.

Given these challenges, striving for "accurate" ratings is not likely to be fruitful. A more practical and effective strategy is to:

1. Define desired performance in terms of the behaviors that are needed to contribute to organizational objectives (see Chapter 4).

2. Measure the presence or absence of these behaviors directly and frequently, using these metrics as a primary source of feedback to help employees improve their performance. Recognize that these measures are inherently limited and don't over-interpret the information from any one source.
3. Develop decision criteria that fit the nature of the decision to be made. Use these decision criteria in place of more traditional performance ratings to inform talent decisions. This idea is discussed in more detail in Chapter 8.

The Ratings Debate

As discussed in Chapter 1, considerable media attention has been devoted to debating whether organizations should continue with formal performance evaluations. Given the challenges with formal evaluations, it is no wonder this question is being raised. The answer depends on how ratings have been used in the past, the extent to which the ratings reflect the organization's culture, and what information is needed to make effective talent decisions. Before deciding whether to use performance ratings, organizations should think through what they hope to achieve and the extent to which these goals are currently being met. Organizations often have assumptions about ratings that are simply not supported by reality. Table 6.3 provides a comparison of common assumptions about performance ratings and the realities present in many organizations.

TABLE 6.3 Assumptions and Realities about Performance Ratings

Assumptions	Realities
Ratings are the best means of providing accurate performance data	Managers and employees frequently say they don't trust that ratings accurately reflect performance. A variety of research shows that the concept of "accuracy" is problematic, in part because no objective standard exists to assess the accuracy of ratings.
Ratings are essential to let employees know "where they stand"	Most employees believe they are above-average performers and will likely resist rating approaches that label them as average and resent receiving a rating that places them in the middle of the rating scale.
Ratings motivate high performers and encourage low performers to improve	High performers like to be recognized for their contributions, but there is no evidence that ratings motivate them to perform better. High performers frequently say that they are most motivated by meaningful work, autonomy, and ability to use their skills. In turn, low performers who receive low ratings are likely to perform worse in the future, not better, especially if they believe the ratings are unfair.

(Continued)

TABLE 6.3 (Continued)

Assumptions	Realities
Ratings are necessary to make compensation decisions	Managers usually have a keen awareness of how their employees are performing and who they need to reward to keep engaged. Managers often "back into" ratings to justify whatever decisions they would like to make. Therefore, ratings don't determine compensation—desired compensation usually determines ratings.
Ratings defend against legal challenges	Most managers are reluctant to give low performance ratings—even to poor performers. It is not uncommon in organizations for ratings that are below average to account for less than 2% of all performance ratings. Consequently, performance ratings can work against employers in legal challenges because the performance appraisals often reflect a pattern of satisfactory ratings for poor performers.
Our organization is a meritocracy, and it is necessary to make distinctions among employees	Most organizations have little variation in performance ratings. If budgets are tight there may be little distinctions in rewards also. Pay-for-performance does not uniformly improve performance and may in some cases hinder it.

In addition to critically evaluating these assumptions, consider the following:

- How much time and energy is spent on the performance rating process? What value is the organization getting from this time and energy? Are there benefits to having ratings, and can we achieve the same benefits without ratings?
- What structures do we have in place to ensure employees are getting coaching and feedback on a regular basis? If we eliminate ratings, will we still have a way to ensure effective performance conversations?
- What is the link between performance and rewards? If we eliminate ratings, how will we communicate reward information to employees? (Making reward decisions without ratings is discussed in more detail in Chapter 8.)

Another consideration is the question of how ratings have been used in the past to defend against legal challenges. While performance ratings are not always required, in-house counsels and external regulatory bodies (e.g., the EEOC) often have strong views about the need for ratings because they provide a consistent way to document performance-based compensation decisions. Documenting performance ratings as justification for rewards does not guarantee protection from challenges, and poor or inconsistent documentation can hurt more than help. To protect against challenges, organizations need to:

- Have a clear rationale for decisions about compensation, rewards, and other actions.

- Communicate those decisions effectively to employees.
- Monitor decisions for potential adverse impact and act if it is discovered.

Organizations can make defensible decisions without performance ratings, but it is prudent to work with internal or external counsel to discuss the implications of changes to the rating process.

Organizations will need to carefully consider their needs, culture, and risk tolerance when deciding whether or not to use ratings. Performance evaluations by themselves appear to have little impact on performance, but organizations often flounder when removing them without a suitable replacement. Culturally, ratings are entrenched in many organizations and cannot be eliminated—in these cases, steps can still be taken to make the evaluation process less burdensome and more valuable, such as:

- Simplify the rating process (e.g., instead of rating each objective and each competency, provide an overall summary rating).
- Do not rate on whether goals were met or exceeded, as this promotes sand-bagging (writing goals that are easily exceeded). Instead rate on overall contributions and impact.
- Reduce narrative descriptions required to support performance ratings and focus on information essential to supporting any resulting decisions.
- Eliminate formal self-assessments. They are time-consuming, and there is no evidence they lead to greater accuracy or better performance. Give employees a voice in the evaluation process by asking them to provide input on accomplishments and development needs—this process can be informal rather than formal.
- Use ratings primarily for decision-making (see Chapter 8 for details) and separate conversations about performance from conversations about decisions. Use performance conversations as an opportunity to discuss strengths and development needs. Use conversations about decisions to explain both the outcome and the process used to make the decision.
- Teach managers how to address poor performance as soon as it is observed rather than waiting for a performance review to force the issue. Make it easier for managers to handle performance challenges and take action with poor performers (see Chapter 9 for more details).

Some organizations have chosen to keep formal reviews in place but eliminate the performance ratings that accompany them. Employees still receive formal feedback at designated times throughout the year, but the feedback is more qualitative (e.g., a discussion of strengths and development needs) instead of being anchored in ratings. Ledford, Benson, and Lawler (2016) report that this practice is on the rise and is usually associated with ongoing feedback. According to their research, organizations have found rating-less reviews moderately helpful for providing effective feedback to employees and supporting effective coaching behavior but less effective for rewarding employees.

★★★

Performance measurement is essential for tracking progress on performance expectations, and it serves as the foundation for effective feedback. Good performance measures are an integral part of work processes. It takes time and effort to measure performance effectively; therefore, organizations should be selective about what is measured and embed measurement into everyday workflows that make it easier for managers and employees to sustain. The effort involved in measuring performance should be outweighed by the value of the insights gained for improving performance.

Although performance evaluation is often a proxy for robust performance measurement, evaluation is more useful for decision-making than performance improvement. Ongoing performance measurement that uses information from multiple sources is the best way to provide timely information to employees and managers to help improve performance. If approached in the spirit of continuous improvement, the act of measuring performance can prevent defensiveness and emotional reactions that inhibit performance. As discussed in more detail in Chapter 8, performance evaluation is better suited to support talent decisions rather than provide performance feedback.

Note

1 We have seen some notable exceptions to the traditional 5-point scale. One organization used a 250-point scale, though ratings below 100 or above 150 were rare. Even so, managers spent many hours arguing whether an employee should be given a 110 versus a 115, despite the fact that the difference in compensation between these two ratings was practically zero.

References

Aguinis, H., Gottfredson, R. K., & Joo, H. (2013). Avoiding a "me" versus "we" dilemma: Using performance management to turn teams into a source of competitive advantage. *Business Horizons, 56*, 503–512.

CEB. (2012). *Driving breakthrough performance in the new work environment.* Arlington, VA: Author.

CEB. (2014). *Performance management process benchmarks.* Arlington, VA: Author.

CIPD. (2016, December). *Could do better? Assessing what works in performance management.* Research Report.

Culbertson, S. S., Henning, J. B., & Payne, S. C. (2013). Performance appraisal satisfaction: The role of feedback and goal orientation. *Journal of Personnel Psychology, 12*, 189–195.

DeNisi, A. S., & Murphy, K. R. (2017). Performance appraisal and performance management: 100 years of progress? *Journal of Applied Psychology, 3*, 421–433.

Greguras, G. J., Robie, C., Schleicher, D. J., & Goff, M. (2003). A field study of the effects of rating purpose on the quality of multisource ratings. *Personnel Psychology, 56*(1), 1–21.

Grubb, A. D. (2015). *Performance management in a high stakes environment: A case study from the FBI.* Presentation at the 2015 SIOP Leading Edge Consortium, Boston, MA.

Harkins, S. G., & Lowe, M. D. (2000). The effects of self-set goals on task performance. *Journal of Applied Social Psychology, 30*, 1–40.

Headey, B., & Wearing, A. (1988). The sense of relative superiority—central to well-being. *Social Indicators Research, 20*, 497–516.

Landy, F. J., & Farr, J. L. (1980). Performance rating. *Psychological Bulletin, 87*, 72–107.

Ledford, G. E., Benson, G., & Lawler, E. E. (2016, August). *Cutting-edge performance management: 244 organizations report on ongoing feedback, ratingless reviews, and crowd-sourced feedback.* World at Work Research, Center for Effective Organizations.

Murphy, K. R., & Cleveland, J. N. (1995). *Understanding performance appraisal: Social, organizational, and goal-oriented perspectives.* Newbury Park, CA: SAGE.

O'Boyle, E. Jr., & Aguinis, H. (2012). The best and the rest: Revisiting the norm of normality of individual performance. *Personnel Psychology, 65*, 79–119.

Pulakos, E. D. (1984). A comparison of rater training programs: Error training and accuracy training. *Journal of Applied Psychology, 69*, 581–588.

Pulakos, E. D. (1986). The development of a training program to increase accuracy with different rating formats. *Organizational Behavior and Human Decision Processes, 38*, 76–91.

Pulakos, E. D. (2009). *Performance management: A new approach for driving business results.* Oxford: Wiley-Blackwell Publishers.

Pulakos, E. D., & O'Leary, R. S. (2009). Defining and measuring results of workplace behavior. In J. L. Farr & N. T. Tippins (Eds.), *Handbook of employee selection.* Mahwah, NJ: Erlbaum.

Rock, D. (2008). SCARF: A brain-based model for collaborating with and influencing others. *NeuroLeadership Journal, 1*, 1–9.

Scullen, S. S., Bergey, P. K., & Aiman-Smith, A. (2010). Forced distribution rating systems and the improvement of workforce potential: A baseline simulation. *Personnel Psychology, 58*, 1–32.

Smither, J., London, M., & Reilly, R. (2005). Does performance improve following multisource feedback? A theoretical model, meta-analysis and review of empirical findings. *Personnel Psychology, 58*, 33–66.

U.S. Army (1993, September). *A leader's guide to after action reviews.* Training Circular 25–20. Washington, DC: Headquarters, Department of the Army.

Warren, T. (2013, November 11). Microsoft axes its controversial employee-ranking system. *The Verge.* Retrieved February 27, 2017, from www.theverge.com/2013/11/12/5094864/microsoft-kills-stack-ranking-internal-structure

7

ENABLE HIGH-QUALITY PERFORMANCE CONVERSATIONS

Effective performance management is fundamentally about frequent and high-quality performance conversations between managers and employees. The most effective conversations include an open and two-way dialog, candid yet supportive feedback, and coaching to improve performance. Unfortunately, good conversations appear to be rare. When interviewing HR professionals for this book, the biggest pain point that each of them cited was lack of effective performance conversations, and especially lack of manager skills in providing effective feedback and coaching.

Many organizations try to combat this problem with a hyper-focus on improving feedback. They attempt to improve the presence and quality of feedback by training managers to:

- get over their fears about giving feedback,
- use techniques for providing feedback constructively,
- provide more frequent informal feedback, and
- develop trusting, solid relationships.

While training can have some positive benefits, it falls short of what's needed to drive effective performance. HR leaders often comment that, "If only we could only get feedback right, everything would improve." However, this is an oversimplified view because feedback by itself does not always increase performance. According to one seminal meta-analysis on feedback (aggregating the results of hundreds of different studies), about one-third of those receiving feedback perform better, one-third perform worse, and one-third don't change one way or the other (Kluger & DeNisi, 1996).

Instead of focusing on helping managers deliver feedback more effectively, organizations should broaden the focus to supporting high-quality performance conversations for both managers and employees. The difference between effective and ineffective conversations is having a clear purpose (why the conversation is happening), ensuring the right content (what is the conversation is about), and using a sound approach (how the conversation is conducted). This chapter provides guidance on structuring the focus, content, and delivery of conversations to make them more effective and on how to build and sustain a climate that is conducive to effective conversations.

Ensuring a Clear Purpose

First and foremost, the purpose of performance conversations should be to help improve performance. Feedback delivered as part of formal performance reviews often fails to meet this criterion—it comes too late to impact performance, and the feedback is given for the purpose of passing judgment or justifying rewards, rather than improving immediate performance. It is no wonder that managers dislike giving reviews and employees dislike receiving them. Feedback that is most useful in driving performance is embedded in the holistic process of setting expectations, tracking progress, and adjusting strategies and behaviors to advance the work and deliver results.

Most conversations are for the purpose of improving the work itself or changing behavior. Being clear on the purpose one is trying to achieve is the first step in determining how to structure the conversation and when and if feedback should be given. Discussing work products or process tends to be less personal, and it is easier to pinpoint problems when they occur and brainstorm solutions. When problems arise, they are best addressed in real time so that they can be corrected.

Conversations about behavioral issues are more challenging. These issues tend to occur less frequently but are important to address when they do, especially when they negatively impact others or block achieving high performance. When the feedback is aimed at core behavioral traits or someone's interpersonal style, it can be difficult to depersonalize. It is important to understand and acknowledge this reality rather than assume all feedback can be made palatable and easy for recipients to receive by simply using the "right" feedback techniques; therefore, feedback providers must carefully weigh the potential benefits of delivering this type of feedback against the potential consequences.

Behavioral issues can take time to diagnose, so feedback is often not given in real time when the behavior in question first occurs. Unless an obvious, extreme behavior is exhibited, it takes effort to observe, understand, and form both a clear conclusion and message about what the person is doing that's ineffective, its impact, and what needs to change. Managers need to assess whether there's a legitimate reason for the behavior and whether it is a consistent habit or a one-off event. This often requires allowing a repeated pattern to emerge to ensure it is attributable to person rather than the situation.

Considering the real discomfort managers have in discussing behavioral challenges, the focus of feedback should be in areas that will most impact one's current performance and future potential, not all areas in which one could potentially improve. Doing this well will mean carefully thinking through how much behaviors are actually impacting performance and whether giving feedback will make a difference. Unless the feedback is high on these criteria, it may not be worth the trouble or distraction to provide it.

Ensuring the Right Content

Given a clear purpose, the next consideration is what to communicate during the performance conversation. Performance conversations should help employees assess their progress toward some goal or expectation. Seeing visible progress toward goal accomplishment is a key factor in driving higher performance. Employees must feel they are making progress to stay motivated and engaged in the pursuit of their goals (CIPD, 2016). Colquitt (2017) suggests that knowledge of progress is even more important than feedback. Discussing progress rather than simply providing feedback changes the dynamic from one of employees receiving judgment from managers to one of a two-way dialog about how things are going, what is getting in the way of progress, and how these barriers can be removed. Conversations about progress also take the pressure off managers to be the sole providers of feedback because other sources of data can be used to provide knowledge of results, a concept that will be discussed in more detail later in this chapter.

When feedback is needed, it is more effective (that is, leads to improved performance) when it is based on strengths rather than weaknesses (e.g., CEB, 2002; Kluger & DeNisi, 1996; London, 2003). This is not to suggest feedback must be sugarcoated. Performance challenges should be dealt with honestly and in a straightforward manner. Yet, many managers tend to notice what goes wrong much more than acknowledge what is being done well. Some believe that too much positive feedback "coddles" employees. For example, one manager told us that he thought compliments should only be given when employees do something extraordinary, but constructive feedback should be given for even the most minor of mistakes. If an employee had written a paper that was generally good but missing a few commas, his feedback would focus on the missing commas rather than the strengths of the paper. Employees found his feedback unhelpful and disliked working for him.

A common feedback myth is that constructive criticism should always be "sandwiched" between two compliments. However, the feedback sandwich does a disservice to the recipient by making it difficult to understand the real message. Feedback can include both compliments and critiques. However, both easily correctable and serious performance problems should be addressed directly. Honest feedback can still be delivered in a considerate manner, and recipients appreciate getting straight talk even if they don't like the message. Compliments and appreciation should stand on their own without recipients having to question if they are simply given to soften the blow of a criticism.

Acknowledgment, thanks, and appreciation for work well done are some of the most powerful, lasting, and engaging rewards available—even more so than pay and other monetary rewards. These rewards tend to be underutilized—not just by managers but also peers and direct reports. Appreciation and thanks should be given when they are warranted and not capriciously. Calling attention to what people have done well, the positive behaviors they demonstrate, and the skills and abilities they apply in their work paves the way for more openness and receptivity when feedback needs to be constructive. A balanced approach to feedback creates a context in which individuals are confident that their strengths are recognized and they are secure in their position, which then helps constructive feedback to be processed less defensively.

When feedback needs to be more constructive, it is more effective when it is about how the work is being accomplished (the process) rather than what results were achieved (the outcomes) (Early, Northcraft, Lee, & Lituchy, 1990). Process feedback is diagnostic and helps the recipient understand the underlying reasons for a result rather than just hearing about the result itself, which is often obvious. For example, telling a project manager she is missing key deadlines is not helpful. She is likely aware of the problem but may not know how to fix it. On the other hand, a discussion about how she is managing the project schedule could be more useful, such as how she is assigning tasks, tracking completion, and holding team members accountable. This type of discussion can lead to concrete suggestions for how to improve.

Regardless of whether it is focused on strengths or improvement needs, feedback is more effective when it is about behaviors and not personal characteristics. A key insight from Kluger's and DeNisi's (1996) research was that feedback about personal characteristics distracts people from the task at hand and can lead to decreased performance—even when the feedback is positive. Behavioral feedback is also more within the recipient's control, which is important for positive change (Deci, 1975). For example, one of us earlier in our careers got feedback after a presentation that we were "too young" to be presenting to such a senior audience. While being called "too young" would be welcome today, at the time it was disengaging. It would have been much more useful to get specific feedback on how the presentation style or content could be improved.

Using a Sound Approach

With a clear purpose and the right content, attention can be given to how the conversation is conducted. A one-size-fits-all approach will not work. Communication strategies should be tailored to the situation. For example, critical incidents require immediate feedback, such as egregious behavior that needs immediate correction, a serious failure that needs to be dealt with right away, or a huge win that needs to be recognized. Timeliness of feedback is key in these situations while everyone's memory is still fresh (van der Kleij, Eggen, Timmers, & Veldkamp, 2012). Real-time feedback is more impactful than delayed feedback, in part because it better enables unpacking what exactly happened within the context in which it occurred and thus enables the specificity that is needed to coach employees for improved future performance. Feedback should also be specific because recipients need to understand exactly what was ineffective, so providing specific information and examples of what happened, and the impact, are important (Ilgen, Fisher, & Taylor, 1979).

A related situation that requires immediate feedback is the everyday teachable moment—the multitude of daily events that provide opportunities for improvement embedded in ongoing work. Teachable moments can be prompted by comments in response to written documents, reactions from colleagues during meetings or in conversations, or reactions from customers when providing service. Even lack of response is a form of feedback—it may indicate lack of interest, engagement, or understanding. These feedback opportunities are not always recognized as such, yet they have the most potential to impact performance.

Using a teachable moment as the impetus for performance conversation is more impactful than waiting until a formal review to provide feedback. Figure 7.1 illustrates this contrast. Formal performance conversations deliver feedback too late for recipients to take action, which can lead to frustration and

---

Scenario: Jessica just finished leading an important customer meeting. Her manager, Maria, thinks Jessica did well for the most part but could use some improvement. She was prepared, had a solid agenda, and successfully engaged the customer and got some key decisions from them. However, she let a few participants dominate the conversation and take things off-track at times, which led to the meeting going way over the scheduled time.

Formal Performance Review	*Teachable Moment*
Maria quickly tells Jessica after the meeting that she "did a pretty good job" and that they will "discuss the feedback in more detail" when they meet for Jessica's performance review. Jessica is glad for the compliment but also nervous because she knows more feedback is coming. She spends a lot of time until the review replaying the meeting in her head, trying to imagine what Maria's feedback might be.	Maria asks Jessica to debrief for a few minutes immediately after the meeting: **Maria:** How do you think it went? **Jessica:** I thought it went ok but long. I really did a lot to prepare … **M:** You did prepare well. The agenda was well organized. Great job with that. Why do you think the meeting went over time?

FIGURE 7.1 Contrasting Formal Performance Reviews with Teachable Moments

At the performance review Maria tells Jessica that she needs to improve her meeting management skills. Jessica is surprised and asks for examples. Maria has forgotten many of the details but remembers the recent customer meeting where the discussion was off-topic. She tells Jessica, "You let some participants dominate the conversation, and it went way over time." Jessica becomes a bit defensive—she doesn't remember the meeting that way and thinks Maria is not giving her credit for a positive outcome or all the other successful meetings she has had throughout the year.

Maria, sensing the defensiveness, moves on to other topics. Thirty minutes later, Jessica leaves the meeting feeling ok, but her confidence is a bit shaken. She doesn't completely agree with Maria's feedback and is worried about how she will judge her performance in the future.

J: Lisa and Tom are real talkers. I wanted everyone to share their views, but those two just went on and on!

M: Yes, they had a lot to say! Everyone was engaged, and you asked good questions. Lisa and Tom did tend to dominate the discussion, and they took the group off-topic a few times. What can you do next time to keep the discussion on track?

J: Maybe I could ask upfront for everyone to spend just 1–2 minutes sharing their ideas.

M: That's a good idea. You could also try . . .

Maria and Jessica spend another few minutes brainstorming. They end the conversation with Maria reinforcing that the meeting was a success overall: they got the decisions they needed. She then asks Jessica to summarize what she will do differently at the next meeting.

Jessica leaves the conversation feeling good. She knows what she did well and has concrete ideas for how to improve. She is confident the next meeting will be even more successful.

FIGURE 7.1   (Continued)

hinder future performance and motivation. In contrast conversations that stem from teachable moments are empowering and can provide concrete ideas for how to improve in the future.

A useful orientation in almost any performance conversation is to use a coaching approach rather than to simply provide feedback (Gregory & Levy, 2015). Coaching goes beyond providing information to others about what they are doing well or could do to improve; it empowers the recipient to uncover root causes of challenges and provides the opportunity for the feedback provider and recipient to jointly identify improvement strategies. Coaching embodies the partnership relationship discussed in Chapter 2. Feedback can be delivered in all the right ways, but without a coaching component, feedback is less likely to lead to behavior change. Box 7.1 illustrates the distinction between traditional feedback and coaching.

BOX 7.1   TRADITIONAL FEEDBACK VERSUS COACHING

Traditional Feedback

MANAGER: "At the last staff meeting, I noticed that you spent a lot of time looking at your phone and didn't join the discussion. This sends a message to others that you are not engaged and that you don't value these meetings. I'd appreciate it if you could keep your phone off and participate more during our meetings. What are your thoughts?"

EMPLOYEE: "Sorry about that—I just have a lot going on right now. I'll do better next time."

MANAGER: "Thank you."

Coaching

MANAGER: "What did you think about our last staff meeting?"

EMPLOYEE: "I thought it was ok."

MANAGER: "Just ok, huh? I noticed that you spent a lot of time looking at your phone and didn't join the discussion. What's going on?"

EMPLOYEE: "Sorry—I just have a lot going on right now. I'll be more attentive next time."

MANAGER: "I appreciate that, but I'd like to better understand what you have going on that makes it hard for you to participate and how we can help the meetings feel more valuable to you."

EMPLOYEE: "Well, to be honest it just didn't seem like most of the discussion was relevant to me. I was stressing about all the emails that were not getting answered while we were sitting there."

MANAGER: "I hear you saying that you didn't find the meeting a good use of time because you don't see how it's relevant to you. Is that right?"

EMPLOYEE: "I'm not sure I'd go that far. I think these meetings are important. It's just that this last one didn't actually pertain to my work that much."

MANAGER: "Got it. The reason I brought this up is that when you don't participate, it sends a message to the others that you don't value our time together, and that's not what we want. Let's talk about what we can do to help you get more value from the meetings and stay engaged. What would make the meetings feel more relevant to you?"

EMPLOYEE: "Well for one thing, maybe we could focus the discussion a bit more. Also, updates from each project would be useful."

MANAGER: "Good feedback, thanks. I can do more to keep people on track. In turn, can you facilitate the discussion to get project updates? What other ideas do you have for making these meetings more valuable?"

EMPLOYEE: "That sounds like a good start. I'll let you know if I think of anything else. Thanks for listening."

Effective coaching builds on effective feedback in the following ways:

- Coaching starts with the idea that the recipient is in the best position to determine how to overcome challenges and improve performance. The coach's role is to facilitate this process, but the recipient must ultimately come to his or her own conclusions if coaching is to succeed. As such, coaching is more empowering than feedback alone, in which the recipient is a more passive recipient of information.
- Coaching focuses on thought-provoking and open-ended questions to drive deeper insights about the root causes of challenges. These "powerful questions" help the feedback recipient develop their own understanding and awareness rather than simply being told what the issue is, which leads to greater buy-in and motivation to change. Example questions might include:
  - What concerns do you have about this situation?
  - What are you most looking forward to?
  - If you could do it over again, what would you change?
- The coach uses direct observations to raise the recipient's awareness of what they are thinking or feeling and how that might be perceived by others. These observations are an authentic assessment from the coach about what they are noticing without judgment attached. They are intended to challenge the recipient's thinking in new ways to help them examine assumptions they may be making. Examples include:
  - It sounds like you don't trust her.
  - Your eyes just lit up when you mentioned that project. How are you feeling about it?
  - I noticed you used the words "train wreck" to describe the customer call. Tell me more about why you think that.
- The coach helps recipients summarize their thoughts and feelings by reflecting back what they are hearing. This helps the recipient better understand their thoughts and feelings, gives them an opportunity to clarify any misunderstandings, and can help move the discussion along if it gets

too detailed and off-track. For example, "I'm hearing that you have too much on your plate and are feeling overwhelmed; is that right?"

- The coach and the coaching recipient work together to determine how to address issues and create a solution together to improve performance. This is different than managers simply telling employees what should be done. Ultimately, the employee must believe in the solution and commit to implementing it.

Coaching will usually take more time than delivering feedback alone. There may be times when delivering simple feedback is preferable because of the nature of the situation or time constraints. However, a coaching approach can improve both performance and the relationship between the employee and manager.

There is no question that managers will have an easier time providing feedback and coaching in the context of a solid relationship (Vancouver & Morrison, 1995; Williams, Miller, Steelman, & Levy, 1999). However, the idea that all managers and employees will be able to develop the type of solid relationships that will enable effective feedback and coaching is unrealistic. Relationships between employees and managers are like any others. Some click easily when the two individuals can find common ground and have similarities in their thinking, values, and views. With others, it is hard to find common ground and develop easy, trusting relationships. Old-school managers have been taught to maintain distance with employees and not get too close. At the extreme, this gets in the way of developing the type of solid, trusting relationships that support feedback.

Regardless of the strength of the relationship, conversation quality can be improved if employees perceive that feedback is accurate and fair. Perceptions of accuracy and fairness are improved when the source is credible (i.e., someone who is very familiar with the recipient's work and able to make well-informed judgments about its quality) and trustworthy (Ilgen, Fisher, & Taylor, 1979; Taylor, Fisher, & Ilgen, 1984), and the feedback is supported with specific examples. Perceived fairness can be increased if others appear to be held to similar standards, the feedback seems objective (e.g., based on observable and measurable behaviors and not just on subjective evaluations), and it does not just focus on what went wrong but also what worked well. When recipients believe feedback is accurate and fair, their performance is more likely to improve (CIPD, 2016).

Enabling Effective Conversations

Creating a climate that fosters effective performance conversations takes time and requires effortful learning and behavior change. Organizations often underestimate the amount of work it takes to drive and embed significant culture change. Aspirations for change must be aligned with what is realistic and practical in each situation. Luckily, wholesale culture change is not required for improving conversations to have a positive impact. Suggested in the following list are more straightforward strategies that have been shown to add value:

1. Don't overcomplicate what managers and employees are asked to do.
2. Keep any desired behavior simple, straightforward, and easy to monitor.
3. Focus on what matters most.

We chose these criteria based on extensive experience attempting to drive complex learning and behavior change in many organizations of varying sizes and learning that keeping things simple offers the most potential for success.

Ensure Formal Processes Help Rather Than Hinder Conversations

Organizations sometimes inadvertently set up processes that undermine effective conversations. Many legacy performance management processes have arbitrary requirements, such as "identify each employee's three top strengths and three top areas for development." These systems have low credibility because employees never know the extent to which their strengths and development areas are real and something to be taken seriously or force-fit to meet arbitrary process requirements. While everyone is stronger in some areas than others, feedback should not be force-fit into some required number of strengths and weaknesses to discuss. What's important is understanding and showing appreciation for everyone's true strengths and identifying areas for development that will most impact performance.

Encourage Regular Check-Ins

Many organizations have moved away from once- or twice-a-year formal reviews in favor of more frequent check-ins. Check-ins work best when they are regularly scheduled as one-on-one frequent meetings to ensure regular communication about work progress and issues (Gregory & Levy, 2011). The distinction between a formal review and a check-in is that check-ins have no documentation or rating requirements, and they are done to enable performance in real time and not evaluate it after the fact. They allow performance information to be exchanged informally and provide a mechanism that makes problem-solving and feedback a regular aspect of work. These are especially useful when managers do not have extensive access to employees' day-to-day performance.

One pitfall to avoid is turning check-ins into "mini performance reviews." This happens when too many "rules" are attached to them, such as requirements to cover particular content and documentation. Managers and employees ultimately resist requirements that add work without adding value. Organizations can support effective check-ins by:

- Allowing for flexibility in the frequency and format; provide helpful tools but not rules, such as sample discussion questions/topics (see Figure 7.2 for an example).
- Encouraging managers to approach these with the goal of coaching, not just providing feedback. This means that the purpose of the check-in is to discuss how things are going and to problem-solve together to address challenges. These discussions should be in the spirit of helping employees improve rather than judging them.
- Holding managers and employees accountable for having regular check-ins by asking them about their effectiveness instead of requiring specific

Topics	For Managers	For Employees
Opening	• Discuss topics to cover during the check-in.	• Discuss topics to cover during the check-in.
Looking Back	• What has been happening since we last spoke? • What has gone well and why? • What could have gone better and why? • What will you do differently in the future? • Offer own observations about performance.	• Review key events since your last meeting. • Highlight accomplishments and things that didn't go as well as planned and your observations about why. • Discuss what you might do differently the next time and what help you need to be successful.
Looking Forward	• What key meetings, due dates, other events do you have coming up? • What are you looking forward to? • What concerns do you have? • What can you do to mitigate these concerns? • Offer your own observations about strategies for success.	• Note any upcoming events and discuss how you think they might go. • Discuss any concerns you have for the future, plans to address these concerns, and any support you might need. • Ask for and listen to ideas about how to succeed in the future.
Closing	• What do you think you will have accomplished by our next meeting? • How can I support you?	• Here's what I plan to do before our next meeting ... • Here's the support I need from you or others ...

FIGURE 7.2   Sample Check-in Discussion Topics and Questions

processes, documentation, or ratings (we discuss this idea more fully in the following sections).

Provide Targeted Training

Training managers in feedback and coaching skills is a common strategy to drive more effective performance because it is concrete, easy to implement, and many off-the-shelf products exist already to support this. Training, especially for new managers, can provide a baseline of knowledge and skill; however, training by itself does not help embed lasting behavior change. It is easy to believe that training adds more value than it actually does because training effectiveness is often evaluated solely by how much participants like it. However, satisfaction with or perceived usefulness of training is largely uncorrelated with learning and behavior change on the job (Alliger, Tannenbaum, Bennett, Traver, & Shotland, 1997). Even though strategies beyond training are needed to drive effective feedback, the baseline knowledge is still helpful. High-impact topics for *all* employees should include:

- Principles for effective conversations (described earlier in this chapter) and an explicit expectation that giving feedback is everyone's responsibility, not just the manager's.
- Tips for how to ask for and receive feedback (Stone & Heen, 2014). Feedback recipients can't control how feedback is delivered, but they can control how they interpret and react to it. A better understanding can lead to greater acceptance and action.
- "Feedforward," which is the powerful technique of asking for forward-looking advice rather than backward-looking feedback (Goldsmith). Feedforward is easier to give than feedback and can lead to useful insight about how to improve. For example, if Jorge asks a colleague for feedback after giving a big presentation, he is likely to hear "you did great," regardless of his actual performance. If instead Jorge asks a colleague to give him some specific advice for how to give a successful presentation in advance, he is likely to get more candid comments (e.g., "get out from behind the podium and engage the audience, make eye contact, don't read your notes"). Jorge can then choose to use these ideas or not, but both he and his colleague will find the conversation easier. The colleague will likely be flattered at being asked for advice, and Jorge will have some ideas he can use to perform effectively.

High-impact topics for managers should include:

- How to diagnose performance issues, understand their root causes, and handle these appropriately (see Chapter 9 for details).

- Coaching techniques, especially how to use teachable moments to improve performance.
- Barriers to feedback (see Box 7.2) and useful strategies to overcome them. This needs to go beyond simple advice to "get over your fear of feedback" and help managers understand other ways to mitigate factors that interfere with effective feedback (e.g., how to use other sources of feedback to supplement feedback from the manager).

BOX 7.2   BARRIERS TO EFFECTIVE FEEDBACK

If the principles for effective feedback are so well known, why don't they happen more often?

Barriers to effective feedback include:

- **Cultural taboos.** Many clients have told us that they have "too nice" cultures, meaning that employees and managers believe that delivering constructive feedback is akin to being "not nice." Therefore, feedback is avoided because it is perceived as clashing with cultural norms.
- **Fear of harming the relationship**. Managers and employees alike avoid giving constructive feedback because they believe it will hurt the relationship with the recipient and result in decreased motivation and performance. What will happen if the employee's performance does not improve or a generally productive employee decides to leave for another job? Managers rely on employees to get work done and for their success, and they are hesitant to risk alienating them, especially when providing feedback is unlikely to improve the recipient's performance.
- **Fear of negative reactions**. In general, people avoid giving feedback due to justifiable concerns that recipients will react badly to it—denying it, making excuses, turning the tables about what the feedback provider is doing wrong, or getting angry and defensive. In the end, it is often easier to simply not give feedback and put up with some amount of ineffective behavior or less-than-optimal performance. However, avoidance creates situations in which issues are ignored and allowed to go on until they sometimes reach a boiling point, when feedback can be communicated poorly or in anger and blindside the recipient. The longer a person goes without getting feedback, the harder it is to bring up a long-standing problem. Managers fear the inevitable reaction of "why didn't you tell me this before!" and so enter a vicious cycle—feedback is delayed for fear of the negative reaction, causing more delays and increasing the likelihood of negative reactions.

- **Lack of time, information, and a foundational relationship to support effective feedback.** Many managers, especially in today's work environment, may have little day-to-day contact with their direct reports and may lack the information needed to provide effective feedback. Related to this and one of the biggest issues facing managers today is simply lack of time to work closely with their employees so they can develop effective relationships that enable providing real-time individualized feedback. As organizations become flatter, more team-oriented, and cost effective, many managers have full-time responsibilities beyond "people management," along with more direct reports, yielding significant challenges for managers in providing effective feedback.

Successful training uses simple concepts that are easy to learn and remember rather than complex models and processes. In-person sessions are always preferred, though web-based sessions can work if group sizes are small and interactivity is built into the session. The opportunity to practice skills with a partner is important. Job aids and other tools can reinforce training concepts and support their use in day-to-day work. Follow-up sessions in which participants try new approaches on the job (sometimes with the support of a learning partner) and then discuss with others what they tried and how it worked can solidify learning. Several HR leaders told us that they used this strategy successfully, and research supports this approach to learning (Latham & Saari, 1979).

Take the Pressure Off Managers

One of the main reasons that effective feedback is rare is that the manager is often the sole source of it, which creates a single point of failure—if the manager is unable or unwilling to give feedback, it won't happen. Managers may not be in the best position to give feedback if they are not observing the employee every day. Additionally, feedback is more likely to be accurate and credible when it comes from multiple sources, which can include others in the organization, customers, external partners, objective metrics, etc. in addition to the manager's observations. When employees get feedback from many sources, the manager's role shifts from sole feedback provider to coach: the manager is there to help the employee collect and interpret feedback and then work in partnership to improve performance in priority areas.

While many organizations use 360-degree feedback as part of the performance review process, this strategy for collecting feedback from other sources can be time-consuming and cumbersome to administer. Moreover, 360-degree ratings collected for performance evaluation are usually not as accurate as those collected for development purposes only (Dalessio, 1998; Toegel & Conger, 2003). Open-ended comments are often more useful than ratings so one option to simplify this process may be to request open-ended comments only and forgo ratings, assuming the goal is development only. If comments can be provided more flexibly and informally throughout the year, employees will have a chance to address any issues prior to the formal review.

Keep 360-degree feedback questions simple and focused on what matters most for improving performance: strengths and priority areas for improvement. It can also be valuable to ask how the employee supports and contributes to the feedback provider's work. Feedback should be requested only from those who work closely with the employee so that the feedback is most relevant to the individual's work. Multi-source feedback can be collected through standard performance management software systems, informally via email, or through the many new cloud-based applications designed for this purpose. A recent study shows that using crowdsourced feedback (i.e., using social media type technology to quickly gather feedback from multiple sources) combined with ongoing feedback from managers has more impact on desired outcomes than traditional formal feedback sessions (Ledford, Benson, & Lawler, 2016).

There are many other sources of naturally occurring feedback information that may be available in different situations, such as:

- Customer survey data or feedback.
- Objective metrics where available (sales, production, error rate, attendance, timeliness of task or project completion, website analytics, etc.).
- Reactions from others in the organization via email, verbally, nonverbally, etc.

We discussed many of these sources of performance information in Chapter 6, as they are also important inputs for measuring performance.

While it takes time to collect feedback from other sources, the payoff can be significant. Employees receiving relevant feedback from different sources takes pressure off managers to gather comprehensive feedback on their own and be the sole provider of feedback to employees. They can shift to helping employees integrate, interpret, and effectively act on the feedback from different sources. Managers can better use their time with employees to identify areas that should be prioritized for performance improvement and career advancement by first helping employees understand the distinction between these and then ensuring they target the most important areas to develop across different time frames.

Measure Conversation Quality and Hold Managers Accountable

Expectations need to be set for managers and employees to engage in meaningful performance conversations (London & Smither, 2002) and hold them accountable by measuring their quality and frequency. The best way to assess quality is to ask employees if the conversations are helpful. Employees may be naturally reluctant to answer these questions honestly for fear of retaliation or harming the relationship. Anonymous pulse surveys can be very valuable for getting honest and frequent assessments of conversation quality. A pulse survey is a very short (typically less than 10 questions) questionnaire that is focused on a single topic. It not only provides useful information about how employees feel, but it is short and easy enough that it can be administered as needed to evaluate multiple topics or reactions to change. It can also be used to hold managers accountable for improvements over time.

To promote accountability and prevent defensiveness, we suggest a progressive approach to sharing pulse survey results with managers. The first time results are shared, it can be done at the organizational or business unit level so that managers become familiar with how results will be reported and can get a sense of the overall feedback climate. On the next administration, managers can be provided with aggregate results from their direct reports so they can see how they are perceived when compared to the organization as a whole. Managers could hopefully obtain support from a coach if needed to make improvements, but at this stage it is best if the manager has the option to keep his or her individual results private. In the next administration, these results would not be private—they would also be shared with the manager's manager (second-level manager). The second-level manager can use the results to hold the manager accountable for improving if needed.

One method to make this process less intimidating for managers is to frame the questions in terms of frequency rather than effectiveness. For example, instead of asking employees to rate manager effectiveness at giving feedback on a 1–5 scale (very ineffective to very effective), ask employees to rate the frequency of effective feedback behaviors (e.g., never, rarely, sometimes, often, very often) or to rate how often behaviors occur to suit them (too often, just right, or too little). Frequency ratings are easier for managers to cope with because they give specific information about what to do more of or less of to get a better result in concrete, behavioral terms. Figure 7.3 shows an example of two pulse surveys on conversation quality.

★★★

Enabling better performance conversations is the single most impactful thing that organizations can do to drive high performance. Good conversations work in tandem with related practices such as good selection, good organizational systems, and clear definitions of success. While improving conversation quality should be only one of many interventions designed to improve performance, it is a high priority for most organizations because good conversations are almost universally lacking.

My manager needs to . . .	A lot less often	A little less often	The same amount as now	A little more often	A lot more often
1. Compliment me when I do something well	☐	☐	☐	☐	☐
2. Tell me when and how I need to improve	☐	☐	☐	☐	☐
3. Give me specific, helpful suggestions to improve my performance	☐	☐	☐	☐	☐
4. Be open and honest when giving feedback	☐	☐	☐	☐	☐
5. Give me useful career advice	☐	☐	☐	☐	☐

My manager . . .	Never	Rarely	Sometimes	Often	Almost Always
1. Provides positive feedback that makes me feel good	☐	☐	☐	☐	☐
2. Provides constructive feedback that is accurate and fair	☐	☐	☐	☐	☐
3. Provides feedback that is helpful for improving my performance	☐	☐	☐	☐	☐
4. Is open and honest when giving feedback	☐	☐	☐	☐	☐
5. Gives me useful career advice	☐	☐	☐	☐	☐

FIGURE 7.3 Sample Pulse Surveys on Conversation Quality

Effective conversations happen when the focus, content, and delivery are thought through and align with evidence-based practices. Training is often the most prominent and in many cases the only means organizations use to improve conversations. However, other approaches are far more effective, such as ensuring systems are in place that support rather than hinder good conversations, leveraging feedback information from multiple sources, measuring perceived usefulness of performance conversations, and holding managers accountable.

References

Alliger, G. M., Tannenbaum, S. I., Bennett, W. Jr., Traver, H., & Shotland, A. (1997). A meta-analysis of the relations among training criteria. *Personnel Psychology, 50*, 341–358.

CEB. (2002). *Building the high-performance workforce: A quantitative analysis of the effectiveness of performance management strategies.* Arlington, VA: Author.

CIPD. (2016, December). *Could do better? Assessing what works in performance management.* Research Report.

Colquitt, A. L. (2017). *Next generation performance management: The triumph of science over myth and superstition.* Charlotte, NC: Information Age Publishing, Inc.

Dalessio, A. T. (1998). Using multi-source feedback for employee development and personnel decisions. In J. W. Smither (Ed.), *Performance appraisal* (pp. 278–330). San Francisco, CA: Jossey-Bass.

Deci, E. L. (1975). *Intrinsic motivation.* New York: Plenum Press.

Early, P. C., Northcraft, G. B., Lee, C., & Lituchy, T. R. (1990). The impact of process and outcome feedback on the relation of goal setting to task performance. *Academy of Management Journal, 33*, 87–105.

Goldsmith, M. (undated). *Try feedforward instead of feedback.* Retrieved from www.marshall-goldsmithfeedforward.com/html/Articles.htm

Gregory, J. B., & Levy, P. E. (2011). It's not me, it's you: A multilevel examination of variables that impact employee coaching relationships. *Consulting Psychology Journal: Practice and Research, 63*, 67–88.

Gregory, J. B., & Levy, P. E. (2015). *Using feedback in organizational consulting.* Washington, DC: American Psychological Association.

Ilgen, D. R., Fisher, C. D., & Taylor, M. S. (1979). Consequences of individual feedback on behavior in organizations. *Journal of Applied Psychology, 64*, 349–371.

Kluger, A. N., & DeNisi, A. (1996). The effects of feedback interventions on performance: A historical review, meta-analysis and a preliminary feedback intervention theory. *Psychological Bulletin, 119*(2), 254–284.

Latham, G. P., & Saari, L. M. (1979). Application of social-learning theory to training supervisors through behavioral modeling. *Journal of Applied Psychology, 64*, 239–246.

Ledford, G. E., Benson, G. S., & Lawler, E. E. III (2016). A study of cutting-edge performance management practices: Ongoing feedback, ratingless reviews and crowdsourced feedback. *World at Work Journal, Second Quarter*, 8–24.

London, M. (2003). *Job feedback: Giving, seeking, and using feedback for performance improvement.* Mahwah, NJ: Erlbaum.

London, M., & Smither, J. W. (2002). Feedback orientation, feedback culture, and the longitudinal performance management process. *Human Resource Management Review, 12*, 81–100.

Stone, D., & Heen, S. (2014). *Thanks for the feedback: The science and art of receiving feedback well (even when it is off base, unfair, poorly delivered, and, frankly, you're not in the mood).* New York: Viking.

Taylor, M. S., Fisher, C. D., & Ilgen, D. R. (1984). Individual's reactions to performance feedback in organizations: Control theory perspective. In K. M. Rowland & G. R.

Ferris (Eds.), *Research in personnel and human resource management* (pp. 81–124). Greenwich, CT: JAI Press.

Toegel, G., & Conger, J. A. (2003). 360-degree assessment: Time for reinvention. *Academy of Management Learning & Education, 2,* 297–311.

Vancouver, J. B., & Morrison, E. W. (1995). Feedback inquiry: The effective of source attributes and individual differences. *Organizational Behavior and Human Decision Processes, 62,* 276–285.

van der Kleij, F. M., Eggen, T. J., Timmers, C. F., & Veldkamp, B. P. (2012). Effects of feedback in a computer-based assessment for learning. *Computers & Education, 58,* 263–272.

Williams, J. R., Miller, C., Steelman, L. A., & Levy, P. E. (1999). Increasing feedback seeking in public contexts: It takes two (or more) to tango. *Journal of Applied Psychology, 84,* 969–976.

8

MAKE SMART TALENT DECISIONS

Despite a sincere desire to eliminate performance ratings, the sticking point for many organizations is how to make talent decisions without them. Performance ratings are the foundation for compensation (including pay increases, bonuses, incentives, etc.), reassignment, promotion, succession management, and even downsizing decisions in most organizations. These decisions have significant consequences for employees, and organizations understandably want to ensure they are consistent and fair. Many organizations find it difficult to imagine how this would be possible without some means of rating performance.

Rewarding employees based on performance is an inherent part of many organizational cultures. The underlying principle is meritocracy: employees who perform better "deserve" more rewards, and poorly performing employees need to either improve immediately or face negative consequences. Meritocracy is ostensibly reasonable: performance is a defensible and job-relevant basis for talent decisions, and rewarding high performance makes good business sense because it encourages those who contribute the most to stay and those who contribute the least to leave.

Despite good intentions, using performance ratings to inform talent decisions is extremely challenging to do well. Ratings often show too little variation to allow for meaningful distinctions, and employees complain that they don't see a strong link between their performance and rewards. According to one CEB study, 65% of employees were dissatisfied with the link between pay and performance in their organizations (CEB, 2010). In the U.S. government's annual *Federal Employee Viewpoint Survey*, conducted by the Office of Personnel Management, the lowest rated item year over year is "Pay raises depend on how well employees perform their jobs," which received only 22% positive ratings in the 2016 survey (OPM, 2016).

Linking performance and rewards is not only difficult, it is risky, leaving organizations vulnerable to litigation. For example, in 2012 Yahoo instituted a forced-ranking system that resulted in hundreds of employees getting laid off after they received poor performance reviews. Several employees have since filed lawsuits, alleging ratings manipulation and gender discrimination. One former employee took aim at the ranking process itself, complaining that in the calibration process ratings were often changed by managers who did not have direct knowledge of employees' work, which made the system unfair (Masunaga & Lien, 2016).

To combat these challenges, many organizations try to strengthen the link between performance and rewards. However, this strategy is usually doomed to failure because a) performance ratings are notoriously inaccurate and may not be a sound basis for rewards, b) the promise of rewards does not necessarily lead to improved performance, and c) performance is only one of many factors that impact reward decisions. A better strategy is to clearly distinguish performance measurement from reward decision processes and ensure employees understand these distinctions. This chapter explores typical approaches to making reward decisions and their pitfalls and presents alternative strategies for making effective performance-related talent decisions.

The Typical Approach

The usual process for linking performance to rewards goes something like this:

- Managers make preliminary performance ratings for each employee. As described in Chapter 6, ratings are usually accompanied by written narratives as justification.
- Managers participate in calibration sessions to discuss their ratings. Calibration is a process whereby managers within a given business unit meet to compare employee ratings, justify them based on available data, and adjust ratings as needed. The goal is for managers to agree to a common standard of performance for each rating level and then objectively weigh each employee's performance against that standard to ensure the rating is fair and applied consistently across employees who may be doing different work.
- Ratings are finalized based on calibration discussions. Often ratings will be changed based on the calibration session, and narratives may also need to be changed to be consistent with the rating.
- HR provides guidelines for translating ratings into outcomes (e.g., an "outstanding" rating results in a pay increase of 5–6%, and a "meets expectations" rating results in a pay increase of 2–3%).
- Managers communicate ratings and rewards back to employees.

Employees and managers alike usually find this process stressful and time-consuming. The most common complaints are:

- Managers who participate in calibration sessions are not equally familiar with the work of all employees under consideration. Consequently, they must rely on written summaries to inform their decisions, and the quality of the narrative and persuasiveness of the individual's manager serve as imperfect proxies for the employee's accomplishments.
- Up to 100 employees or more to be considered within a given calibration session, making the process very time-consuming and tedious. This problem is compounded when distinctions must be made among the entire group of employees, resulting in long debates over relatively minor differences in ratings (e.g., 3.2 versus a 3.3) and subsequent rewards.
- Rating guidelines are not always in sync with budget realities. For example, one executive confided to us that ratings were often lowered not because of employees' performance but because budget limitations constrained the money available for raises. Many high-performing employees could not receive the highest ratings because the budget simply would not allow for it. Attempting to make ratings and rewards consistent results in mixed messages to employees—either managers need to lower performance ratings to match budgets or they need to decouple ratings and rewards, which goes against organizational guidelines for "pay-for-performance."
- When ratings are changed during calibration, managers are left with the task of explaining to employees why they were rated and rewarded at a lower level than expected. We have heard more than one employee complain that his or her manager "passed the buck" for the lowered rating by saying something to the effect of, "I wanted to give you a higher rating but it was changed during the calibration process." It is not surprising that many employees complain that calibration is a "black box" and that they don't see a clear link between their performance and rewards.
- Managers frequently lack the knowledge and skills to communicate reward decisions effectively to employees, resulting in confusion and perceptions of unfairness when employees don't understand how decisions were made.

Why Linking Performance and Rewards Is So Challenging

Linking performance to rewards is so difficult because:

1. It is challenging to make meaningful distinctions in performance.
2. Pay-for-performance does not always lead to better performance.
3. Business goals and realities often outweigh performance evaluation when making talent decisions.

The Difficulty of Making Performance Distinctions

Like the forced-ranking approach discussed in Chapter 6, most reward structures have been based on the now-questionable assumption that performance is normally distributed; and hence, both performance levels and rewards can be readily distinguished among employees. However, rather than following a normal distribution, with a small proportion of very high- and low-performing employees, recent research shows that performance frequently follows a Pareto or power law distribution. Ratings distributed in this manner show most employees performing below the arithmetic mean, and about 20% of the population significantly outperforming their peers (O'Boyle & Aguinis, 2012). This means that it is relatively easy to distinguish the top performers from the majority of employees, but distinguishing among the majority of employees not in the top ~20% will be very difficult. Ironically, most employees believe they are above-average performers and may resist performance ratings that imply they are less than average. Figure 8.1 shows these contrasts.

Organizational leaders want to reward based on curve "B" because they assume this curve represents actual performance. Many organizations put out guidance for pay increases that mirror this distribution. In contrast, most employees believe they perform and should be rewarded in accordance with curve "C." A more accurate means of distributing rewards might follow curve "A" because it is difficult to distinguish among the vast majority of employees, while "star" performers are adding significantly more value than their peers;

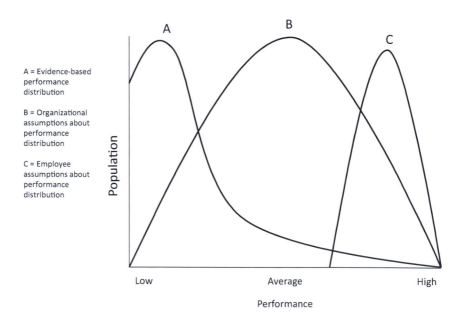

FIGURE 8.1   Three Perspectives on Performance Distributions

however, employees are likely to resist this structure if they are accustomed to a more traditional reward structure.

Beyond disconnects in assumptions about rating distributions, it is difficult for managers to make accurate distinctions in performance that lead to differentiated rewards. Part of the problem stems from not being able to consolidate hundreds of examples of performance over time into an accurate rating, as discussed in Chapter 6. Employees perform differently in different areas, such as planning versus communication, and their performance even within an area is not always consistent day-to-day. This situation is made more difficult because managers see only a small fraction of each person's actual performance. Part of the problem stems from motivation. Managers inflate ratings in response to powerful social and political factors—they want to look good, do not want to jeopardize relationships with their direct reports, etc.

Because of human information processing limitations, managers will have more difficulties accurately distinguishing performance levels between employees as the judgments become more specific and nuanced. For example, it is nearly impossible to accurately rank order 100 employees based on their performance. Making accurate distinctions using a 7- or 9-point scale is challenging because this number of rating levels starts splitting hairs and forcing raters to make distinctions at too fine a level if they are considering many performance instances and many employees. Realistically, managers will typically have their top "go-to" trusted agents, and these individuals will be advanced and most generously rewarded. Then, there will be a set of "doing-fine employees" who are meeting expectations and can expect average rewards but will not be propelled ahead, and finally, there may be employees who should be counseled out. Good managers will counsel them out; less effective managers may simply let them go along. Managers should be able to accurately distinguish employees using 3- to 5-rating levels; however, the extent to which these distinctions are fully merit-based will depend on how much the manager focuses on relevant performance versus their own biases and preferences.

Pay-for-Performance Does Not Always Lead to Better Performance

Pay-for-performance is based on the assumption that external rewards will motivate higher performance. Does this assumption hold up? The research on this question is mixed. About half the studies indicate a positive relationship and the other half show no relationship (Rynes, Gerhart, & Parks, 2005). Pay can be a motivator under certain circumstances:

- There is enough pay at risk to be meaningful to employees. For example, Google has a strong history of pay-for-performance and substantial funding to make distinctions among employees (Bock, 2015). In contrast, many organizations have small budgets for merit increases—averaging 2–3% a year, which makes it difficult to reward people differently. A common rule of thumb is that there needs to be at least 10% salary available in variable pay to make pay-for-performance stakes attractive enough to be motivating.

- Employees perceive a clear link between their efforts and the reward. This link is easier to see in production or sales jobs (e.g., where output can be clearly measured and results have a clear link to defined rewards—producing X items will lead to Y pay). However, sometimes inadvertent biases or preferences of managers lead them to elevate some employees over others for reasons that are not always performance- or merit-based, which can weaken the perceived link between effort and rewards.
- Tasks are fairly routine and straightforward, requiring little creativity and intrinsic motivation to do well (Deci, Koestner, & Ryan, 2001).
- Employees believe they have substantial control over the results they produce. For example, highly interdependent jobs or jobs that are greatly impacted by external factors are poor candidates for pay-for-performance because employees may expend a great deal of effort and not achieve positive results.

There are also several risks to pay-for-performance. First, the motivational effects of rewards are short lived. While feeling underpaid can be demotivating, cognitive dissonance from feeling overpaid is temporary. Organizations need to pay employees enough so that they feel fairly compensated in line with what their skills are worth in the labor market, but additional rewards may provide diminishing returns. Employees quickly habituate to pay increases—they adjust to the higher pay and the motivational effects of the increase can't be sustained without future rewards.

Second, external rewards can interfere with intrinsic motivation, which can negatively affect performance (Pink, 2009). For example, Lepper, Greene, and Nisbett (1973) showed that preschoolers who were rewarded for drawing showed less interest in drawing two weeks later. Ariely, Gneezy, Lowenstein, and Mazar (2005) found that adults in India who were paid a significant sum performed worse on a series of game-like tasks than those paid a smaller sum. Creativity can also be dampened when attempting to provide rewards for innovative solutions. For example, when given a problem-solving task that required a creative solution, individuals who were promised a reward performed worse than those who were not promised any payment (Glucksberg, 1962). When extrinsic rewards replace intrinsic rewards, it can interfere with an individual's natural drive to excel and dampens innovation (Deci, Ryan, & Koestner, 1999).

Third, there is a risk of unintended consequences. With a lot of pay at stake, employees and managers may try to game the system. For example, as described in Chapter 4, Wells Fargo employees were creating fraudulent customer accounts to earn bonuses. Aguinis (2013) provides another, more humorous, example. Executives at the food maker Green Giant instituted a new bonus plan that rewarded employees for removing insects from vegetables during processing. Initially, they were pleased that performance apparently increased: employees were finding more insects after the plan was introduced. However, they were later chagrinned to learn that employees were actually bringing insects from home and planting them on the vegetables! Needless to say, the bonus plan was discontinued. When too much is at stake, employees may hyper-focus on achieving specific goals and ignore other important aspects of their work or even act unethically to attain desired rewards.

A final risk is a practical one: pay-for-performance is hard to do well. It takes significant amounts of time and energy to ensure performance ratings are fair and rewards are distributed accordingly. However, ratings are never likely to be 100% accurate or fair by purely objective standards because fallible human judgments that come with imprecision and biases will always impact these decisions. The time and effort to administer pay-for-performance systems may not be worth it, especially in the absence of clear evidence that pay-for-performance leads to improved performance. For example, the U.S. federal government has tried for years to implement pay-for-performance, and it has been largely a colossal failure. See Box 8.1 for one of the most noteworthy examples. These systems are also risky and have been the target of numerous legal challenges, especially when they result in systematic differences among various groups. For example, Google has been accused by the U.S. Department of Labor for gender discrimination in pay and has faced numerous legal challenges related to this issue (Lam, 2017).

BOX 8.1 PITFALLS OF PAY-FOR-PERFORMANCE IN GOVERNMENT

The National Security Personnel System (NSPS) was an ill-fated pay-for-performance system for U.S. Department of Defense (DoD) civilians. NSPS was implemented in 2006, and as of May 2008 covered 182,000 employees (GAO, 2008). This ambitious plan was intended to replace the practice under the current General Schedule system of giving automatic pay increases to all employees and instead base raises on a rigorous performance evaluation process. DoD executives hailed NSPS as a means for driving increased accountability and performance in government. They sincerely believed employees would benefit under the plan because high performers would receive greater rewards than they did previously and lower performers would be motivated to improve their performance or seek employment elsewhere. Despite its promise, NSPS was a colossal failure, and Congress eventually repealed it in 2009.

DoD invested millions of dollars in designing and implementing NSPS and millions more were spent on pay increases and bonuses. Some of the most talented government executives and consulting experts worked together throughout the project to help ensure its success. They created an entirely new performance management approach and software to evaluate employees and collect data needed to link performance to pay. All employees and managers had to undergo extensive training to learn how to use the new software. They conducted several studies to evaluate the effectiveness of the approach and make refinements in response to feedback.

How did so much investment lead to such a poor outcome? Media reports have focused on two major issues: resistance from labor unions and inequities in pay. Several analyses revealed that white employees and employees from certain agencies received higher pay increases and bonuses than others (Losey, 2008). Employees had generally negative perceptions of the system that only worsened as they gained experience using it (GAO, 2008). Some of the most common concerns cited were:

- Documentation required for the system was heavier than what was required previously. Managers and employees had to write lengthy justifications for their ratings. Software programs were filled with glitches and resulted in lost work. The process left everyone feeling frustrated.
- The calibration process by which supervisors would meet to discuss ratings and recalibrate them to a common standard was cumbersome and viewed as unfair. Calibration groups could cover as many as 100 employees or more. Participating managers were often unfamiliar with employees in these groups and relied heavily on written narratives to make decisions. Often this process would result in ratings being changed, and managers then had to explain to employees why their rating was lower than expected. In turn, employees felt that the calibration process was a "black box" in which decisions were made with little knowledge of what employees actually contributed.
- Guidance from DoD leaders that most employees should be rated a "3" on a 5-point scale was at odds with prior practices. Given that most employees were used to receiving higher ratings, they deeply resented being rated as "only average" even though the rating label for a 3 was "Valued Performer." As one employee confided to us, "It's an insult to be labeled as only 'valued' when before I always got 4's and 5's." It is interesting to note that studies later demonstrated that employees generally fared better financially with NSPS than they did under the GS system, but the reactions to NSPS were far more negative.

Since the repeal of NSPS, DoD has gone back to the GS system. Raises are largely based on tenure, and overall performance and results have been largely consistent, regardless of the performance management approach. Other efforts have been made to implement large-scale pay-for-performance in the U.S. federal government, but none has resulted in demonstrably better performance.

Business Realities Have a Greater Impact On Rewards Than Performance

Figure 8.2 shows example relationships among different talent decisions, including pay increases, bonuses, promotions, and downsizing. One could imagine adding several other decisions to this graphic: identifying development needs, succession planning, selections for special assignments, etc. While performance is a component of all these decisions, it is only one consideration among many. For example, pay increases and bonuses are constrained by annual budgets. The pay increase available to any employee will be based on how that individual is paid relative to the market (e.g., the best performing janitor may receive a paltry raise compared with a mediocre computer programmer, if the programmer's skills are in high demand and he or she is paid low relative to the job market) as well as internal equity considerations (e.g., where the individual falls on a salary curve relative to his or her job—even if performance is equal, those

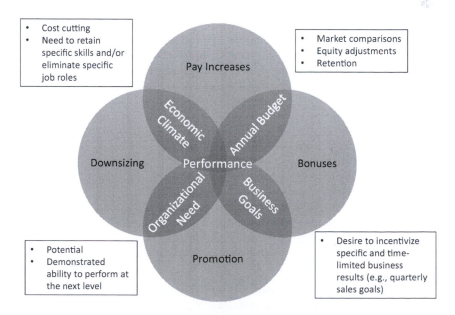

FIGURE 8.2   Relationships Between Performance and Talent Decisions

lower on the curve may get a bigger increase than those higher on the curve simply because people at the high end have "maxed out" their salary potential).

Similarly, performance may be a key consideration in determining who to promote, but larger considerations are organizational need for individuals in higher-level positions and the employee's potential to perform effectively in a new job level. In fact, a common complaint is an over-reliance on past performance in promotion decisions—high-performing individual contributors may not make effective leaders. Promoting someone as a "reward" for high performance often leads to disaster, and complaints about bosses who were promoted based on technical rather than leadership skills are ubiquitous.

These examples illustrate that performance is often the least important component of talent decisions but is often assumed to be the most important. This is the reason that so often employees say they don't see a link between performance and rewards—in fact this link is tenuous at best.

Implications for Making Reward Decisions

Taken together, these findings suggest several implications for making reward decisions:

1. Make fewer rather than more distinctions in rewards; for example, three categories of rewards. Instead of trying to distinguish among all employees, identify the top performers who are providing substantially more value and reward them accordingly. Provide moderate rewards to the vast majority of employees whose performance cannot be distinguished. Offer no rewards to the small number of employees who fail to meet standards and instead ensure they are on a Performance Improvement Plan (see Chapter 9 for details).
2. Proceed with caution when it comes to implementing pay-for-performance. Consider whether it even makes sense given organizational culture, potential resistance from employees and labor unions, and organizational budgets. If the budget does not allow for meaningful distinctions, an alternative is to provide the same raise to everyone who is at least performing successfully and then use other means (including non-monetary incentives) to reward those who have made more significant contributions: spot bonuses, stock options, extra paid time off, awards, praise and recognition, additional responsibilities, special assignments, etc. If pay-for-performance is viable from a budget standpoint, ensure performance measurement is structured in a way that allows employees to control their results and see a clear link between what they produce and how it is rewarded. Evaluate pay decisions regularly to ensure no adverse impact exists.
3. Give employees clear messages about how talent decisions are made and the various factors that inform each decision. Use appropriate and business-relevant criteria for making each decision and make those criteria

transparent to employees. Instead of asking employees if they see a link between performance and rewards, ask if employees believe decisions are fair and consistent with business needs.

Making Smart Talent Decisions With or Without Performance Ratings

The primary reason many organizations are reluctant to go "rating-less" is because they have difficulty envisioning how they will make talent, and especially pay, decisions without performance ratings. However, managers often admit that they do not use performance ratings to make decisions. Instead, they try to fit their ratings to the decisions they have already made (Pulakos, Mueller-Hanson, Arad, & Moye, 2015). Most managers have strong views about how their employees are performing and who their "go-to" people are, who has expectations for a raise, or who is at risk for leaving if they do not receive a big enough raise. They then identify the rating that is needed to get the desired outcome. This approach helps them manage issues that are peripheral to the performance management process itself, such as (a) attrition risk, (b) internal or external equity, and even (c) whose turn it is for a larger increase this year, given relatively small raise pools of 2–3% that are common today. Because managers need to motivate high performance from their teams, it is not surprising to find them pushing all the levers they have available to keep team members collectively engaged and productive.

While ratings may not be necessary for decision-making, they may be so entrenched in the organizational culture that change will be difficult. Moreover, if managers are not skilled at providing effective feedback, the rating at least can provide employees a sense of how they are doing.

Some organizations have successfully figured out how to make talent decisions without ratings. There are two primary approaches for doing so: 1) allow managers to make their own judgments about raises, and 2) use decision criteria that are distinct from performance ratings. With the first approach, managers are given reward guidelines and a budget to work with and then given discretion over how to use this budget to make pay decisions. Guidelines may include performance-based as well as equity considerations. Box 8.2 shows an example of how one organization used this approach.

BOX 8.2   PAY-FOR-PERFORMANCE WITHOUT PERFORMANCE RATINGS

Gamma Partners[1] is a medium-sized professional services organization. The organization transformed their performance management approach and removed performance ratings, but they still wanted to distribute pay increases and bonuses based in part on performance.

Gamma's first step was to create a compensation philosophy document that was shared with all staff members. This document described the pay and benefits available to staff members and how decisions about compensation were made. For each decision, Gamma laid out the various factors that were taken into consideration, for example:

- Annual pay increases were tied each year to the budget, which put a ceiling on average raises. Other considerations included internal equity and market comparisons.
- Available funds for bonuses were determined by how much the organization met its overall revenue and profit goals for the year. Once the overall pool was determined, individual bonus amounts were determined by the employee's job level, team performance, and individual performance.
- Promotions were based on demonstrated ability to perform successfully at the next level. Role descriptions defined the criteria that were important for each job role and level.

To distribute pay raises and bonuses, Gamma would first determine the total budget available for each major business unit. Within each business unit, managers used an iterative process to determine specific amounts for each employee:

- A spreadsheet was provided for the business unit so that managers could see the impact of raising or lowering an individual's salary increase or bonus on the overall budget (see example at the end of this Box).
- Equity or market adjustments were added to individual salaries if an analysis showed that the individuals were underpaid relative to their peers with similar tenure or the market as a whole.
- Each manager then recommended specific amounts for his or her direct reports. They discussed their recommendations as a group, but did not engage in formal calibration. Amounts were adjusted as needed to bring the total business unit within budget guidelines. The business unit vice president made final determinations when disagreements arose.
- Business unit vice presidents repeated this process for their direct reports, with the organization's president.

This process was relatively quick and conflicts were minimal. Once finalized, managers communicated salary and bonus information to employees and referenced the compensation philosophy to explain how decisions were made. Reward conversations were short and straightforward. Employees were satisfied with the process and said they understood why they received the salary and bonus they did, even if they were not always pleased with the outcome.

Sample Salary Increase Worksheet

Employee Name	Current Salary	Proposed Increase	New Salary
Batiste, Eduardo	$50,000.00	$1,500.00	$51,500.00
Heald, Mary	$75,000.00	$1,125.00	$76,125.00
Johnson, Tyrell	$137,500.00	$5,500.00	$143,000.00
Mulvaney, Christine	$98,000.00	$3,500.00	$101,500.00
Scott, James	$87,500.00	$2,150.00	$89,650.00
Total	$448,000.00	$13,775.00	$461,775.00
Budgeted Amount (3%)		$13,440.00	$461,440.00
Variance		-$335.00	-$335.00

Note: This worksheet indicates that further salary adjustments are needed to bring the total in line with the budgeted amount.

The advantage of letting managers make these decisions is that it allows for those closest to the work to determine rewards. If all members of a group are performing equally well, the manager may decide to give them similar raises. In contrast, if a few employees are making outstanding contributions, the manager may decide to provide bigger rewards to those individuals. This approach streamlines reward decisions by eliminating unneeded bureaucracy such as lengthy calibration discussions. The disadvantage of this approach is that it puts a great deal of power into the hands of managers who may make biased decisions.

The fundamental question of whether this approach is viable is one of trust in managers' capabilities to make effective and fair reward decisions in the best interest of the business. When this trust is lacking, numerous checks and approvals are needed. Often, decisions are taken out of the hands of managers, in favor of predetermined decision rules. When managers can be trusted to make effective reward decisions, however, they can be aided by certain types of materials and guidelines, such as:

- A written compensation philosophy that defines how decisions are made in the organization.

- Structured criteria with which to guide decisions (see the next section for details).
- Executive oversight of the process to ensure decisions are defensible and consistent with business priorities.
- Training for managers on how to communicate reward decisions to employees.

A second, related approach to making talent decisions without traditional ratings is to use distinct guidelines for each different type of decision. Each decision is made to accomplish different business objectives and is therefore based on different criteria. For example:

- Pay decisions are intended to ensure the right employees (those making the most valuable contributions to the business) are retained.
- Bonus decisions are intended to incentivize short-term performance that may or may not be sustained over time. A one-time payment allows the organization to recognize a significant accomplishment without an ongoing financial commitment.
- Promotion decisions are intended to fill specific roles in the organization with individuals who have the best possible chance for success. For example, a business wanting to increase market share in Asia will seek leaders for that region who have the experience and skills needed to grow the business there. Individuals who were successful performers in other regions and roles may not be the best fit for this role.

These criteria should fit with the purpose of the decision as relevant to business needs. Table 8.1 shows an example of criteria for pay increases. As shown in this example, the amount of pay increase is based on a) performance, b) impact of the individual on the business, and c) importance or scarcity of skills. While effective performance is a must-have for the highest increase, it is not sufficient. The level of contributions as well as the uniqueness of the skillset and the difficulty of replacing the employee are also important. Although these criteria can set general guidelines for distributing pay increases, overall business goals and budget constraints will ultimately determine how much money is available and how it will be distributed.

An example set of criteria for promotion is presented in Table 8.2. Again, performance is a factor in this decision but not the most important one. The purpose of this decision is to select individuals who are most likely to succeed in new roles. Key considerations are demonstrated knowledge and skills, willingness to take on new responsibilities, and critical past experiences that prepare the individual for the new role.

TABLE 8.1 Example Pay Increase Criteria

Category	Skills, Performance, and Contributions	Replacement Difficulty*
1 5%–7% Increase	Possesses critical or unique technical skills and knowledge, which if lost would have a long-term business impact. Performance consistently exceeds expectations. Contributions have a significant impact on the team, customers, or other groups.	**Extremely difficult** to replace at the same performance level without tremendous expense and time.
2 3%–4% Increase	Possesses essential and current technical skills and knowledge, which if lost would cause disruption to the business. Performance fully meets or exceeds expectations. Makes solid, reliable, and meaningful contributions.	**Difficult** to replace at the same performance level without considerable disruption to the business.
3 1%–2% Increase	Developing required technical skills and knowledge, or skills are narrow in scope. Performance mostly meets expectations. With guidance and coaching, contribution remains steady and/or is improving. May include newly hired or promoted employees, possibly in the position for less than 6–12 months, for whom it is not yet possible to give an accurate evaluation.	**Somewhat difficult** to replace at the same performance level without some disruption to the business.
4 No Increase	Deficient technical skills and knowledge. Performance does not meet expectations; a performance improvement plan should be established.	**Little difficulty** to replace.

*Note: Replacement difficulty based on scarcity of specific technical skills or breadth of knowledge.

Some organizations publish these criteria while other keep them secret. In the interest of transparency, it is best to publish these criteria so that employees are more informed about how decisions are made. As the next section explains, employees are more accepting of decisions when they understand how they were made.

TABLE 8.2 Example Promotion Criteria for Individual Contributors

Criteria for Promotion to Senior Technical Contributor	*Criteria for Promotion to First-Line Supervisor*
• Performance currently meets or exceeds expectations • Has developed more advanced technical knowledge and skills than those required for current position • Has successfully completed complex tasks or projects • Has demonstrated technical leadership by providing effective technical guidance and mentoring to others • Is willing to take on additional responsibilities associated with performing more complex and high-level technical work	• Performance currently meets or exceeds expectations • Has successfully led projects or tasks that involved assigning, monitoring, and evaluating work of others • Has successfully provided effective feedback and coaching to others; has strong communication and interpersonal skills • Has enough technical expertise to be credible to the group s/he would supervise • Is willing to take on additional responsibilities associated with managing others

Communicating Decisions

Managers often lack the skills to effectively communicate reward decisions to employees; however, effective communication has a significant impact on how those decisions are perceived. Employees who are satisfied with how their organization handles pay and performance linkages are more likely to want to stay with the organization and more likely to continue putting effort into their jobs (CEB, 2010). Years of organizational justice research have shown that perceptions of the fairness of both the outcome and the process used to arrive at the outcome are important predictors of employee satisfaction (e.g., Folger & Konovsky, 1989). Of course, most employees would prefer positive outcomes (e.g., a big raise) over negative outcomes (e.g., little or no raise) but will maintain a positive attitude about the organization and their manager if the process used to arrive at the outcome is perceived as fair (Colquitt et al., 2013; McFarlin & Sweeney, 1992).

While many organizations strive to emphasize the link between employee performance and rewards in communications, this approach can backfire. Because most employees believe their performance is above average, they are unlikely to feel good about being told that their raise is based on their performance unless the raise is very high. Focusing communication solely on performance as the driver of rewards will likely reinforce perceptions that the process was unfair because most people would rather believe that the performance evaluation process is flawed than believe that their own performance is average or deficient.

Employees perceive performance ratings and reward outcomes differently, and communication approaches need to take these differences into account. When employees receive a performance rating, they often interpret it as a judgment about their very worthiness as a human being. It does not matter what numbering or labeling system is used, employees have a negative reaction to feeling judged. It threatens their perceived status, which can be more stressful than experiencing physical pain (Rock, 2008). The psychological processes that underlie these beliefs are deeply rooted in evolution. Early humans survived by forming social groups and cooperating. Group membership provided safety, and acceptance into the group was essential for survival. The higher the status, the greater the acceptance. Loss of status meant risk of social rejection and potentially death. These links are still strong in our lizard brains; threats to status are threats to our very existence, which is why both managers and employees struggle with performance rating communications. However, employees can more easily accept a less than desirable outcome (e.g., a smaller raise) if they understand the process that was used to arrive at that outcome <u>and</u> if that outcome is not solely tied to their value (i.e., performance rating) but also impacted by business realities and budget constraints.

This research suggests that the best approach to communicating reward decisions is to do it separately from performance conversations and to explain the various factors that go into these decisions. As described in Chapter 6, performance conversations are most effective when they happen on an ongoing basis and are done to help employees improve performance. Periodically it is also valuable to discuss performance trends, career goals, and development needs. Reward conversations should be distinct and occur when the reward is about to be distributed.

Effective reward conversations are:

- Straightforward: they provide the facts about the outcome and the process used to arrive at that outcome.
- Moderately detailed: they provide enough information for employees to understand decision criteria but not so much detail that the manager sounds like he or she is trying to defend the decision.
- Focused on business goals: talent decisions ultimately serve business goals, and employees appreciate understanding these linkages.

Despite a manager's best efforts, employees may still question or complain about reward outcomes. It may not be possible to please everyone, but how the manager handles this disagreement can help prevent the problem from escalating. See Box 8.3 for tips on conducting reward conversations.

BOX 8.3   TIPS FOR COMMUNICATING REWARD DECISIONS

1. Communicate both the outcome and the process used to get to the outcome. For example:

    • "Your raise this year is X%. We make raise decisions based on our overall budget for the year and then factor in market considerations and individual performance. Managers in Y business unit met to discuss raises to ensure they are consistent and fair."

2. Put the decision in context:

    • Describe how the general business climate (e.g., overall financial performance of the business) and any other significant factors (e.g., labor market trends) impact decisions.

3. Communicate the impact of performance directly—don't use distribution guidelines as an excuse:

    • Note how performance impacted the decision in plain language (e.g., "This raise is based in part on your performance over the past year, which *exceeded expectations/was solid/fell a bit short of expectations* as we discussed previously."

    • Keep discussion of the link between pay and performance very short and to the point; schedule a follow-up conversation if needed to go into more detail about performance issues.

4. Be prepared to address questions about how to increase rewards in the future:

    • Be honest and realistic in your answers.
    • Look for non-monetary reward opportunities.

5. If employees express disappointment or frustration:

    • Let the employee's concerns be heard and acknowledge their disappointment and frustration.
    • Reiterate the decision process and the business basis for the decision.
    • Do not be drawn into debates about what others received.
    • Discuss what the employee might do to get a better outcome in the future (e.g., upgrade skills, take on more responsibility).

★★★

Supporting talent decisions, especially reward decisions, is a key reason many organizations cite for engaging in formal performance management processes. Many organizations assume that ratings are essential for a fair and legally defensible approach, but the reality is that performance ratings are not essential for making talent decisions. In fact, they can sometimes contribute to poor decisions or risk to the organization, for example, if faulty assumptions are made about how performance is distributed or how directly performance ratings can be linked to rewards. Reward decisions are typically heavily dependent on business realities, whereas performance ratings are often based more on psychological factors, such as not wanting to damage relationships with employees or not wanting the team to look good to others.

Rather than over-rely on ratings as a basis for linking performance to rewards, it is typically more effective to use criteria that are focused on the specific decision that needs to be made (e.g., who is best equipped to perform in a new role, who made the most significant contribution to the team, etc.). Making these criteria explicit and transparent to employees and training managers on how to communicate decisions effectively is essential for employees to perceive there is due process and fairness in decision-making. When employees understand the process used to arrive at reward decisions and the factors that impact decisions, they will be much more likely to accept these decisions even if they are disappointed by the actual result.

Note

1 Gamma Partners is a pseudonym.

References

Aguinis, H. (2013). *Performance management* (3rd ed.). Boston, MA: Pearson.

Ariely, D., Gneezy, U., Lowenstein, G., & Mazar, N. (2005, July 23). Large stakes and big mistakes. *Federal Reserve Bank of Boston Working Paper No. 05-11.* Retrieved from http://citeseerx.ist.psu.edu/viewdoc/download?doi=10.1.1.362.1828&rep=rep1&type=pdf

Bock, L. (2015). *Work rules! Insights from Google that will transform how you live and lead.* New York: Twelve.

CEB. (2010). *Creating a pay-for-performance organization.* Arlington, VA: Author.

Colquitt, J. A., Scott, B. A., Rodell, J. B., Long, D. M., Zapata, C. P., Conlon, D. E., & Wesson, M. J. (2013). Justice at the millennium, a decade later: A meta-analytic test of social exchange and affect-based perspectives. *Journal of Applied Psychology, 98,* 199–236.

Deci, E. L., Koestner, R., & Ryan, R. M. (2001). Extrinsic rewards and intrinsic motivation in education: Reconsidered once again. *Review of Educational Research, 71*(1), 1–27.

Deci, E. L., Ryan, R. M., & Koestner, R. (1999). A meta-analytic review of experiments examining the effects of extrinsic rewards on intrinsic motivation. *Psychological Bulletin, 125,* 627–668.

Folger, R., & Konovsky, M. A. (1989). Effects of procedural and distributive justice on reactions to pay raise decisions. *Academy of Management Journal, 32,* 115–130.

Glucksberg, S. (1962). The influence of strength of drive on functional fixedness and perceptual recognition. *Journal of Experimental Psychology, 63*, 36–41.

Government Accountability Office—GAO. (2008, September). DOD needs to improve implementation of and address employee concerns about its national security personnel system. GAO-08-773. Retrieved from www.gao.gov/assets/290/280547.pdf

Lam, B. (2017, April 7). The Department of Labor accuses Google of gender pay discrimination. *The Atlantic.* Retrieved from www.theatlantic.com/business/archive/2017/04/dol-google-pay-discrimination/522411/

Lepper, M., Greene, D., & Nisbett, R. (1973). Undermining children's intrinsic interest with extrinsic rewards: A test of the 'overjustification' hypothesis. *Journal of Personality and Social Psychology, 28*, 129–137.

Losey, S. (2008, August 11). Is DoD's new pay system fair? *Federal Times.*

Masunaga, S., & Lien, T. (2016, February 2). Yahoo ex-employee sues, alleging manipulation of performance reviews and gender bias. *Los Angeles Times.* Retrieved from www.latimes.com/business/technology/la-fi-tn-yahoo-lawsuit-20160202-story.html

McFarlin, D. B., & Sweeney, P. D. (1992). Distributive and procedural justice as predictors of satisfaction with personal and organizational outcomes. *Academy of Management Journal, 35*, 626–637.

O'Boyle, E. Jr., & Aguinis, H. (2012). The best and the rest: Revisiting the norm of normality of individual performance. *Personnel Psychology, 65*, 79–119.

OPM. (2016). *Office of personnel management 2016 federal employee viewpoint survey results.* Retrieved from www.fedview.opm.gov/

Pink, D. H. (2009). *Drive: The surprising truth about what motivates us.* New York: Riverhead Books.

Pulakos, E. D., Mueller-Hanson, R. A., Arad, S., & Moye, N. (2015). Performance management can be fixed: An on-the-job experiential learning approach for complex behavior change. *Industrial and Organizational Psychology: Perspectives on Science and Practice, 8*, 51–76.

Rock, D. (2008). SCARF: A brain-based model for collaborating with and influencing others. *NeuroLeadership Journal, 1*, 1–9.

Rynes, S., Gerhart, B., & Parks, L. (2005). Personnel psychology: Performance evaluation and pay for performance. *Annual Review of Psychology*, 572–600.

9

ADDRESS POOR PERFORMANCE HEAD-ON

Organizational failure to deal with poor performance is one of the single biggest complaints employees have about performance management. On the annual *Federal Employee Viewpoint Survey* conducted by the Office of Personnel Management, it is consistently the second-lowest rated item. Only 29% of employees in 2016 agreed that "In my work unit, steps are taken to deal with a poor performer who cannot or will not improve" (OPM, 2016). This dismal result is second only to employee perceptions about the lack of a relationship between performance and rewards (as described in Chapter 8). Poor performance hurts morale, sends the wrong message about accountability, and costs organizations billions in lost productivity. One survey suggested that 15–25% of employees are not performing to standard (Tyler, 2004). Yet, in most organizations, 95–99% of employees are rated as meeting expectations or higher on their performance reviews.

It is ironic that for all the time and effort spent on formal performance management activities, managers do not use the performance management system to handle or provide consequences for poor performers. The question is why. First and foremost, managers avoid giving low ratings for all the reasons discussed in Chapter 6: fear of harming relationships, desire to make themselves look good (poorly performing employees might reflect negatively on the manager), and organizational norms for providing high ratings. These blockers hinder managers from taking immediate steps to manage poor performance as it occurs. While some situations self-correct or get resolved over time, others fester and eventually deteriorate to an urgent state that requires additional formal processes that sit outside the regular performance management system because the manager has not provided feedback or otherwise attended to issues along the way.

Formal processes for managing poor performance are commonly referred to as Performance Improvement Processes, or PIPs, and they tend to be quite long and can be arduous. Once a performance problem has escalated, PIPs require managers to prepare written documentation that clearly explains performance failures. Employees must then be given an opportunity period (e.g., often 30–90 days) in which to improve, and subsequent performance must be closely monitored and documented to show whether it is meeting expectations, or, if not, exactly where failures are continuing. This process typically requires multiple meetings with HR and in-house counsel and multiple drafts of performance memos. Organizations fear lawsuits, especially if they have faced prior challenges, which also leads to caution in managing performance issues. This can be especially difficult in union environments or government organizations where further restrictions are in place. PIPs thus provide the formal due process and protections organizations need to make a termination decision if needed.

Managing through a PIP is time-consuming for the organization and manager and has significant potential consequences for the employee; therefore, it should not be undertaken lightly. The paperwork and time required can leave managers feeling that it is simply too hard to deal with poor performers, the organization does not support them, or that it's impossible to fire people. They sometimes look for other strategies—job rotations, promotion opportunities in other units, etc. to get poor performers out. The difficulty of managing poor performers can create a vicious cycle of managers not dealing with performance issues until they become significant, which then triggers a lengthy process, which then makes managers further avoid dealing with poor performance. What gets lost in the mix are the strategies managers can employ to more productively handle poor performance situations. A formal PIP should be used as a last resort when reaching a negative tipping point in which the employee's chances of achieving minimum standards of success are more unlikely than likely.

Well before a PIP comes into play, the first step in effectively managing poor performance is providing real-time, specific feedback as performance occurs—a point reinforced countless times throughout this book. Nipping poor performance in the bud by providing a few instances of solid feedback will address many performance issues. For those cases in which this does not work, managers then should consider what will be most beneficial for themselves, the team, and the employee as a next step. The manager may decide to hold onto less-than-stellar performers at least for some time, if the team is understaffed and facing tight deadlines, there is a tight labor market, or it takes a very long time to replace staff. A poor performer in one area may also have unique skills in other areas, so managers can sometimes reorganize the work to leverage important skills while also mitigating problems for themselves and others that result from ineffective performance in some areas. Finally, just because someone is not performing well in one situation does not mean there are no jobs or contexts in which they will perform well, and sometimes the best answer *is* to transfer the person to another situation. Although transferring staff to other teams or redesigning jobs can be viewed as dodging performance problems, these strategies can in fact be productive.

Discussions of handling poor performance are sometimes oversimplified, possibly perpetuated by employee survey questions that ask whether or not managers are effectively dealing with poor performers. In reality, handling poor performers is often not cut and dry and instead involves much more subtle nuances and complexities. There are relatively few cases of performance being so obviously poor that it needs to be managed out of the organization, and there is often more going on in these cases than what appears on the surface. Examples of complex performance problems include:

- The ineffective performer who is highly skilled in some areas but struggles in others.
- The employee who falls short of expectations but can be developed to perform successfully with time and effort.
- The employee who is underperforming but still filling a vital role that is difficult to replace.

Managing complex performance issues such as these are not straightforward but they do need to be managed in a timely manner, actively, and success- fully to avoid poor morale and attrition among higher performers, poor team or organization performance, and productivity losses. This chapter provides examples and insights for how to better address performance challenges before they get to the point of no return.

Poor Performance Defined

What is poor performance? For the purposes of this chapter, poor performance is a pattern of failing to meet one or more critical job expectations even after rou- tine feedback and coaching. Poor performance is not a simple mistake or "one- off" event in which the employee failed. For example, poor performance is not:

- Sales people who occasionally miss quarterly targets but who otherwise usually hit them.
- Hourly employees who are occasionally late to work but still generally adhere to attendance policies.
- Employees with odd or eccentric personalities who usually get along fine with others and complete tasks effectively.
- Employees with diverse perspectives that do not always fit with organiza- tional traditions and ways of doing things.

Poor performance comes in many forms but can be broadly categorized as either challenges with behaviors or task completion. Table 9.1 lists examples of chal- lenges in each category. Distinguishing significant issues from the day-to-day

TABLE 9.1 Examples of Performance Challenges

Behavioral Challenges	Task Performance Challenges
• Actions inconsistent with organizational values (e.g., lack of integrity, customer focus) • Unethical behavior—lying, cheating, stealing, etc. • Lack of initiative—waiting to be told what to do before acting • Lack of perseverance—giving up when faced with routine challenges • Lack of resilience—being easily upset by change or everyday problems to the point where it interferes with the individual's ability to get things done and is disruptive to others • Disruptive interpersonal behaviors—arguing, bullying, insulting, interrupting • Poor communication skills—withholding information, lack of clarity • Intolerance of diversity—making disparaging remarks or treating others disrespectfully due to differences in race, ethnicity, religion, gender, sexual orientation, age, background, etc.	• Failure to perform required tasks on time or at all • Work that is of poor quality and requires a lot of rework • Making significant errors when completing work • Slow production—producing far less work than peers in similar roles • Poor efficiency—using too many resources (time, money, supplies, etc.) to get things done; makes poor use of time • Inability to handle complexity or ambiguity—can complete straightforward tasks but cannot handle situations that deviate from the norm • Lack of independence—needs more guidance than others to complete tasks; requires step-by-step instructions for completing work and cannot use judgment to determine how to get things done on his or her own

ups and downs is important because dealing with poor performance requires investment from the manager to address well. Managers need to be intentional in prioritizing where they will lean in to actively manage performance and where they won't. This requires carefully evaluating each person and planning how to handle each situation in which managers need to do more work. For example, an employee who is frequently late but otherwise doing a good job may not need to be handled as a "performance problem" if the manager and others can work around this issue and the employee is providing value without being disruptive. Too often, however, the opposite is true with managers failing to act on issues until irreparable damage is done—frustration from coworkers, lowered morale, and significant negative impacts on the business.

Attention and Proper Diagnosis

Managing employee performance requires attending to and monitoring employee outcomes, behaviors, and attitudes. In many cases, managers simply are not attuned to what is happening in the environment or personally with employees, even when signs of disengagement or distraction are clear. Thus, a critical first step in managing poor performance is to carefully diagnose its root cause(s) to better tailor the solutions.

Performance problems have three major root causes:

1.   Environment: something outside of the employee's control is prevent-
     ing optimal performance. For example, onerous policies and procedures,
     uncooperative colleagues, organizational structures that inhibit communi-
     cation, maladaptive cultures, lack of resources, poorly designed workflows
     and business processes, workload/tasks not appropriate for the employee's
     role, etc.
2.   Lack of capabilities: the employee lacks the knowledge and skills necessary
     to perform the essential functions of the role. For example, if a new tech-
     nology system is introduced and employees are not properly trained to use
     it, their performance will suffer.
3.   Lack of will: the employee lacks motivation to perform effectively. For
     example, employees may be unwilling to work cooperatively with organi-
     zational rivals, hurting their ability to perform tasks requiring collabora-
     tion. Lack of will may also be a temporary situation due to personal factors
     or difficulties employees may be dealing with outside of work. It is very
     important to separate motivational factors that stem from work and may
     require changes on the job from outside factors that have nothing to do
     with work. In the latter case, most managers will work with employees,
     especially good performers, to help them get through these temporary
     personal situations.

When employees are not meeting expectations, there is a natural tendency to point to lack of skill or will as the root cause. However, this orientation ignores the substantial influence of context on performance and may overesti-mate the employee's ability to improve. Many powerful factors sit outside the employee's control that significantly contribute to performance misses. In fact, environmental factors are the biggest drivers of poor performance and, at least theoretically, what the organization has the most power to change. It may not be possible to change an employee's level of capability or attitude. Figure 9.1 shows examples of potential root causes of performance challenges.

Tools such as the example provided in Figure 9.2 can help managers diag-nose and address potential causes of poor performance. Aside from environ-mental causes, managers also need to consider whether or not they can address capability gaps or attitude and behavioral issues. Figure 9.3 provides some tips for addressing problems stemming from a lack of skill or will.

An important question to ask when addressing lack of skill or will is whether the employee is in the right role. How often has an organization hired an employee with high hopes only to quickly find that the individual is unable to perform the essential functions of the job? These employees will likely eventually

Type of Challenge	Possible Causes		
	Lack of Will	Lack of Skill	Environment
Behavioral (e.g., poor attitude, interpersonal challenges, lack of initiative)	• Personal values conflict with organizational values • Fear (of failure, looking foolish, the unknown, etc.) • Resentment—perceived slights that lead to aggression	• Lack of education about organizational values • Lack of awareness of own actions and their impact • Lack of experience or maturity • Lack of confidence • Poor communication and interpersonal skills	• Poor role models • Lack of support for those who speak up about concerns • Lack of accountability that perpetuates a culture that tolerates maladaptive behaviors
Task performance (e.g., late, sloppy, or incomplete work; poor production or efficiency; lack of independence)	• Lack of willingness to put in effort • Belief that assignments are unimportant • Feeling overwhelmed • Habit of procrastination • Dislike of assigned tasks • Belief that other tasks are higher priority	• Low attention to detail • Lack of experience • Lack of job knowledge or skill • Poor organization and time management skills • Lack of understanding or work priorities • Low cognitive abilities	• Workload too heavy • Instructions and expectations not clear • Lack of resources; equipment and technology failures • Poor match between employee abilities and job requirements • Policies, procedures, or processes make getting things done difficult

FIGURE 9.1   Potential Causes of Performance Challenges

Step	Actions	Examples
Describe the Situation	Describe the specific problematic behaviors and their impact. Note: hold off on trying to interpret why the behavior is happening.	Jill is constantly asking questions she knows the answer to, meetings with her go on too long, and she regularly checks in to confirm if she is doing things correctly. Colleagues describe her as "needy" and "attention-seeking." The impact is that peers and senior leaders avoid her and are growing increasingly unhappy with her performance. She has gotten some feedback but has not changed.

FIGURE 9.2   Example Tool for Diagnosing Performance Challenges

Step	Actions	Examples
Gather Data	Observe the employee in different situations and with different people. Note any differences and where the individual excels and struggles.	Managers and peers find fault with Jill, but her direct reports describe her as the best team leader they have ever had. They appreciate the time and attention she gives them.
Make an Initial Diagnosis	Determine if the issue is lack of will, skill, environment, or a combination. Ask questions to better diagnose the issue.	Jill is aware of her need for reassurance but does not understand the impact on others. She is new to her role and is still unsure of expectations. Her goals often conflict with those of her peers; she senses the tension but is not sure of the cause. These problems stem from a combination of lack of skill, maturity, and environmental factors.
Choose a Course of Action	Determine what specifically needs to change and how. Identify a desired resolution and a path to an end state (e.g., if no improvement, do a PIP or consider reassignment).	Jill's manager tells her that she needs to become more independent in her work—limit her questions and requests for time. Her manager commits to setting clearer expectations and providing better feedback about how she is doing so she is not left to wonder. Her role is modified slightly to make peer interactions more likely to succeed.
Evaluate and Adapt	Assess the results of the initial action, determine their effectiveness, adjust as needed, and move to desired end state).	Jill improves, though managers still find her a bit difficult. However, she has improved enough that they no longer avoid her, and remaining challenges can be worked around (e.g., set time limits for meetings).

FIGURE 9.2   (Continued)

be reassigned or let go, costing the organization time and money in the process. Because these problems can be mitigated by hiring the right people in the first place, the importance of good selection practices cannot be overstated. Good selection does more to prevent performance problems than remedial efforts to build skills or change attitudes after the fact. A sound selection system begins by clearly defining the knowledge, skills, abilities, and other characteristics employees need to possess on day one to successfully perform essential job functions. Assessing candidates for these attributes with reliable and valid methods (e.g., tests, structured interviews, simulations, work samples, and so on) increases the

Lack of Will	Lack of Skill
Ask powerful questions to get to the root cause of the problem • What's holding you back/what's your real concern? • What are you afraid of? • What do you want to achieve for others? For yourself?	Provide additional training/guidance • Classes • Written materials • Show examples of effective and ineffective performance • Pair up with a mentor; observe a pro in action
Challenge thinking • Be direct—label what you are noticing (e.g., "It sounds like you think paperwork is not important—is that right?") • Provide an alternative perspective if needed	Emphasize practice • Start small to build confidence • Be deliberate in practicing what the employee struggles with the most
Help make the link to broader goals • Show them how desired behaviors fit with organizational purpose and priorities • Show them how desired behaviors help them personally and professionally	Find a support system • Create a reminder system • Build in work arounds/accommodations if issue is relatively minor Consider if the individual is in the right role • Restructure role or reassign if needed
Consider if the individual is in the right role • Restructure role or reassign if needed	

FIGURE 9.3   Example Techniques for Handling Lack of Will or Skill

likelihood that new employees start with the right capabilities for the role. The need for good selection applies equally to newly hired employees as well as employees who are being promoted or transferred into new roles.

A precursor to effective selection is accurately defining the job requirements to gain a full understanding of the individual capabilities and experience that are needed to succeed. For example, one organization created new product management roles that required both subject-matter expertise and product management experience. When this combination of skills was difficult to find, priority was placed on product management experience. Those hired ended up performing poorly and eventually new roles had to be created to fill gaps in subject-matter expertise so the company could compete effectively.

Managing performance effectively thus entails multifaceted systems and activities that go beyond providing feedback, coaching, and helping employees. It also requires having effective selection systems in place to support managers, having job roles defined properly for which fully capable employees can be hired, ensuring employees are competitively and fairly compensated, along with many other factors—some of which sit with the managers themselves but many of which are part of the larger context within which managers and employees are operating.

A Case Study in Diagnosing Poor Performance

Health Services Group (HSG),[1] a medium-sized healthcare provider, was experiencing some classic performance challenges. Required documentation was frequently late and of poor quality. Patients complained about poor service and long wait times. Health and safety violations were a regular occurrence, putting patients and employees at risk. The organization handled these challenges in a traditional way: employee performance was evaluated with a 5-point rating scale. Low performers received low ratings, and managers provided extra training and guidance to these employees to help them improve. Employees who had significant performance problems were placed on a PIP. Employees who could not improve while on the PIP were eventually fired.

These measures yielded marginal gains on an individual basis. Some of the mediocre employees improved with extra training and coaching, and some of the employees on a PIP improved to the point that their performance was considered acceptable. However, many employees did not improve, and performance on the whole in the organization was lower than desired. Unlike many other organizations, these performance challenges were not because managers failed to give tough feedback, hold poor performers accountable, or go through the process of documentation and creating a PIP. Instead the problem stemmed from a failure to diagnose and address the root causes of the performance issues.

Realizing that the traditional approach was not working, the organization worked department by department to analyze the current environment and identify underlying reasons for the performance challenges. Like many complex challenges, HSG discovered that the underlying causes of poor performance were multifaceted:

- Ineffective workflows and business processes made it difficult to track when documentation was completed and made follow up challenging.
- Technology problems and limitations resulted in difficulty completing required documentation and inability to effectively use data in decision-making.
- Chronic staffing shortages led to over-work for supervisors who tried to fill in the gaps. In turn this led to lack of adequate supervision, training, and implementation of safety procedures for new staff.

- Budget constraints kept wages low, which made it difficult to attract and retain the most qualified applicants. Some applicants who were hired lacked the skills or willingness to perform effectively.

Not all of these issues were ones that HSG could control. For example, budgets were determined by negotiated insurance reimbursement rates, which were not able to be changed. Government rules and regulations made documentation complex and time-consuming to complete. Other problems were within HSG's control, and they prioritized several initiatives designed to address the biggest performance issues:

- Invest in a new technology system that would streamline documentation, make it easier to track, and result in more useful data. Redesign workflows and business processes to make them easier to follow.
- Ramp up hiring efforts to address staffing shortages and emphasize career growth and benefits to compensate for lower wages.
- Add more first-line supervisors to reduce the span of control and allow more time for training and direct supervision. Provide more tools to supervisors to better equip them to train and support their staff.
- Revise the performance evaluation process to provide more real-time performance measurement and feedback, identify when staff members are underperforming, and give remedial support when needed.
- Retain the PIP process to put poor performers on notice and address chronic lack of skill/will issues.

Implementing these changes resulted in slow but steady organizational improvements. Some employees still failed to meet expectations; however, they were the exception rather than the rule. In addition to improving organizational performance, HSG also got better at identifying and diagnosing the impact of context on performance. Armed with this information, they could respond more quickly to future issues and tailor interventions to the root cause of performance problems.

The Importance of Context

As this case study illustrates, the external environment or context can have a greater impact on performance than individual skills or attitudes. Employees who shine in one context may struggle in another. As described in Chapter 2, one study showed that 46% of stock analysts who were star performers at their prior companies did poorly after moving to another firm (Groysberg, Nanda, & Nohria, 2004). What happened that so dramatically changed their performance? It may be that some of them were unmotivated when they switched to the new firm, but more likely is that contextual factors that optimized their performance in their old firms were not present or different in the new firms.

Contextual factors that impact performance can include but are not limited to:

- The boss. There is a well-known adage that employees leave their managers more than they leave their organizations. It seems as if everyone has a "bad manager" story—either from their own experience or from hearing others' experiences. Google added credibility and teeth to the notion that managers have a significant impact on team performance in their Project Oxygen study (Bryant, 2011). In this study, the best managers were those who were good coaches, empowered their team members, demonstrated concern for employee well-being, helped with career development, and communicated effectively, among other attributes. In other words, they were effective at the most important performance management behaviors. Managers who lack these capabilities have less effective teams, and those who demonstrate negative behaviors (toxic leaders) can—even worse— actively hurt employee performance.

- Culture. The organization's culture impacts performance in two major ways. The first is an issue of fit—some cultures may work well for some employees but not others. For example, employees who do best with a high degree of structure and certainty may struggle in a highly flexible and dynamic environment. Second is the issue of maladaptive cultures, which create an environment that broadly impairs performance. For example, by many accounts, Enron's culture promoted excess and a lax attitude to adequate control mechanisms. In this culture, ethical breaches were allowed to flourish, leading to the company's ultimate demise.

- Organizational structure. Organizational structures can inhibit communication and collaboration and impact productivity. For example, one of our past clients had a strong structural separation between the sales and service teams. When the sales team sold a new product, they failed to involve the service team in planning its installation and support. As a result, service technicians were constantly under pressure to deliver on unrealistic promises made by the sales team, and they often fell short of performance targets. It was not until the sales and service teams were restructured to enable more effective collaboration that performance improved.

- Position requirements. Some positions have challenging requirements that are difficult to meet. These requirements may be by design (e.g., an astronaut is a challenging position for which only a few people qualify, but high requirements nonetheless exist to ensure safety and success) or by chance. For example, workload requirements may be so heavy that otherwise effective employees struggle to keep up. Working long hours can lead to lower performance because errors tend to increase and productivity goes down when employees are overworked and under too much stress.

- Work processes, policies, and procedures. Inefficient work practices or poorly conceived policies and procedures can inhibit employees from getting things done. For example, in one organization with whom we worked, making a purchase of any amount required extensive written justifications and multiple approvals. As a result, supplies frequently ran out, equipment broke down because maintenance was delayed, and employee productivity suffered.
- External factors (e.g., economy, laws, politics, etc.). Sometimes despite an organization's best efforts, external factors conspire to make life difficult. For example, legislated budget cuts often leave government organizations and private sector contractors with fewer resources, which in turn creates challenges for employees to meet performance targets. Despite admonitions to "do more with less," performance usually suffers when more work needs to be done with less money and fewer people to help.

Mitigating Legal Risks

Organizations may be reluctant to address performance challenges for fear of litigation. These concerns are well founded. Wrongful termination lawsuits have been on the rise, and defending against lawsuits, regardless of the outcome, is costly and emotionally taxing. The best defense is to engage in sound decision-making practices; that is, make decisions based on job-related, not discriminatory, reasons that are consistent with business needs (Aguinis, 2013). A legally defensible performance management approach includes:

- A well-defined process that is applied consistently to employees. This does not mean that the system needs to be rigid. Rather, the processes used to define expectations, measure performance, and allocate rewards and consequences should be clear, transparent, and applied consistently to all employees.
- Consistency between written guidelines and actual practices. For example, if organizational policies dictate that all employees get an annual review, then failing to provide a review puts the organization at risk.
- Job-relevant performance standards. Consistent with the guidance provided in Chapter 6, measuring performance against these standards should be reliable and valid, and managers should be provided with written instructions for how to evaluate performance.
- Documenting specific examples of performance that fail to meet expectations and ensuring that performance reviews, ratings, etc. show a consistent pattern of poor performance before taking negative actions. One of the biggest legal pitfalls for organizations is when employees have a long history of positive performance reviews only to be demoted or fired after a single negative review. Employees have successfully argued that the negative review was a pretext for discrimination, citing the long history of

positive reviews. These challenges are tough to defend against, and organizations are safer to ensure a sustained pattern of negative performance is documented before taking adverse action.

- Providing employees with clear feedback about what they need to do to improve and an opportunity to respond to the feedback.
- Allowing employees an opportunity to improve and providing additional coaching, training, etc. if needed to help them be successful.
- Dealing with performance problems early—as soon as they are detected. For example, if a new employee lacks the skills to be successful, it is better to terminate his or her employment right away, especially if there is a defined probation period. An early termination can be easily explained as a faulty hire. A delayed termination is more difficult to justify. Once the employee is past any formal probation period, it is prudent to provide an opportunity period before taking action.
- Treating all employees with dignity and respect, regardless of performance challenges. Poorly performing employees cause organizations serious disruption, and managers may be understandably angry with them. However, many lawsuits are fueled by anger and resentment. If an employee feels fairly and kindly treated, he or she will be less likely to pursue legal action, even if demoted or terminated.

Following these practices does not guarantee that organizations won't be challenged, but it can make challenges less likely to succeed. Werner and Bolino (1997) evaluated 295 U.S. court decisions involving performance management. They concluded that the courts were more likely to rule in favor of organizations when performance reviews were job relevant, included written instructions to individuals evaluating performance, and allowed employees an opportunity to review evaluation results.

If All Else Fails . . .

If employees have been given good feedback, steps are taken to help them improve, and factors outside of the employee's control are addressed, but performance is still not meeting minimum expectations, then implementing a PIP will likely be the best option (see Box 9.1 for tips on doing this well). Streamlining the requirements for documenting and handling PIPs should be considered so managers are not discouraged from using these processes when appropriate. This is not to suggest that organizations act hastily or carelessly. An appropriate due process is necessary when an employee's performance has become sufficiently ineffective that material action is considered that may harm the employee's current income or career. Thus, the goal of streamlining the PIP process is to facilitate action while keeping in place essential protections that are needed to ensure fairness and mitigate any legal issues.

BOX 9.1   TIPS FOR EFFECTIVE PIPS

- Train managers to address and document examples of performance challenges as soon as they occur rather than waiting until a formal review to address the issue.
- Provide a simple template for managers to use when writing a PIP. The template should include a clear and straightforward description of how performance failed to meet expectations (with specific examples), what the employee needs to do differently to perform successfully, the time frame for improvement, and what the possible consequences are for a failure to improve.
- Provide the least amount of review and oversight needed to get the PIP implemented. Too many organizations drag out the creation of the PIP, requiring multiple rounds of review, revision, and sign-offs. While it is a good idea to consult with HR or legal counsel (in stickier situations) before finalizing the PIP, this process should not result in too much of a delay. The adage, *don't let the perfect be the enemy of the good* applies here.

★★★

Poor performance is a significant problem in any organization. It is costly, lowers morale, and undermines productivity. Yet, poor performance can go unaddressed because managers are reluctant, uncomfortable, or lack capabilities to effectively manage it. Managers often perceive their only option is to engage in a burdensome and heavy-handed PIP process, the sole purpose of which is to protect the organization in case of litigation. Use of PIPs should be a last resort, however, after solid performance management attempts have failed, rather than as the primary means for addressing issues. Addressing poor performance begins with diagnosing the root causes of the performance issues. An often-overlooked cause is the environment and much more attention is needed here. Organizations should first seek to fully analyze, understand, and address environmental barriers before taking action to improve skill or motivational deficits.

Careful consideration needs to be given to the effort that will be required to improve skill and motivational issues. Tackling those that can be addressed easily makes sense, but other strategies such as redesigning jobs or transferring staff into other roles can also be effective mechanisms for successfully managing performance. Using these strategies does not mean the manager is ignoring the problem, as some might believe, but it requires managers to be skilled in understanding job requirements and matching them to employee capabilities and preferences. Moreover, if managers are effectively managing performance in the ways described here, they will mitigate risk from legal challenges, which is best protected against by following sound performance management practices and ensuring decisions are fair, job-relevant, and non-discriminatory.

Note

1 Health Services Group is a pseudonym.

References

Aguinis, H. (2013). *Performance management* (3rd ed.). Boston, MA: Pearson.

Bryant, A. (2011, March 12). Google's quest to build a better boss. *New York Times*. Retrieved from www.nytimes.com/2011/03/13/business/13hire.html?mcubz=3

Groysberg, B., Nanda, A., & Nohria, N. (2004, May). The risky business of hiring stars. *Harvard Business Review*. Retrieved from https://hbr.org/2004/05/the-risky-business-of-hiring-stars.

OPM. (2016). *Office of personnel management 2016 federal employee viewpoint survey results*. Retrieved from www.fedview.opm.gov/

Tyler, K. (2004). One bad apple: Before the whole bunch spoils, train managers to deal with poor performance. *HR Magazine, 49,* 77–86.

Werner, J. M., & Bolino, M. C. (1997). Explaining U.S. courts of appeals decisions involving performance appraisal: Accuracy, fairness, and validation. *Personnel Psychology, 50,* 1–24.

PART III

Sustaining the Change

10

THE HOLY GRAIL OF BEHAVIOR CHANGE

In 1987, the Aluminum Company of America (Alcoa) appointed a new CEO, Paul O'Neill, in the hopes that he could turn the struggling organization around. Alcoa's critics charged that product quality was declining along with profitability. Past leaders had tried to improve effectiveness and efficiency with dismal results. Alcoa's board hoped that O'Neill could improve productivity and quality, but he surprised investors and analysts by announcing that the company's focus would be on improving workplace safety. Despite initial concerns from Wall Street and company executives, O'Neill's strategy paid off. By the time he left Alcoa in 2000, the organization's market value increased from $3 billion in 1986 to $27.53 billion, while net income increased from $200 million to $1.484 billion (Duhigg, 2012).

How did O'Neill achieve such extraordinary results? As Charles Duhigg reports in his book, *The Power of Habit: Why We Do What We Do*, safety was a "keystone habit" that led to a chain reaction of many other positive behaviors at Alcoa, which ultimately led to higher performance. For example, O'Neill required that any workplace injury be reported to him within 24 hours along with a plan for making sure it never happened again. This rapid reporting requirement meant that communication between all levels of leadership had to improve. Floor managers needed to ensure workers reported incidents quickly and that they had suggestions at the ready for improving safety. In turn, floor managers needed to be able to quickly communicate up the chain, which led to improvements in communication systems. O'Neill also required that manufacturing processes be analyzed so improvements could be made to prevent future accidents. Union representatives and managers, who had previously been resistant to improvement efforts when the focus was on increasing productivity, embraced these process improvement efforts because their primary purpose was to improve safety, a value upon which everyone agreed. As a result, processes improved, yielding less waste, fewer injuries, and increased production and quality.

As illustrated in the Alcoa example, changing key manager and employee behaviors can have a big impact on an organization's success. The heart of performance management transformation has always been and continues to be behavior change to improve performance, although previous attempts to achieve this goal have usually fallen short. Some behavior changes are reasonably simple, such as learning how to use a new automated system to more easily collect and share performance management information. Other behavior changes are extremely complex, such as learning to give useful but difficult developmental feedback on a regular basis that will leave employees feeling motivated and engaged in their work. It is the latter type of behavior change that is most important and has the most potential to impact performance outcomes.

A key lesson to take from the Alcoa story is that choosing which behaviors to change is paramount. Had Paul O'Neill chosen to focus on increasing productivity, he would have faced significant resistance, as others before him had. Had he chosen to focus on simply improving communication, the effort likely would have fallen flat. "Improving communication" is far too vague and intangible for most people to take specific action. Instead he focused on improving safety, which was something that everyone agreed was important and was also tangible and easily understood. Therefore, behavior change must start by identifying the right behaviors to change—they must be important to the business and to meeting performance goals and at the same time be concrete and easily understood. Addressing these keystone behaviors can yield positive changes in other behaviors, such as Alcoa improving communication and efficiency along with improving safety.

Complex performance management behavior change is challenging because it is not well understood and tends to be oversimplified. For example, a common misconception is that driving informal feedback is simply a matter of scheduling more feedback sessions or prompting managers to talk to staff more regularly. While more frequent feedback is not a bad thing, effective performance management is rooted in developing productive work relationships that are characterized by open communication and trust, which in turn enable productive, real-time feedback, coaching, and development to occur naturally as part of daily work. Focusing only on improving feedback behavior is too narrow, too vague, and does not emphasize the importance of changing behaviors that have a clear and direct link to the business. Lasting change entails rethinking manager and employee roles and how we approach and perform work holistically day-to-day—and it goes well beyond simply learning how to say the right thing to deliver better feedback in isolated situations. Complex performance management behavior change requires time and investment learning how to enable high performance in partnership with others.

Research has confirmed what we all know from common sense and experience—that managers play a critical role in driving effective performance and employee engagement. One research study conducted by CEB in 2004 showed that performance and engagement are substantially higher in the presence of several key manager behaviors: setting clear expectations, providing regular informal feedback, and helping employees develop and succeed. Another study was Google's Project Oxygen (Bryant, 2011), which identified eight habits of highly effective managers, including making time for one-on-one meetings, helping employees solve problems, coaching employees, and helping employees develop. Google managers who demonstrated these behaviors had teams that performed better, stayed longer, and had better attitudes about their work. Google began teaching the eight habits in training programs, as well as in coaching and performance review sessions with individual managers. These efforts yielded significant improvement in 75% of Google's least effective managers. Taken together, these studies demonstrate the strong effects of manager behavior on employee performance, engagement, and important bottom-line results, and they support the idea that key behaviors can be learned with proper training and coaching.

When comparing the impact of manager behaviors to the impact of formal performance management system features (which is neutral to negative), it is not surprising that behavior change is a primary goal of transformation. The manager behaviors targeted for development include:

- Set clear expectations, ensuring employees understand priorities, success criteria or standards, and exactly what is expected.
- Flexibly revise expectations in real time as changes occur, so that employees are always clear on what they should be doing and what good looks like.
- Identify credible information sources so that employees can measure their progress and use this information to improve.
- Provide informal feedback day-to-day to praise, coach, or course-correct performance on an ongoing basis.
- Check in regularly with employees so that the manager stays in touch with what is happening and can guide employees through delivering performance to achieve outcomes, as needed.
- Coach employees and help them solve problems so they can be successful on the job.

Employees, too, can learn performance management behaviors that will facilitate their own performance as well as that of their team. In the end, achieving success requires good partnership between managers and employees and between peers on a team, especially given the trends toward flatter organizations in which more work is accomplished in collaboration with coworkers than has been the case in the past (CEB, 2012). To build a high-performance culture, employees need to do their part to engage in effective performance management behaviors (Pulakos et al., 2015), such as:

- Ask for expectations to be clarified if needed to understand priorities and what good looks like.
- Revisit expectations with their managers when performance is blocked or the situation changes.
- Set expectations with peers when working together about who is doing what, by when, and what good looks like.
- Ask for and receive feedback from managers and other colleagues.
- Use feedback effectively to course correct or improve areas consistently noted.
- Provide feedback to others in ways that will be useful to them and help them improve.
- Coach and assist colleagues who are encountering challenges in their work.

The goal of performance management behavior change is to fundamentally shift how we conceive of and execute performance management activities. Historically, performance management has been viewed as a set of low-value, intermittent formal steps that are typically cued by an automated system. The desired change involves both a mindset and behavioral shift—from thinking about performance management as a formal HR system to engaging in performance management behaviors on a daily basis that enable high performance. Figure 10.1 illustrates this change.

Many new commercially available training and development programs claim to deliver performance management behavior change. These programs are not misguided in theory, but they often have less impact in practice than expected. While numerous theories, models, and strategies offer ideas that should contribute to successful behavior change, the reality is that efforts

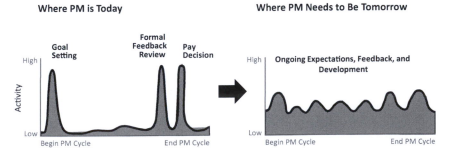

FIGURE 10.1   Performance Management Today and Tomorrow

© Elaine D. Pulakos, reprinted with permission

directed at embedding effective performance management behaviors have resulted in insufficient traction and momentum to substantially impact performance outcomes. In the remainder of this chapter, we will review what we know from research about learning and behavior change. We will then discuss lessons learned from behavior change implementations that provide insights about how to best enable success.

The Heart of Behavior Change

Some managers are naturals at the behaviors that drive performance—their personality, skills, and experience help them intuitively know how to engage employees and coach them through performance delivery in ways that advance both learning and results. Most people are not naturals, however, and they need to be intentional about learning and practicing behaviors that drive performance until these become the automatic way they approach work. Behavior change is like learning a new skill—it could be a sport, such as golf or baseball; how to drive a car with stick shift rather than an automatic transmission; how to play an instrument; or learn to ride a bike. In the beginning, you need to be intentional about every movement. You fall off the bike, stall the car, or drive your golf ball into a sand trap. Eventually with sufficient practice and coaching, you develop enough muscle memory that the skill comes more easily without as much intentional thought. When deep learning occurs, your golf swing, driving a stick shift, playing the piano, etc. become automatic and embedded—you do these things without even thinking about them. Of course, those with natural talent, coordination, or athletic ability will pick things up more easily and do them more effortlessly than most. Nonetheless, most people can learn a new skill or behavior with intention and repeated practice, although this is not always easy, as many lifelong golfers will attest!

The implications for behavior change in organizations are that it will take time, intentionality, and repeated practice to form new habits for engaging with others. What adds complexity to organizationally driven behavior change is that the impetus often comes from HR and, in the best case, the organization's leaders. Even then, behavior change requires a sincere interest and investment to stay the course from those individuals who are making the change. Put simply, behavior change programs do not work unless learners are self-motivated, invest time, and commit to making personal change. Managers need to be as passionate about being great managers who drive performance as they are about being great golfers. Further, this needs to be a high enough priority for the manager's time that it trumps other demands.

The question then becomes how to help managers become invested in their own performance management behavior change. An important aspect of motivating change is communicating the "WIIFM" (what's in it for me). Successfully done, this wins people over and creates the motivation and ownership that is required for success. The first and foremost benefit of performance management behavior change for managers is that the team will perform more effectively and deliver increased results. Managers will more clearly see the WIIFM if the target behavior for change is one that has a direct link to achieving an important business goal (e.g., improve customer service, increase sales, speed up decisions). Performance improvements make the manager look good and potentially enhance his or her ability to be promoted. Performance management behaviors can then help achieve this goal. These behaviors in turn cultivate a culture in which employees feel valued and motivated, which positively impacts their engagement, reduces intention to quit, and, again, makes the manager look good.

Despite the strong WIIFM for managers, not all managers are willing to embrace, commit to, and drive their own behavior change. When performance has more to do with contextual or environmental factors outside the manager's control, managers will be less willing to invest in behavior change than those who believe their actions can directly impact their and the team's success. Also, some managers will be skeptical that these efforts will make a difference, in which case an educational campaign and individual discussions to persuade managers about the benefits may need to precede implementation of behavior change processes.

Characteristics of Effective Behavior Change Programs

Deep learning that is required to change behavior needs to go beyond passive learning methods, such as e-learning, classroom learning, and active learning methods that are typically provided through simulated practice (e.g., role plays). Complex behavior change requires practice in a meaningful context over time to understand how to translate and apply new concepts to real situations. On-the-job, experiential learning is the foundation of successful performance management behavior change because work inherently contains important drivers that are needed to embed change (Davache, Kiefer, Rock, & Rock, 2010), as follows:

* The tasks for which managers are responsible on the job inherently capture their attention and have built-in relevance and ownership, which are important to hardwire learning.
* Practicing new concepts as part of real work helps learners see how these concepts manifest and play out across different people and situations, which provides contextualization, personalization, and varied learning experiences that are essential for deep learning.
* Naturally occurring work provides spaced opportunities for practice that is important to solidify learning.
* Learning as part of real work incorporates important social elements: learning generation by participants, connectedness, and opportunities for positive feedback as skills are honed.

CEB (2015) identified three common barriers that impede managers and employees from extracting effective learning on the job:

1. Inability to recognize and leverage relevant learning opportunities.
2. Not understanding that effective learning requires intentional practice, reflection, and feedback.
3. Lack of time and expertise to effectively structure experiences to gain value from on-the-job learning.

The list provided below is a checklist of features against which to evaluate programs aimed at performance management behavior change. Ask yourself . . . to what extent does this program:

- Use readily available, routine work activities to support learning.
- Drive deliberate, repetitive practice (Ericsson, Krampe, & Tesch-Romer, 1993) that leads to adaptation of new behavior.
- Help learners reflect on what they are learning, adjust, and solidify effective behavior (e.g., provide specific reflection questions at key points).
- Provide feedback on how learners are behaving and changing in the eyes of others.
- Cue learners on what outcomes indicate effective behavior change (Fitts & Posner, 1967).

The preceding discussion provides insight into why meaningful behavior change is hard—it is a process that requires sustained time and effort rather than a quick win, once-and-done activity. Because of the effort required, individuals need to see evidence of payoffs—in other words, the golf ball needs to start getting closer to the hole rather than land in the water or sand trap, the car with a stick shift needs to stop stalling on an incline, etc. Behavior change programs tend to focus on *how to enable* new behaviors but have fallen short in *how to motivate* learners to persevere until change is embedded. An important aspect of this piece is reinforcing learners and helping them see progress. Without this, there is risk that motivation will wane and other things will be prioritized, interfering with the type of lasting behavior change that builds a high-performance culture.

Performance management behavior change introduces complexities beyond those encountered with behavior change efforts outside of work:

- The first stems from the fact that many managers and employees will have already solidified many ineffective performance management behaviors, such as "check-the-box" behavior patterns that are characteristic of traditional performance management processes. It is important to recognize that we are not dealing with a blank slate in which effective techniques can be learned from the start. Instead, effective behavior change will likely require a longer process of un-doing past learning and rebuilding new thinking and skills.

- Irrespective of the ultimate potential for behavior change to contribute to higher engagement and performance, the second challenge is that busy managers and employees may find it difficult to shift from their current habits to more informal, ongoing behaviors that are likely to take more time and skill than what they do today.

- Finally, also adding complexity is the requirement for change *en masse*. It is hard enough to achieve effective behavior change when an individual is internally driven to meet his or her own unique goals, but it is exponentially harder when the change is being driven externally across many different individuals who bring different levels of commitment and willingness to invest their limited time in change that may not be personally important to them—in which case it will not be successful in the end.

Scalable behavior change programs that so many organizations implement today are interesting to participants, but like so many other organizational learning interventions, they fall short of driving meaningful, lasting change. This raises the important question of what ROI organizations are realizing from performance management behavior change interventions and what—if anything—can be done to make improvements?

A Strategy for Behavior Change Success

In researching this book, we spoke with several leading expert practitioners and researchers about their performance management implementation experiences. To a person, they all said that the greatest need in organizations today is better coaching and feedback behavior from managers; however, they also noted the lack of evidence supporting the idea that meaningful performance management behavior change can be broadly achieved. Thus, behavior change is like the Holy Grail—a solution that is much sought after but that remains elusive.

Most training interventions aimed at performance management behavior change treat the target behaviors (e.g., real-time feedback, agile goal setting, coaching, etc.) as the end goal, rather than as a means to achieving the more important end goal of driving high performance. This is an important nuance to understand because it lies at the heart of why behavior change programs likely fail so often. First, while nice to know, most managers and employees will not be compelled to make a significant, long-term investment in learning effective feedback and coaching techniques. These are vague, intangible concepts for many people that may not hold high value, especially in the face of other pressing business priorities. In contrast, both managers and employees readily see the importance of tangible business outcomes and invest significant time and personal effort to achieve these, as demonstrated in the Alcoa example.

The implication is that focusing on performance management behavior change for its own sake is unlikely to provide an effective platform for embedding new keystone habits. Instead, the best way to embed behavior change is to implement it in conjunction with specific performance improvement goals. In this way, behavior change is leveraged as it is intended—as an enabler of important performance outcomes.

Implementation of performance management behavior change would then entail first selecting a performance outcome that is important for an individual or team to achieve (e.g., develop more consultative relationships with customers, speed up communication between groups, push decision-making down to lower levels). If improving customer relationships was the goal, for example, employees and managers would need to have more honest conversations about current customer relationships, employees would need to be given more real-time feedback on their customer service skills, and managers would need to provide coaching to help employees improve. Coupling performance management behavior change with specific, meaningful performance improvement goals is important for gaining the traction that is needed to embed new behaviors. Depending on the goal selected, other behavior changes beyond performance management behaviors may be required as well.

One approach that helps accelerate performance management behavior and culture change is to engage whole teams in learning and changing together as they drive toward specific performance outcomes, which increases the likelihood of developing the momentum and sustainability that's needed to embed change. For this approach to be successful, it needs to be led by a manager who is committed and motivated to drive the team's success. A meaningful performance outcome needs to be selected around which the team can rally; for example, increasing customer satisfaction by 20%. The team then needs to be intentional about what they will do to achieve this by setting clear expectations and adjusting as the situation may change, practicing real-time feedback, and everyone pitching in to help each other achieve the goal. Success achieving one goal is likely to motivate further effort and investment in behavior change. Additional goals can be set, and the process continued until effective performance management behavior defines how the team accomplishes its work. Good supporting materials can help managers drive the change, such as modules that provide step-by-step instructions for engaging others in practicing target behaviors and automated tools that facilitate giving and receiving feedback on these. This type of guided in-work training can work well to support individual efforts but is exponentially more powerful when done with the entire team working together.

Interventions beyond the learning program itself can reinforce behavior change. For example, periodic pulse surveys can assess engagement and show impacts on important team attitudes. Feedback from pulse surveys can be provided to individual managers or used to monitor trends. Another technique to reinforce change leverages success stories. As an example, Cargill established a quarterly communications cascade that initially featured senior leader success stories about implementing change in their teams. However, this later evolved into identifying the "most engaging" managers from their engagement survey results and interviewing these individuals to learn about their practices, tips, and results from engaging in effective behavior with their teams. These were then used to inspire others about the possibilities and give them ideas they could try in their teams.

★★★

Behavior change can be extremely powerful but requires sustained effort from managers and teams if the change is to be impactful and robust. It is important to start with the right target for the change—it must be tangible and have a direct link to important business priorities. It is important to be realistic about the inherent challenges and effort that is needed to achieve lasting behavior change that will drive performance. We have not seen many situations in which the motivation and sustained effort has existed to embed lasting behavior change, which is why so many behavior change programs fall short in delivering expected results. If the appetite does not exist to see behavior change through, this does not mean that improvements in performance management are not possible. In fact, very encouraging data reported by the Center for Effective Organizations (see Chapter 11) showed that even one or two process changes in the areas of implementing real-time or crowdsourced feedback can yield positive outcomes (Ledford, Benson, & Lawler, 2016).

If there is aspiration to invest in performance management behavior change, this can be best accomplished by treating target behaviors as the means to achieve important business outcomes, rather than as end goals themselves. Repeated use of effective performance management behaviors to achieve specific performance goals will eventually hardwire these behaviors into the way work is naturally performed. While this can be done by managers working with their employees individually, the impact will be exponentially greater if behavior change is tackled as a team sport rather than an individual sport, with everyone working together to drive and reinforce it. Even with this type of support to facilitate behavior change, it is important to remain realistic about how much change is possible in what time frame and set expectations accordingly.

References

Bryant, A. (2011, March 12). Google's quest to build a better boss. *New York Times*. Retrieved from www.nytimes.com/2011/03/13/business/13hire.html? pagewanted=all&_r=0

CEB. (2004). *Driving employee performance and retention through engagement: A quantitative analysis of the effectiveness of employee engagement strategies* (Catalog No. CLC12PV0PD). Arlington, VA: Author.

CEB. (2012). *Driving breakthrough performance in the new work environment* (Catalog No. CLC4570512SYN). Arlington, VA: Author.

CEB. (2015). *Building a productive learning culture: More learning through less learning* (Catalog No. LDR1622915SYN). Arlington, VA: Author.

Davache, L., Kiefer, T., Rock, D., & Rock, L. (2010). Learning that lasts through AGES. *NeuroLeadership Journal, 3,* 1–11.

Duhigg, C. (2012). *The power of habit: Why we do what we do.* New York: Random House.

Ericsson, K. A., Krampe, R. T., & Tesch-Romer, C. (1993). The role of deliberate practice in the acquisition of expert performance. *Psychological Review, 100,* 363–406. doi:10.1037/0033-295X.100.3.363

Fitts, P. M., & Posner, M. I. (1967). *Human performance.* Oxford: Brooks and Cole.

Ledford, G. E., Benson, G. S., & Lawler, E. E., III. (2016). *A study of cutting-edge performance management practices: Ongoing feedback, ratingless reviews and crowdsourced feedback.* Retrieved from www.worldatwork.org

Pulakos, E. D., Mueller-Hanson, R. M., Arad, S., & Moye, N. (2015). Performance management can be fixed: An on-the-job experiential learning approach for complex behavior change. *Industrial and Organizational Psychology, 8,* 51–76.

11

A CHANGE MANAGEMENT APPROACH TO IMPLEMENTATION

A solid design is important for performance management transformation; however, success ultimately rests on the effectiveness of its implementation. What does effective performance management implementation look like? Consider these examples:

- Company A decided to drive change through branding and communication. They wrote many flowery speeches and spent significant time on developing a logo, writing marketing slogans, designing posters, etc. to get employees and managers on-board with the new program. The effort never ended up going anywhere, no change was realized, and the campaigns eventually became a big joke in the organization. At the root of this failure was no clear or compelling vision to rally around—the campaign was focused on the idea of change but not the substance of it. Not only did no change occur, but the HR team leading the effort lost credibility and had difficulty implementing future initiatives.
- Company B dramatically changed the performance rating process in a way that positively impacted people's pay, leaving implementers quite surprised when employees had negative reactions to the new process. Even though pay changes were positive, the rating scale was defined in a way that made employees feel less successful. In this case, failure to think through employees' emotional reactions to their performance ratings undermined what could have been a very positive change.
- In Company C, a core group of employees developed a thorough plan for performance management reform to include securing funds to execute it. However, they did not include key stakeholders in the process, who were then angry at being left out. They also failed to account for how the change

they were planning might derail due to significant business challenges and layoffs. The entire effort went down in flames. Failure to get buy-in for performance management reform when there were much bigger fish to fry in addressing business challenges was a recipe for disaster. There was no burning platform for this particular change now.

• In Company D, change was implemented using a "test and learn approach" to improving performance conversations. A core design team met with key stakeholders to get input. They consulted with outside experts and put together a preliminary proposal. They got broad input on the proposal and implemented it in stages—pilot testing various aspects with small groups, making changes, and doing more testing before rolling it out to the broader organization. The entire change effort took over three years, and stakeholders complained that progress was too slow. The effort was ultimately successful but under pressure throughout the process because realistic expectations were not set for what the change would entail.

These examples show the multitude of factors that can impact implementation success—having a compelling vision, a strong business case, a solid design fit for purpose, buy-in from stakeholders, effective communications, and proven change enablement strategies. Performance management transformation is like any other major change management initiative and requires similar approaches. Established change management models provide insights about how to orchestrate performance management reform so that it is well understood and achieves its goals (Kotter, 1995; Bridges & Bridges, 2016; Heath & Heath, 2010; Cohen, 2005). However, the unique challenges of performance management lead to important differences in how some of these reform efforts are implemented. In the following sections, we present key principles and guidelines for implementing performance management change that draw from and build upon established change models.

Where to Begin

A successful change process starts by answering three important questions about the need for change:

• What exactly needs to change and why; what business problem will this change solve?
• When is the right timing for change?
• What does success look like?

Organizations often initiate performance management changes to quell noise about the current system or keep up with the newest "flavor of the day" trend that everyone else is implementing. Examples include competency models, cascading goals, and, most recently, rating-less reviews and behavior change. Unfortunately, many organizations have adopted fads anointed as "best practices" only to learn that these did not work as anticipated because not enough attention was paid to assessing the fit of the new practice for the organization or implementing it effectively. This has led to a repeated pattern of performance management change that produces little ROI or lasting process improvement (Pulakos & O'Leary, 2011). It's not surprising that skepticism and lack of enthusiasm are often the responses when the topic turns to yet another new and improved performance management process.

The purpose of performance management change must be anchored in a compelling business need. Simply changing the performance management approach to keep up with the latest trends is not enough to make a compelling business case. However, anchoring the change in tangible business outcomes (e.g., increasing innovation, reducing bureaucracy so that decisions can be made faster, improving market share) will make the case for change clear and compelling. Managers and employees will be more likely to support the effort if it has specific potential benefits for them in the form of a better work experience.

Determining What to Change

One of the biggest challenges with performance management is that there is little ground truth about what works best—ratings or no ratings, cascading goals or no cascading goals, 360-degree ratings or ratings from managers only, and so forth—and no playbooks that guarantee implementation success. However, case studies and benchmarking research provide useful insights about the frequency and perceived effectiveness of different performance management features. As one example, a recent study conducted by the Center for Effective Organizations (CEO) found that of 244 companies surveyed, 97% had adopted real-time feedback, 51% had adopted rating-less reviews, and 27% had adopted crowdsourced feedback. (Ledford, Benson, & Lawler, 2016). In some companies, these new practices were added to more traditional processes (e.g., cascading goals, 360-degree ratings, competency assessments, etc.); however, implementation of real-time feedback and rating-less reviews together were associated with decreased use of legacy practices. The combination of all three new practices yielded the most positive impact on several outcomes, including strategic alignment, motivating employees, developing employees, and rewarding top talent. Combining real-time and crowdsourced feedback was found to be more effective than real-time feedback alone or real-time feedback combined with rating-less reviews. Comparisons with prior benchmarking studies showed the three new performance management practices to be more effective overall than traditional practices.

While benchmarking research is useful for identifying trends and gaining insights into what other organizations are experiencing, implementation success depends on evaluating what will work best within each organization's individual context. The following questions provide a starting point for diagnosing what types of change should be considered in a given context (see Chapter 1 for additional guidance):

- What would genuinely add more value by being fixed, how much value, and how do we know this? If you don't have answers here, it's important to get them.
- How much is the organization willing to invest?
- How much appetite and energy are there for performance management change?

The first question is designed to uncover aspirations about what could be. The last two questions are important to ground planning in practical realities. Biting off the right amount of change that adds value, respects people's time, and can be implemented effectively is essential for success.

Selling Change and Managing Expectations

Like other change management efforts, performance management transformation requires engaging stakeholders, gaining their buy-in and support, and managing their expectations. Stakeholders often come to the performance management change effort with their own ideas about what works best based on their experience and engrained ways of doing things, which can present further challenges. Several techniques and strategies are reviewed in the rest of this section that will be helpful for negotiating the process of selling change and managing expectations about change.

A solid business case can provide the backbone for selling change and enabling implementation. It translates aspirations, ideas, and plans into a specific proposal to invest in performance management. The business case should include the changes that will be made, expected outcomes, a high-level plan and time frames, costs, and risk mitigation. The following questions will help in evaluating whether or not there is a sufficiently compelling business case for change:

- Are the outcomes we expect from change realistic in our context?
- Have we painted a sufficiently clear picture of what good looks like so that others can understand the aspiration? How much does this resonate?
- To what extent will the anticipated ROI of change justify the financial investment?

Change often requires meeting others where they are and bringing them on a journey to a new state. If, for example, leaders embrace elaborate rating processes and believe they are needed for pay decisions, then no matter the reality, targeting this area for reform will be challenging. A better strategy would be to show value and progress in addressing agreed-upon pain points. Once confidence and trust are earned, it may then be possible to initiate discussion of how rating processes could be similarly evolved to add more value.

Changes that result in others thinking and behaving differently take much more time than changing the mechanics of a process. Changing forms or steps can often be accomplished in a few weeks, whereas making lasting behavior, mindset, or culture changes can take years. Even simple mind shifts, such as changing the view of performance management from an administrative HR process to a tool for driving high performance, will be hard for some to grasp. A reasonable expectation is to build incremental change over time, rather than think about implementation as a once-and-done effort. Achieving even a small amount of incremental change is valuable. Starting small, showing proof of concept, impact, and positive success stories builds momentum. Consistency, repetition, reinforcement, and patience are important in driving attitude and behavior change.

It is important to set realistic expectations about what is required for successful change and how much change will occur in what time frame. If the goal is behavior change, stakeholders often underestimate the time and effort this will take. When unrealistic expectations are then not met, HR can suffer credibility losses and organizational members can become cynical and unwilling to invest in further change efforts. Cynicism has been a common outcome from performance management change efforts that promise improvements but then deliver burdensome processes that people hate. Newer trends that tackle key performance management pain points head-on have brought renewed hope about the potential for positive change. With such high hopes, it is especially important to understand the extent of leadership appetite and support for change that exists, the investment needed, and what outcomes and time frames are realistic, as these factors shape what should be attempted and can be successfully accomplished.

Balancing Customization With Consistency

While performance management should be customized to align with the organization's strategy and goals, reward structures, business model(s), and management philosophy, some level of consistency with effective practices is needed to ensure the process is evidence-based. Further considerations are the extent to which the same process should be uniformly applied across the organization or if further customization is needed for individual business units. While it is easier to administer, monitor, and control one process with standard content, policies, and technology systems, different approaches may actually be needed to optimize performance in different business units (Church, Ginther, Levine, & Rotolo, 2015). For example, knowledge work, sales, and production are fundamentally different types of work. The have different performance metrics (e.g., innovation advancements, volume of sales or percentage of renewals, phone calls handled per day), time frames for goal accomplishment (years, months, days, respectively), opportunities to observe performance, and skill requirements, all of which have implications for performance management design that is aimed at driving high performance.

The question of what degree of tailoring is needed and will be permitted is critically important to evaluate from the start, not only from a process development perspective but from an implementation and maintenance perspective. It would not be practical to implement entirely bespoke and unique processes for each division, group, or team. One strategy that can work well, however, is to modularize different components so that these can be easily implemented through configuration flexibilities to address local needs. For example, a 360 could or could not be included, different templates, rating scales, or data display options could be provided that support use of different types of performance measurement data, and so forth. In sum, evaluating implementation requirements entails being clear on the goals for change, thinking through all of the requirements from the start, and understanding the downstream implementation and maintenance consequences end-to-end.

Overcoming Impediments to Change

Political, social, motivational, or practical factors can either enable or undermine implementation success and should be carefully considered as part of the change management effort. As discussed in Chapter 9, the impact of environmental factors on performance has been given insufficient attention. While some of these factors can be mitigated, others are extremely powerful success blockers that should not be underestimated. Politically toxic environments, passive-aggressive cultures, and leadership failures can bring down even the best teams and performers in ways that no performance management intervention can save. Understanding what outcomes are realistic is critical for both designing change and setting expectations for what change can achieve.

The level of manager capability in the organization becomes increasingly important to the extent that the change relies on manager behavior to implement successfully, such as driving more effective feedback, adjusting expectations in real time, and so forth. These changes require managers to possess a number of skills—some are related to performance management behavior and others are related to technical, business, or subject-matter expertise—both types of skills are needed to advise, diagnose, and course-correct performance. But beyond having requisite skills, managers need to believe in driving high performance as an important concept, and the organizational culture needs to support it. Imagine how an effort aimed at robust behavior change might play out in the following environment:

> *Managers take a pragmatic approach to performance management that plays to people's strengths rather than attempts to maximize each person's performance. They carve up work and make assignments that enable them to overlook development areas that are unlikely to change while still ensuring work gets done. They understand that focusing on what people can't do well simply demotivates them.*

In a culture that ascribes to this mindset, how likely is it that change effort to drive high performance will resonate and be successfully adopted? Instead, a better approach might be to focus on performance optimization—how to shape the environment to maximize chances for success.

Assessing the extent to which environmental factors will derail performance management change is essential, as it makes no sense to invest in change that is doomed to fail from the start. If very significant barriers to success exist in the environment, they should be tackled first before expending time and resources on designing change initiatives or building business cases to support them.

A Checklist for Successful Performance Management Change

Implementing a new performance management process and tools is reasonably straightforward and often once-and-done. But implementing change to systemically drive improved performance requires a longer-term commitment. In the remainder of this section, we summarize aspects of change that are most important for implementation of performance management processes that drive performance.

1. **Connect change to business priorities**. Change must be anchored in an urgent business priority in which performance improvement is needed. Business goals can then be used as a call to action to drive implementation of new performance management processes (e.g., real-time feedback, flexible goal setting, etc.) hand in hand with driving actual performance improvements in a specific focal area. Techniques that drive performance like real-time feedback and more agile goal setting are not end goals in and of themselves but rather enablers of high performance. They need to be seamlessly integrated into ongoing work and practiced repeatedly within the given work context until they are embedded, which has significant implications for the implementation strategy. Implementation thus becomes the process of practicing the application of new techniques in context to embed them in ongoing work. With enough practice, the

behaviors that enable high performance will eventually become the way work is naturally approached and performed.

2. **Clearly define behaviors to change**. Once the target behaviors for change are identified, they must clearly be defined and contrasted with current behaviors. For example, if innovation is the target, the current behaviors that block innovation need to be identified. These might include overly harsh criticism of every new idea or lack of willingness to try new approaches for fear of failing. Replacement behaviors then need to be defined, such as encouraging new ideas, discussing possibilities instead of limitations, and permission to try new approaches and accepting their risk. Performance management behaviors then support and enable the new replacement behaviors and discourage the old behaviors (e.g., managers give feedback that encourages rather than inhibits new ideas). As noted in point 1, performance management behaviors are not the end goal but rather the means for fostering desired performance outcomes.

3. **Make sure the environment will support the change before asking employees to change their behavior**. As we have discussed at several points in this book, behaviors that enable performance can be undermined by strong environmental impediments that block success. For example, if employees need to make decisions faster yet they face an ocean of red tape in getting anything done, change efforts that focus on performance management behavior only will fail. Cleaning up the red tape to gain efficiencies is needed before asking employees to change their behavior.

4. **Ensure relevant leaders personally support change**. Too many change efforts come from HR, and business leaders demonstrate public ambivalence for them. Leaders need to believe that making a given change is the right thing to do. They must earnestly support it, change their own behavior, and hold others accountable. If leaders are not willing to do this, the change effort is probably not worth trying because it will fail and waste resources along the way.

5. **Use a Kaizen approach**. There are two major types of change—revolution and evolution. Revolution has its place when unacceptable behaviors or outcomes require immediate action; for example, unethical or corrupt behavior. For most performance management change, evolution is likely to be a better strategy. Kaizen is an approach that can help organizations evolve. The basic principle is to make small improvements and build on them over time. Kaizen begins with small, non–threatening questions that prompt more creative thinking. For example, "What small action could I take to improve the quality of feedback?" Small questions lead to taking small steps and then building upon them to take bigger steps. For example, to improve feedback quality, a manager might start with just giving one sincere compliment to one employee each day (Maurer, 2014).

6. **Pay attention to the mechanics**. Even if a more in-depth implementation process is planned, initial training for employees and managers on the nuts and bolts of how to use a new approach and expectations of them is important as a first step. The most effective training strategy is to provide bite-sized, just-in-time training—teach each piece when it is needed, keep it short and to the point, and reinforce it with job aids or other resources that are readily accessible.

7. **Measure and provide feedback**. Change efforts must be measured to know if anything has improved. A few caveats are in order about this principle. First, measures must be meaningful and targeted to assessing the desired change as directly as possible. For example, if the change is improving the quality of performance conversations, then measure success by asking employees about the quality of their conversations with managers. Second, feedback from measurement is best used to coach and improve, not as a hammer. If the feedback is tied to a reward or punishment, people will game the system and the feedback will become useless.

8. **Allow enough time to show success**. It is important to allow enough time between implementation and assessment of impact to draw accurate conclusions about success. Be careful of the "thermostat effect" when measuring the impact of change. The thermostat effect refers to the fact that change needs enough time to take effect before it can be successfully detected. Continuing to turn up the heat in a large, cold room will eventually make the room unbearably hot, because it takes time for enough heat to build up to register the change in temperature on the thermostat. Likewise, a robust program to improve the quality of feedback may take several cycles of evaluation surveys before employees collectively perceive enough difference to register a change.

9. **Do not overdo marketing aspects at the expense of making progress**. "Overdoing it" means spending an inordinate amount of time trying to come up with the perfect logo, marketing slogan, posters, etc. A few well-done graphics can help communicate the change, but too much time spent agonizing over irrelevant details can distract from progress. Emphasize the change itself, not the slogan. If employees perceive that the change is all fluff and no substance, they are more likely to mock the effort.

10. **Do not let technology dictate process**. Numerous performance management technology platforms are available that provide a full range of features and options, most with traditional performance management workflows built in. While it can be tempting to adopt these standard features, they may not meet the needs of the organization or facilitate more progressive performance management strategies. Make sure the technology is easy to use for managers and employees and that minimal steps and handoffs are needed to accomplish each major activity. Resist the temptation to add in more complexity than is needed simply because features

are available. Before shopping for technology, have your ideal process and must-have features clearly defined and buy the technology that meets your needs rather than adapting your needs to the technology available.

Putting It All Together: A Case Study on Effective Change

The Nation's First Insurance example discussed in this section shows how a change effort might unfold that follows these principles and incorporates many of the suggestions made throughout this book to effectively manage performance. It focuses on a specific performance issue that was urgent to address and translates recommended performance management techniques and strategies into concrete steps, expectations, and outcomes that align the team around addressing the issue.

Nation's First Insurance (NFI)[1] is a well-established, mature organization that has long been a market leader in their industry. Recently, however, newer competitors have emerged and are eroding NFI's market share. These competitors offer the same basic product, but at better prices and with better support services. The culture is cautious and conservative:

- Everyone is "nice" and candid feedback is rare.
- Poor performance is rampant and not dealt with because managers do not want to be perceived as "too harsh."
- Customer service is poor, resulting in numerous complaints, and customer defections to competitors.
- High-performing employees have left in frustration because they are tired of getting the same rewards as poorer performing coworkers.
- The CEO is concerned about these problems and has proposed implementing forced distribution performance ratings and firing the bottom 10% every year until the poor performers are purged.

The Chief HR Officer (CHRO) has concerns about the CEO's strategy and thinks the answer is to first better understand the root causes of poor performance and try to fix them. The CEO has no objection but is skeptical of how effective this will be. He wants faster results to get rid of poor performers and turn the company around. However, the CEO agrees to give HR three months to study the problem and propose a solution for the entire executive team to evaluate.

HR begins by conducting focus groups with customer service employees and managers to identify why customer service is poor and gather ideas to improve it (e.g., decisions are too slow because multiple approvals are required for even small concessions). HR then meets with managers to identify process changes to remove blockers to better service (e.g., improving communication and escalation procedures so that customer issues can be addressed faster). They also discuss what employee behaviors will need to change and how (i.e., new standards for responsiveness to customer queries).

HR and senior customer service managers jointly propose short- and long-term solutions to the executive team. The short-term actions are designed to be implemented quickly and yield immediate, small improvements. The longer-term actions will require more research before full solutions can be designed, but presenting them at this stage allows for preliminary feedback from the executive team.

The short-term suggestions include:

- Addressing environmental blockers to fast customer service (e.g., remove extra approval layers that are not needed, empower customer service reps to make decisions about small discounts and refunds).
- Implementing new performance criteria more directly tailored to customer service jobs, including:

  - Objective standards (e.g., respond to customer inquiries within one business day).
  - Behavioral standards (e.g., handle customer challenges at the lowest possible level; thoroughly examine options available to you to solve customer problems before escalating).

Longer-term suggestions include:

- Purchasing new customer management technology that allows transactions to be processed faster.
- Improving leadership training for customer service managers.
- Eliminating some of the traditional components of the broader performance management approach (e.g., annual SMART objectives and ratings on generic competencies) that take up a lot of time but don't appear to be valuable for this group.

The executive team agrees to try out the short-term solutions over the next six months to assess their effectiveness. The HR and customer service leaders ask the executives to personally commit to supporting the effort by 1) authoring some communications about the changes, 2) speaking directly to employee groups, and 3) holding subordinate managers personally accountable for supporting the effort. They also get the executives to agree on what success looks like. Because it will take a while for changes to show results, they agree that, in six months, success will be that new performance criteria are fully implemented, a method of measuring employee progress against the criteria are established, and every employee will have feedback about how they are doing with respect to expectations.

Over the next six months, HR and the customer service leaders work together to craft a change management plan that includes the following components:

- Communicate changes via multiple methods: presentations from executives and managers, emails, and job aids. Ensure expectations are crystal clear and linked to business goals (e.g., "we need to increase speed and flexibility of customer service to win back market share we are losing to competitors").
- Provide short, web-based training about the new performance criteria—what it is and how results will be measured (e.g., call metrics, renewal rates, customer feedback surveys, periodic supervisor monitoring of calls).
- Give managers new tools to communicate and give feedback on these new expectations (e.g., checklists, coaching guides).
- Show managers how they can quickly take action with employees who are not meeting expectations (e.g., provide additional training and coaching, document issues, put employees on notice if no improvement).
- Measure progress of the change itself—employee feedback on performance conversation quality, number of terminations due to poor performance, customer service surveys that speak to flexibility and speed of service.
- Evaluate trends and adjust the plan if needed, paying attention to data collected in real time.
- Take action quickly if data is not trending toward expected results.

After six months, all employees and managers had been trained and were using new criteria and getting performance feedback every month, if not more often. In the beginning, many employees struggled to meet the new standards, and a few quit in frustration, causing short-term staffing issues. By the end of the six months, new employees were hired to fill the gaps, and managers were starting to see steady performance improvements in most employees. Employees were initially wary of the new requirements but eventually came to appreciate the more regular feedback. Small increases were observed in customer satisfaction ratings, though customer retention numbers were unchanged (mainly because customers renew annually so it would take up to 12 months to see the full impact of the change). The executive team felt the effort was promising and anticipated that with more time and additional effort, results would continue to improve. Given the early wins, HR garnered increased credibility that made the executive team more open to some of the longer-term proposed changes.

★★★

Just as there is no one performance management approach that is effective across all situations, there is no one implementation strategy that can be applied to all performance management processes. Following proven change management techniques and principles to include developing and selling the business case, engaging stakeholders effectively, developing effective communications, enabling the workforce in new practices, and evaluating results will help guide successful performance management implementations and facilitate positive outcomes. Most important to effective implementation, however, is thorough diagnosis of the organizational situation and local needs as well as realistic assessment of what can be effectively implemented in the given context that will enable value-added performance management activities for both managers and employees.

Note

1 Nation's First Insurance (NFI) is a pseudonym.

References

Bridges, W., & Bridges, S. (2016). *Managing transitions: Making the most of change*. Boston, MA: Perseus Book Group.

Church, A. H., Ginther, N. M., Levine, R., & Rotolo, C. T. (2015). Going beyond the fix: Taking performance management to the next level. *Industrial and Organizational Psychology, 8*, 121–129.

Cohen, D. (2005, March–April). *The heart of change field guide: Tools and tactics for leading change in your organization*. Boston, MA: Harvard Business Review Press.

Heath, D., & Heath, C. (2010). *Switch: How to change things when change is hard*. New York: Broadway Books.

Kotter, J. P. (1995). Leading change: Why transformation efforts fail. *Harvard Business Review*, 59–67.

Ledford, G. E., Benson, G., & Lawler, E. E. (2016, August). *Cutting-edge performance management: 244 organizations report on ongoing feedback, ratingless reviews, and crowd-sourced feedback*. World at Work Research, Center for Effective Organizations.

Maurer, R. (2014). *One small step can change your life: The Kaizen way*. New York: Workman Publishing Company.

Pulakos, E. D., & O'Leary, R. S. (2011). Why is performance management so broken? *Industrial and Organizational Psychology, 4*, 146–164.

12

THE PATH FORWARD

Performance management is undergoing revolutionary transformation. Gone are the days of employees and organizations blindly accepting tedious procedures, awkward conversations, and bad data. Increasingly becoming more focal are simplicity, ongoing high-quality performance conversations, and better talent insights. In short, organizations are demanding performance management that actually improves performance. The journey is not easy, but we know what it takes to get there.

Fundamental Shifts Needed for Better Performance Management

Figure 12.1 illustrates the contrast between traditional burdensome performance management practices and more beneficial ones that are the vision for the future. Performance management is burdensome today because it is time-consuming, complex, demotivating, and yields poor information that is virtually useless for gaining talent insights and improving performance. The beneficial future state is streamlined, empowering, engaging, and yields useful information that informs talent decisions and actually drives performance. At the core of this transformation are several fundamental shifts in our collective mindset about what performance management means and how we need to approach work differently to get there. These shifts summarize the key themes in this book and represent the disruptions needed to drive meaningful change.

From Many Purposes to a Singular Focus on Enabling Performance

Performance management today almost always serves multiple purposes: inform talent decisions, help employees develop, give people clear feedback, and defend against challenges; and some are in conflict (e.g., development requires honest

Current State   Future State

Purpose
• PM serves multiple, conflicting purposes: develop and engage employees, make talent decisions, protect against legal challenges, and hold employees accountable to meet their goals

Purpose
• PM has a singular focus on enabling performance needed to meet business goals. All components of its design and implementation must serve this purpose or they should not be included

Principles
• Over-engineered controls
• Uniform standards of greatness
• Performance evaluation
• Performance-driven talent decisions
• Manage employee performance
• PM disconnected from day-to-day work

Principles
• Flexible and dynamic approach
• Job-relevant definitions of success
• Performance measurement
• Business-driven talent decisions
• Manage performance context
• PM is how work gets done

Outcomes
Time-consuming, complex process that is demotivating and provides little business value

Outcomes
Streamlined approach that is empowering and engaging and yields useful information to help improve performance

FIGURE 12.1 Current Versus Future State of Performance Management

reflection of strengths and development needs that is suppressed when ratings are used as the basis for rewards). Any talent management system that tries to do too much gets diffused and loses focus—to the point that nothing gets done well or the system collapses from its own weight. To address this challenge, critics have called for the elimination of ratings and increased frequency of feedback. However, these strategies are overly simplistic and do not adequately support what organizations need performance management to achieve.

To enable performance, we need to begin by clearly aligning performance management activities to business strategy and goals—what are the key challenges the business (or team) is facing? What are the most important behaviors in the specific context for driving success? As a practical matter, organizational members cannot attend to too many things at once, so it is imperative to prioritize what matters most. Performance management activities that are directly aimed at driving high performance cut through the complexity and distraction that characterize today's work environments. Activities that do not squarely focus on the sole purpose of enabling performance should not be included in performance management processes. This clarity of purpose drives every aspect of a new performance management design and serves as the litmus test for evaluating any proposed intervention.

From Over-Engineered Controls to a Flexible and Dynamic Approach

The core of managing performance is to engage in an iterative process of setting clear expectations, measuring progress, and having effective conversations.

These activities can't be constrained to a yearly cycle that is disconnected from actual work. They must be integrated into the work itself and allowed to be applied flexibly. This means that organizations will need to let go of over-engineered processes and burdensome documentation requirements, as well as embrace flexibility and change.

Performance management processes are often overly complex due to mistrust: a fundamental belief that managers and employees will fail to do the right thing without numerous requirements and controls that take away the possibility of error. Although this mistrust is not entirely without merit, a truly valuable approach to performance management must be flexible enough to accommodate change and fit the unique requirements of different departments, functions, and regions in an organization. Allowing more flexibility necessitates giving up some control. It also requires HR to operate as more of a strategic partner than compliance enforcer.

From Uniform Standards of Greatness to Job-Relevant Definitions of Success

Organizations frequently define success with one-size-fits-all competency models that assume the ideal employee is one who excels in every area: communication, collaboration, critical thinking, technical expertise, achieving results, etc. However, the ideal employee is one whose profile of capabilities is most needed by the business to accomplish its goals. Different businesses have different priorities and business models and therefore need different attributes from their employees to successfully perform. Recent research has shown the importance of defining the organizational and role context in terms of critical challenges employees will face. Matching employees to roles they are most equipped to handle based on these context factors yields three times higher prediction of success than use of general competency models to predict job performance (Johnson, 2017). Performance management approaches likewise need to account for real differences in the performance requirements of different roles rather than force fit common standards of success on all employees.

Effective performance management requires defining what success looks like for each job or role, which in turn helps determine the performance standards to which employees should be held accountable. For example, fast food restaurants need employees who can work efficiently. Gourmet restaurants need employees who can provide exceptional service. The organization's strategy is best supported when expectations for success are aligned with those employee characteristics that are most needed to deliver on the strategy. Not everyone has to be good at everything, but the profile of employee capabilities needs to be a good match with the profile of role requirements.

From Performance Evaluation to Performance Measurement

Performance measurement is distinct from performance evaluation. Measurement is ongoing collection and analysis of behaviors and results that help employees improve performance. Evaluation is a backward-looking judgment about performance that is used to inform decision-making. Performance evaluation should not be substituted for performance measurement if the goal is to improve performance. Performance measurement helps employees improve by providing real-time knowledge of results, enabling employees to adjust future actions to improve outcomes.

Whereas performance evaluation can inform talent decisions, a focus on measurement will have a greater impact on improving performance and solves the ubiquitous problem of lack of effective feedback. Good measurement methods communicate feedback from the environment without the manager having to be the sole source of it. This approach takes pressure off managers and empowers the employee to seek out performance information and use it to improve. As automation continues to increase in organizations, the challenges organizations have collecting and summarizing performance measures today are likely to decrease.

From Performance-Driven Talent Decisions to Business-Driven Talent Decisions

Organizations strive to link performance and rewards, but most employees do not see a strong linkage between the two because many other factors impact reward decisions aside from pure performance measures. Instead of trying to strengthen the link between performance and rewards, organizations should embrace the distinctions. Talent decisions are first and foremost business decisions. Each has its own purpose and therefore different criteria should be used for different types of decisions. Performance is one factor in the decision, but many other factors may be more important (e.g., organizational budgets put a limit on compensation). Clearly defining criteria for different types of decisions and communicating them to employees is the best way to make sound decisions that are fair, consistent with business necessity, and acceptable to employees.

From Managing Employee Performance to Managing the Performance Context

Behavior is a function of the person and environment (Lewin, 1936); that is, performance is a result of not only an individual's talents and motivation but also the extent to which the environment supports or inhibits performance. The importance of the environment is largely ignored in the typical approach to performance management. Individual goals are set and performance is evaluated as if each employee had full control over the results. This is rarely the case, of course. Instead of focusing on performance problems as individual issues, organizations should consider the larger environmental context in which the problem occurs. If performance falls short of expectations, the first place to fix it is the environment. Employees can only succeed in an environment that provides the right structure, expectations, and resources. Once these are addressed, employee motives and capabilities will then determine the level of performance.

From PM Disconnected from Day-to-Day Work to PM as How Work Gets Done

Performance management (PM) activities and behaviors are a means to an end, and not the end itself. Behaviors such as setting effective expectations, measuring progress, and providing effective coaching and feedback must be in service of achieving business-relevant performance outcomes. Therefore, managers should not be taught to provide feedback and coaching in isolation. Rather they should be taught how to facilitate and enable accomplishing important performance goals, using feedback and coaching techniques. For example, instead of teaching managers how to give effective feedback, teach them how to enable a specific performance outcome like customer service, using performance management practices to support it (e.g., set expectations about what good service is, measure service effectiveness, and discuss how to use customer feedback to improve future service). With a focus on the performance outcome of interest, managers and employees will be more motivated and engaged in change efforts.

Developing these skills comes from experience and not simply training. Experience-based learning requires an intentional focus on the skill to be learned, deliberate practice in which the skill is performed on the job in multiple iterations, progress measurement, and reflection and feedback. The end goal is to embed performance management behaviors in day-to-day work so that they become a natural part of how work gets done rather than as a separate process that takes time without adding value.

Future Directions

What's next for performance management? As part of our research for this book, we sought perspectives on this question from HR leaders, researchers, and practitioners. In this section, we summarize these perspectives along with our own experiences to offer our best prognostications about future trends in performance management.

A Resolution to the Ratings Debate

Most of our interviewees said they thought many organizations would not be able to function without ratings. They are too entrenched in the culture, and replacing them with ongoing conversations is simply too much of a change. Some organizations that have eliminated ratings will go back again because they will find that people are not getting feedback. Only those few organizations that can embed very strong feedback and coaching behavior into their cultures may forever be able to abandon ratings. Many organizations that we have worked with contemplated removing ratings but ultimately decided it was too big of a leap.

This is not to suggest that ratings will not evolve. Organizations are not looking to preserve the status quo. Eventually, some organizations will chart a new path entirely that balances useful performance measurement and feedback with good decision-making. Our belief is that the new path will entail using performance data to inform decisions but that decision criteria will be better tailored to the business purposes for which they serve, as described in detail in Chapter 8.

In a sense, both sides of the ratings debate are right. We believe that the next evolution of performance management will get rid of ratings as we know them today—a perfunctory, check-the-box activity that does not accurately measure performance or provide useful feedback. In this way ratings will be gone, but in another way they will remain, as organizations will still use quantifiable measures to evaluate talent. Future organizations will use more nuanced and sophisticated criteria for making talent decisions that are informed by performance measures but that also consider important business constraints and goals.

Achieving Lasting Behavior Change

If the results of behavior change programs have been disappointing to date, it is not for lack of trying. New training programs and services are emerging every day that purport to drive meaningful behavior changes. To date little evidence exists that these programs result in meaningful changes in manager and employee behavior. A key problem with much of the training offered is that it is disconnected from day-to-day work, and it treats performance management behavior change as an end goal, rather than as a means to an end, integrated with achieving important business goals. Reimagining behavior change training as a strategy for achieving specific performance outcomes is more likely to yield positive change.

Behavior change is like a cathedral—it takes a long, long time to build. Organizations are impatient and grow weary of efforts that take time. A mindset shift that views behavior change as a multi-year journey that needs to be reinforced over and over again versus once-and-done is essential to see significant impact.

What is the next frontier for behavior change? It is noteworthy that practicing mindfulness is gaining traction as a popular organizational intervention to enable performance. We mention this because the key tenants of mindfulness—the practice of being present, being aware of what is happening in the moment, pausing to control fight-or-flight reactions, and using this awareness to make better decisions—may correspondingly enable effective performance management behavior. For example:

- Managers can be more in tune with whether the expectations they are setting are timely, meaningful to employees, and understood by them. They can pause in the moment to check understanding and offer clarification.
- Employees can be more in tune with explicit and implicit feedback cues. They will be better equipped to take in information and separate the message from their reaction to it. Recognizing feedback as it occurs will help them pause and ask clarifying questions if needed to better understand it and use it to improve performance.
- Managers will increase their awareness of their impact on employee performance and develop better coaching skills to help employees overcome challenges.

Whether or not training and the practice of mindfulness will prove effective for enabling effective performance or simply end up as the next business fad has yet to be seen, but at least on a conceptual level, it seems to have potential for enabling effective performance management behavior as long as these techniques can be tied to achieving concrete, tangible performance outcomes.

Meaningful Measurement Instead of Mindless Evaluation

Performance evaluation is fundamentally flawed. Over 100 years of serious research and experimentation has failed to produce an accurate means of evaluating performance. It is time to go in a different direction. Instead of evaluation, organizations should focus on measurement. Measurement is observing and reporting back behavior and results to provide information needed for employees to improve.

Not every job can be measured objectively today, but every job can be observed, and these observations can form the foundation of performance measurement. Observations have limitations of course, and acknowledging these limitations will make the results both more useful and more acceptable. Both objective and subjective performance measures are sources of data that are collected and analyzed for the purpose of improving performance. Performance measurement is therefore not a definitive judgment about an employee's worthiness as performance evaluation is often viewed. Rather it is a source of information that needs to be interpreted in context.

If the idea of performance evaluation fades away, will competencies go with it? Competencies are often used in performance evaluation and are a widely accepted means of defining success. Although initially hailed as the future of talent management, competencies have not been as useful as hoped. They are often too complex and too generic, and there are usually way too many of them. Employees don't always understand what they mean or how to use them. Organizations often try to address this problem by creating vast libraries of job-relevant competencies. These are hard to maintain, however, and often collapse of their own weight.

It is time for competencies to evolve. One organization we spoke with has eliminated them and replaced them with values and habits; values being the enduring characteristics expected organization wide (integrity, appreciation for diversity, etc.) and habits being the key behaviors needed for success in a given role. Another organization uses competencies to communicate broad expectations but more specific behavioral standards to measure performance. These alternative views of competencies are likely the start of more changes that will hopefully result in more useful means of defining success.

With continuing automation of work processes will come increasingly robust and accessible performance measurement dashboards that meaningfully integrate and summarize multiple types of performance data on each employee. Individual manager biases and political and social factors that make human rating data so flawed and useless today will be replaced with more precise and objective automated performance measurement. The question is whether or not automation will allow for comprehensive measurement, reflecting all of the important aspects of technical and behavioral performance—and chances are certain that it will. This will be a game-changer with profound implications not only for performance management as we know it today but for work processes, privacy, and talent insights, as email is analyzed, work behavior is taped, big data tools provide talent insights, and coaching is done by automated playback of actual performance. Technology can deliver most of these things today, so the question is how long will it take for today's performance management processes to become entirely obsolete?

The Rise of Teams and Self-Management

In traditionally structured organizations, managers have the primary responsibility for managing performance. However, the nature of work is fundamentally shifting. Organizations have more of a matrix structure with employees reporting to several different managers or project leaders, none of whom have a full understanding of the employee's day-to-day work. More work is done in teams, and teams tend to be fluid. Employees may be members of multiple teams, each with its own performance expectations and measures. The gig economy is producing many free agents who don't have a permanent organization or manager and may have several simultaneous engagements.

These trends will make it difficult for many traditional approaches to performance management to work. Instead, teams will need to set collective expectations and hold members accountable. In many instances, employees will need to manage their own performance. They will engage in contracting to set expectations with different stakeholders, they will need to seek their own sources of feedback, and their accomplishments will determine their future opportunities.

To support these trends, organizations will need to provide more tools to support team and self-management. They will need to communicate clearer insight into organizational goals and priorities to facilitate individuals proposing how they will contribute. Better methods of measuring results in real time need to be developed so that teams and individuals can track their progress and adjust to get better outcomes without having to rely on a manager to do it for them. Feedback will need to come from multiple sources rather than managers alone. Taken together, these changes can empower teams and individuals to drive their own performance and engagement. Increasing automation of work processes will again produce much more accessible and robust tools and data that will enable this.

A Greater Understanding of the Power of Context

As Peter Drucker famously said, "Culture eats strategy for breakfast." When it comes to performance management, it is sometimes easy to forget how it can shape and be shaped by the organization's culture (London & Mone, 2014). A better understanding of the connection between performance management and culture will be critical to enhancing both. For example, the frequency and quality of performance conversations between employees and managers is an indicator of trust, relationships, and communication in the organization. Focusing on improving conversation frequency and quality can have secondary effects on the larger organizational culture. Likewise, organizational cultures characterized by a high degree of camaraderie and trust will make it more likely that these conversations will be welcomed.

Future research can help shed light on how to better use performance management to shape culture and vice versa. For example:

- Which organizational cultural attributes are most and least conducive to progressive ideas about performance management?
- How do significant changes to the performance management system impact the organization's culture?
- If the organization seeks a cultural change, in what ways will the performance management approach contribute to or inhibit this change?
- How can the performance management approach be altered to drive culture change in a proactive rather than reactive way?

Exploring the answers to these questions can provide a more complete and nuanced understanding of how performance management works, and how it can be better positioned to add value to organizations.

Linking Performance Management to Business Outcomes

Research evidence showing that performance management leads to better business outcomes is very sparse (DeNisi & Smith, 2014). In the short run, if performance management is to survive, it must start to show a positive impact on results that executives care about: increased revenue and profits, decreased costs, and so forth. Even evidence of indirect effects would be an improvement. For example, if better performance conversations lead to increased employee engagement, which in turn lead to increased retention of high performers, the ultimate business outcome could be decreased hiring and training costs. Collecting data to support this chain of inferences is not as rigorous as conducting empirical research in the laboratory, but it is far more valuable for showing the potential value of real-world interventions.

Business leaders are already demanding that new practices show evidence of effectiveness before implementing them, and this demand will only increase. HR will need to do its homework to show how research supports proposed activities. A potential benefit of this strategy will be that performance management practices become simpler. If a given practice does not show tangible benefits, it may be abandoned.

HR leaders will need help in these endeavors. Organizational research is hard to do well, and many practitioners are not schooled in the latest research methods. Academics can help by providing expertise if they work in partnership with practitioners who understand organizational politics and realities. Together they can better understand what works and what doesn't—and how to design an approach that yields better results. Better performance management research may help close the ubiquitous science-practice gap that so many professionals wrestle with.

The Path Forward: From Complacency to Action

Good performance management is needed now more than ever. Organizations must improve performance to meet current goals, and a better performance management system can help them close this gap. Done well performance management aligns individual actions to focus on organizational priorities, it provides employees with insights about their performance so that they can improve it, and it yields good data with which to inform sound talent decisions.

Too often performance management is not done well, but many organizations are hesitant to change, fearing the disruption it will bring. They are complacent with the status quo, not realizing the high cost of inaction.

Performance management done poorly is extremely expensive: it is incredibly time-consuming (e.g., Deloitte found they were spending 2 million hours a year in performance management activities with little business value); it can be demotivating and disengaging, even to high performers (e.g., Culbertson, Henning, & Payne, 2013); and it yields unreliable and inaccurate data, leading to poor talent decisions. No other business practice likely gets so much investment for so little return. Organizations need to move from complacency to action by prioritizing performance management transformation.

While no single recipe for success exists when it comes to designing a good performance management approach, the principles and examples presented in this book are a good place to start. We hope you use these ideas, build and improve upon them, and tailor them to meet the unique needs and culture in your organization. Performance management need no longer be a necessary evil. It can and should be transformed to a value-added business driver. We hope you seize this opportunity to make a difference for your organization and the people in it. The next success story we read could be yours.

References

Culbertson, S. S., Henning, J. B., & Payne, S. C. (2013). Performance appraisal satisfaction: The role of feedback and goal orientation. *Journal of Personnel Psychology, 12,* 189–195.

DeNisi, A., & Smith, C. E. (2014). Performance appraisal, performance management, and firm-level performance. *Academy of Management Annals, 8,* 127–179.

Johnson, J. W. (2017, April). Predicting leader performance from personality: Context is essential. In J. W. Johnson (Chair), *Don't take quotes or personality assessment validities out of context.* Symposium conducted at the 32nd Annual Conference of the Society for Industrial and Organizational Psychology, Orlando, FL.

Lewin, K. (1936). *Principles of topological psychology.* New York: McGraw-Hill.

London, M., & Mone, E. M. (2014). Performance management processes that reflect and shape organizational culture and climate. In B. Schneider & K. M. Barbera (Eds.), *The Oxford handbook of organizational climate and culture.* Oxford: Oxford University Press.

INDEX